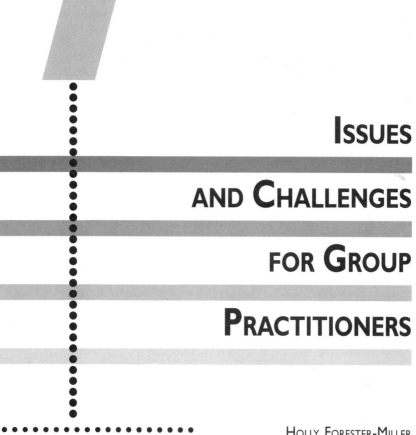

ISSUES

AND CHALLENGES

FOR GROUP

PRACTITIONERS

HOLLY FORESTER-MILLER
NORTH CAROLINA CENTRAL UNIVERSITY

JEFFREY A. KOTTLER
UNIVERSITY OF NEVADA–LAS VEGAS

LOVE PUBLISHING COMPANY®
Denver • London • Sydney

• • • • • • • • • • • • • • • • • •

*W*ith love to Gary, without whose support and patience this book would not be possible, Veronica and Bradley, who bring balance to my life and remind me to have lots of fun, and Charlie, who always seemed to be there with encouragement when I needed it most.

H.F.-M.

Published by Love Publishing Company
Denver, Colorado 80222

Library of Congress Catalog Card Number 96-78053

Copyright © 1997 Love Publishing Company
Printed in the U.S.A.
ISBN 0-89108-251-4

CONTENTS

MEET THE EDITORS

Holly Forester-Miller, Ph.D., is an Associate Professor and Counselor Education Program Coordinator at North Carolina Central University in Durham. She has published and presented internationally in the areas of group work, ethics, and the mind-body connection. Her study of the Tao and its application to group work is an extension of her exploration into understanding the mind-body connection.

Jeffrey A. Kottler, Ph.D., is a Professor of Counseling and Educational Psychology at the University of Nevada–Las Vegas. He is the author of numerous books, including *Advanced Group Leadership, On Being a Therapist, Growing a Therapist,* and *The Language of Tears.*

MEET THE CONTRIBUTORS

Loretta Bradley is Past-President of the Association for Counselor Education and Supervision. She currently is a Professor and Coordinator of Counselor Education at Texas Tech University.

Jesse A. Brinson is an Associate Professor in the Department of Counseling and Educational Psychology, University of Nevada–Las Vegas. His research interests include multicultural issues and substance abuse counseling.

Linda F. Campbell, of the Department of Counseling and Human Development Services, University of Georgia, is Director of the Center for Counseling and Personal Evaluation. Her current research interests are in psychotherapy outcome.

Valerie Conkey is an Outpatient Therapist at the Western District Guidance Center in Parkersburg, West Virginia.

Robert K. Conyne is a Professor of Counseling at the University of Cincinnati. He specializes in teaching, researching, and practicing group work.

Wendy Drewery, of the Department of Education Studies at the University of Waikato in Hamilton, New Zealand, specializes in social constructivism and theoretical analysis.

Allan Dye is a Professor and Chair in the Department of Graduate Studies in Counseling at Rollins College in Winter Park, Florida.

LeeAnn Eschbach is a Counselor Educator in the Counseling and Human Services Department at the University of Scranton, Pennsylvania. She teaches group counseling and other graduate courses.

Samuel T. Gladding is a Professor of Counselor Education and Assistant to the President at Wake Forest University in Winston-Salem, North Carolina.

Paul Granello is the Director of Adult Mental Health at Worthington Center, Inc. in Parkersburg, West Virginia.

Charles F. Gressard is the Counselor Education Program Director at the College of William & Mary. His research interests are in the areas of substance abuse and spirituality.

Richard J. Hazler is a Professor in the Department of Counselor Education at Ohio University.

Arthur M. Horne is in the Department of Counseling and Human Development Services at the University of Georgia. He has done consulting throughout the world, including in New Zealand and Russia.

Elaine Jarchow serves as Dean of the College of Education at Texas Tech University. Her research areas include curriculum change in international settings and women in administrative roles.

Chuck Kormanski, of the Career Development and Placement Service at the Penn State Altoona Campus, is involved in counseling college students, organizational consulting, team building, and conducting research in group development.

Courtland Lee is a Professor and Coordinator of the Counselor Education Program at the University of Virginia. He is President of the American Counseling Association.

Patricia A. Markos is an Assistant Professor at the University of Nevada–Las Vegas. She specializes in rehabilitation counseling and is pursuing research in the area of homelessness. She has considerable interest in the creative arts.

Gerald Monk, of the Department of Education Studies at the University of Waikato in Hamilton, New Zealand, specializes in narrative therapy, narrative mediation, social constructivism, and multicultural issues.

Kathryn Norsworthy is an Associate Professor in the Department of Graduate Studies in Counseling at Rollins College in Winter Park, Florida.

Jennifer M. Rand is a Counselor with Cincinnati Counseling Service, Inc. She leads psycho-education groups for adults and children.

Lynn S. Rapin is a Private Practice Psychologist in Cincinnati, Ohio, and an Adjunct Associate Professor of Counseling at the University of Cincinnati. She specializes in working with managers and task groups.

Rebecca Powell Stanard is the Director of Community Support Services of Health Recovery Services in Marietta, Ohio.

John Winslade, of the Department of Education Studies at the University of Waikato in Hamilton, New Zealand, specializes in narrative therapy, narrative mediation, and social constructivism.

INTRODUCTION:

CORE ISSUES AND DYNAMICS

IN GROUP LEADERSHIP

HOLLY FORESTER-MILLER AND JEFFREY A. KOTTLER

*C*onsider the following situation: You are in charge of an important committee for your institution or agency. Your group's task is to evaluate certain key policies and procedures of the organization and to make recommendations for change. Depending on your employment setting, the policies or procedures you are to review may vary: In a community agency setting you might review the intake process for staffing a case; in a school setting you might review the policy for referring those cases that are beyond your resources; in a university department you might consider admissions criteria. Whatever setting you are in, and whichever task you are undertaking, similar dynamics occur.

This is the first time your group has met in awhile. Generally, the group members have worked well together, agreeing to disagree and working out process issues to everyone's satisfaction. Recently, though, several new members joined the group, dramatically altering the dynamics. One new member in particular seems to have a hidden agenda. He is very opinionated and dogmatic and seems unwilling to listen to others' opinions. Shades of gray elude him, and he tends to see most things as right or wrong. You are amazed at how easily he can draw the whole group off task. The other group members allow this person to manipulate and control them, but all the while they fume and feel resentful. Nobody will confront his inappropriate behavior or take action to keep the discussion focused constructively.

After today's long, unproductive meeting, you ask yourself a number of questions: What is this conflict really about? How are the dynamics that are playing out in the meetings representative of power struggles occurring within the larger organization? What can be done to alter the destructive pattern that has become established? What can I do during the next meeting to help the group get back on track? What can I do to stay centered and present in the meetings? How can I best deal with such an obstructive participant? How can I help the group become more cohesive so that we can accomplish our objectives?

Although this example describes a situation specific to a task group, the same issues and dynamics often exist in counseling groups, therapy groups, and psychoeducational groups. Each week group leaders must face a host of issues and challenges for which they are not sufficiently prepared. Although many of these conflicts and struggles take place in sessions with clients, just as often group leaders are embroiled in difficult situations with colleagues. In both cases, they find themselves trying to make sense of what is happening in the group and trying to figure out what they might do to help the group function more effectively.

As a means of gaining a better understanding of how group leaders can function most effectively, we asked experienced group leaders to identify and discuss the issues they have found most challenging during their careers. In each chapter, the authors provide a personal introduction to the subject in which they discuss their struggles with the issues they have identified as most significant. Then they explore what others have written about the topic. Finally, they discuss their own ideas as well as applications to group leadership. They discuss the implications of these ideas for group work.

The first two chapters address the person of the group practitioner. Chapter 1, written by Allan Dye and Kathryn Norsworthy, looks at the journey involved in becoming an effective group leader. The authors reveal themselves, both personally and professionally, as they explain their paths to becoming advanced group leaders. They share the trials and errors, serendipity, and stages of their development. Their tales shed light on how advanced techniques develop and on the characteristics of these cutting-edge behaviors. Their stories will help other group leaders to put their journeys into perspective and to assess where they are along the way.

Chapter 2, by Jeffrey Kottler and Patricia Markos, explores the group leader's uses of self. The authors discuss the concept of self and the multiplicity of selves in each of us. They give lively examples of the self-talk and self-awareness that exist in the practitioner's mind. Further, they explain the array of therapeutic options that are available to the "experiencing self."

The focus then shifts from the person and development of the leader to the skills needed for working with various populations. In Chapter 3, Jesse Brinson and Courtland Lee offer helpful suggestions on how to become a more culturally responsive group leader. They set out guidelines for facilitating cultural responsiveness that are beyond what is taught in graduate school.

In Chapter 4, Arthur Horne and Linda Campbell discuss the proverbial round peg in a square hole—the resistant or difficult group member. They offer an approach to viewing these typically "dreaded" clients that emphasizes particular leadership skills and characteristics that they have found helpful, especially when dealing with group members who are acting out.

From special populations, the focus shifts to a discussion of special approaches to group work. In Chapter 5, Samuel Gladding describes a number of creative ways leaders can enliven and deepen group sessions. He gives examples of creative arts techniques that can be used in each stage of the process, ranging from collaborative poetry writing to movement exercises and musical improvisation. In Chapter 6, Holly Forester-Miller and Charles Gressard discuss applications of the ancient Chinese wisdom of the Tao to group work. They discuss how the Tao te Ching has been a source of guidance for them in their development as effective group leaders, and they provide specific examples of how they have found solutions to leadership struggles by turning to the ways of the Tao. They also share ideas and exercises that can help others get started in applying the Tao to their group practice.

The next three chapters focus on issues directly related to leading groups in organizational settings. In Chapter 7, Robert Conyne, Lynn Rapin, and Jennifer Rand explore the impact of the leader's interventions on the quality of task group functioning. They present a task group performance model for leaders that depicts three intervention choice components: type of leader intervention, level of leader intervention, and function of leader intervention. They then provide cases for the reader to evaluate as a means of enhancing his or her task group leader intervention techniques.

In Chapter 8, Chuck Kormanski and LeeAnn Eschbach discuss the relationship between group leadership and process consultation. They provide examples of journeys in which individuals learn to transfer their group leadership skills to process consultation and process facilitation and offer a set of process consultation guidelines to help group leaders who choose to make this journey.

In Chapter 9, Loretta Bradley and Elaine Jarchow discuss the relationship of their roles as leaders in the macro sense, as an association president and a college dean, to the roles of group leaders at the more traditional micro level. They stress the leader's role, the personal characteristics of leaders, and the leadership ethic. Through the use of case studies, they focus on the importance of integrity, trust, vision, and synergy in leadership roles.

With Chapter 10, the focus shifts to discussion of a new theoretical model, narrative group work, which allows the group leader to bridge the gap between events occurring at the individual level and events that occur on the larger sociocultural stage. The authors, Gerald Monk, Wendy Drewery, and John Winslade, provide concrete examples of ways in which narrative ideas can be applied in group work. The narrative approach contributes a new way of thinking about how problems arise and how solutions are formed.

The book ends almost where it started, with discussion of the journey involved in becoming an effective group leader, but in Chapter 11 the focus is on being the mentor. Richard Hazler, Rebecca Powell Stanard, Valerie Conkey, and Paul Granello identify the issues involved in mentoring group leaders and explore the factors that make for successful mentoring. They openly share their personal experiences, providing examples of being mentored and of being mentors.

Being a group leader is an awesome responsibility. It involves many factors that do not exist in the same form in individual counseling. Group leaders must attend to so many sources of information, so many dynamics and challenges, and so many different agendas that the pressure to keep things under control often feels overwhelming. This book provides both the experienced group leader and the beginner with an in-depth exploration into issues that have often been ignored by traditional texts and coursework. We hope that the chapters contained herein will inspire group leaders to be more clear-headed and intentional, yet also more intuitive and creative, in the ways they lead groups. We begin with a discussion of the journey involved in becoming a more effective group practitioner.

1

BECOMING AN EFFECTIVE

GROUP COUNSELOR:

THE JOURNEY

ALLAN DYE AND KATHRYN NORSWORTHY

*T*he editors of this book used a cross-generational method when composing the team of contributing authors. They selected a senior author for each chapter and asked each of those authors to "mentor a younger or less published colleague" in writing his or her chapter. The editors are to be applauded for choosing a strategy that allows fresh thoughts to be heard. Moreover, this feature was particularly appropriate for a book about group counseling, since co-leading with a more experienced practitioner is one of the most common means of acquiring advanced group skills. The tradition of handing down, person-to-person, from one professional generation to the next is well established in counseling and therapy.

At the same time, I (Allan Dye) do not define my collaboration with my co-author by the term "mentor." Both of us have had mentors, of course, one or two apiece—individuals whose professional characteristics we chose to emulate, by whom we were inspired, and whom we also respected as persons. As we talked about our professional heroes and heroines as we prepared to write this chapter, we noticed that each of us had actively chosen our mentors, usually without their knowledge or consent. Now that both of us may, ourselves, well be qualified by seniority and position for the title "mentor," neither of us aspires to hold that title, let alone describe to others how it may be successfully acquired. We do not think we are suffering from false modesty or are unwilling to accept a title we may have earned. We merely believe that the authentic and vital spirit of the term "mentor" requires that it is a title that can only be conferred; it cannot be taken, and seeking it is a behavioral contradiction.

The opportunity to collaborate in writing this chapter was serendipitous for us. We have been colleagues for 4 years, spinning busily in separate circles of teaching and program development but highly aware of our similar philosophies and interests. We had been on the alert for a project that would permit us to work together creatively when the invitation came to write this chapter. This circumstance, too, is fitting, for serendipity accounts for a great deal of how both of us have come to acquire advanced group counseling skills. That is, neither of us can say that we set out in the beginning of our careers with a clear view of how to become skilled in group work or that we learned all of what we know about group theory and methods in certain specific ways. We can say, however, that for a long period of time each of us has been eager to acquire competencies in working with groups and for that reason, as well as others, we have participated repeatedly as group members and have made one effort after another as group counselors to provide an effective experience for others. From time to time, seemingly by chance, we have learned about therapeutic group processes through the countless interactions we have experienced and witnessed, some of which have contributed to desirable change. We have noticed upon reflection that some patterns in counseling and therapy groups are relatively predictable and that some interventions are usually more effective than others.

Our original intention for this chapter had been to discuss advanced skills that we have found useful in group therapy. However, although it is true that some methods are more intricate and complex than others, we soon realized that it is the practitioner who becomes "advanced," not the skill, and that in describing the process of becoming skilled it is necessary to discuss the individual's personal as well as professional development. We do not presume to know how to construct a comprehensive model for achieving an advanced skill level in conducting group counseling and therapy, though we have several well-formed opinions about specific kinds of experience that can be useful. Short of having a comprehensive model, we are aware that each of us and other experienced colleagues have much in common, including a history of trial-and-error in working with groups.

The following are brief, personal accounts, first by the senior author and followed by the junior author, of our individual histories in group work: participating, conducting, studying, teaching, writing. We offer them not because they are extraordinary or exemplary but because each illustrates the process of wishing, intending, acting, learning, and then trying again.

ALLAN DYE: FROM UN-LEADER TO PERPETUAL ENGAGEMENT

I conducted my first group in 1964 during my second year as a counselor educator at Purdue University. As part of the curriculum for a National Defense Education Act Counseling and Guidance Institute, "process groups" were set up to enhance the graduate students' personal development by providing a weekly small group experience. The group members were to meet in a particular room for 2 hours each week, during which time they were to discuss anything they pleased, but in the present tense whenever possible. From the experience of conducting such a group, I remember the confusion, frustration, resentment, seemingly endless small talk, first disclosures, changing impressions of one another, pointed conflicts, and the beginnings of friendships that have endured.

My career has been as a counselor educator exclusively, and since that first group adventure I have conducted many other groups—graduate students in training, counseling and therapy groups for adults and adolescents having situational difficulties, human relations training groups with adults and adolescents, counseling groups for managers and supervisors, personal development groups for leaders in training, weekend encounter groups for agency staff members, therapy groups using primarily Gestalt methods, and demonstration groups of various kinds. Teaching and training in group theory and practice has been a major component of my professional life and one of the ways I have defined myself.

Much of what I attempted over the years worked quite well; some did not work at all. Regardless of the outcome, I think every significant effort I made to accomplish some objective using a group format enabled me to learn something, whether or not I was aware of it at the time. For example, during a weekend human relations workshop sometime during the mid-1970s, I was leading a small group consisting of members who were to have had prior experience with Gestalt methods. The small group was scheduled to meet four times during the Friday-through-Sunday workshop, with each session to last approximately 2 hours. During the second session, three members were distraught and weeping, each because of a recent, personal tragedy. As the group struggled to respond, another member calmly announced that he regarded such emotional displays as "phony and theatrical," not the sort of "genuinely therapeutic work" he wanted this group to do. Dismayed by his indifference toward the other members and furious at him because of his ill-timed, unfounded interruption, I told him to leave the group and not return. I stewed for several days after the workshop, wondering if I had done the right thing. Was I wrong to remove the member abruptly and without waiting for the group to decide what should be done? Why was I so angry, and how might I have remained calm until I could think the matter through more carefully? Had it really been necessary for me to protect the group from the member whose perspective was so different?

Many weeks passed before I could point to several important things I had learned from the experience. To begin with, I had discovered that weekend workshops can produce intensive emotional experiences, and the practice of self-selection may not ensure that participants are sufficiently informed about what they may experience. Moreover, the possibility always exists that an individual may not be suitable for a particular group—and this incompatibility may become evident only after the group is under way. I also discovered that I cannot always be calm, alert to everything that happens, totally accepting of all member behavior and attitudes, and completely certain about all the choices I make. This event helped me to more fully acknowledge an important reality: Although reflection on my behavior may cause me to be pleased or distressed, approving or disdainful, I cannot act in the present according to how I may judge my behavior in the future. I must be content with doing the best I can in the moment.

LEADER AS MEMBER (THE UN-LEADER)

Sensitivity and humanistic interpersonal relations were the order of the day when I was first learning (actually, teaching myself) to do group work in the mid- and late 1960s; moreover, at that time, no model of active group leadership had achieved prominence. This combination produced an emphasis upon egalitarian leadership and stressed the shared humanness of everyone present. The notion was that the leader should participate as "just another member." In exploring this modality, I tried to avoid thinking like a counselor, diverted group members from attributing expertise to me, and concentrated on being friendly and interested in others; I thought that being equal and having problems in common was what made the group a valuable experience for everybody.

Several things went wrong. For one, I seemed unable to stop noticing when someone's request for feedback was avoided, when there were conspicuous inconsistencies between a member's behavior and explanations, when two members' perceptions of the same events were different but they treated them as though they were identical. I saw countless opportunities to clarify, to acknowledge similarities and differences, to model active listening, and so on. Still, I held my counselor behaviors at bay in the spirit of universality. Other things also did not work well. I noticed that there were usually people in the group I did not much like and others who did not seem to particularly care for me. And there were often times when some members insisted that I act like a leader whether I wanted to or not. On occasions when I consented to perform an act of leadership or intervention, the same individuals became annoyed and resentful.

I learned that the notion that I could simply be a friendly and unpretentious member of the group and avoid any ambition or invitation to act like a counselor was faulty. It became apparent to me that nothing much of worth was going to happen until somebody provided some focus, encouragement, and perhaps direction to the group members on how to interact differently.

Another strategy I tried was to offer to work in the group on some of my own personal problems and concerns of the moment. In part, I was attempting to model and thereby encourage others' disclosure. I thought members might approve of me, identify with me, or accept me more readily if I acknowledged a dilemma and asked for help. This strategy, too, failed miserably. For one thing, I was never fully convinced that a group in which I held the leadership role was the proper, most appropriate place to ask for personal assistance. It was not a matter of my feeling superior to anybody else or feeling more sophisticated in problem solving. Even though I could not explain it at the time, my hunch was that there were more effective ways of leading a group.

In addition to my discomfort from this cognitive dissonance related to role conflict, I remember having the impression that some people seemed disapproving of the nature of one of the problems I presented. They seemed to think that I should not have had that particular problem in the first place. The problem I discussed was not serious enough, in their opinion. I think they expected something far more interesting from someone who had led other groups, who had studied counseling and therapy, and who should, therefore, be able to avoid the usual and ordinary pitfalls that bedeviled mere mortals such as themselves.

A more substantial difficulty with this strategy became apparent to me at a session in which I was truly distressed about something going on in my life. In talking about it in the group, I became quite self-involved and felt very sorry for myself. I lost completely my focus on everything and everybody else and simply wallowed in my self-pity. I was unable to extract myself and felt frustrated that nobody would help me. The members of the group were sympathetic but bewildered. I remember feeling foolish and incompetent.

During this period of my being an un-leader, group members commonly gave advice and instruction to one another and to me. I was always annoyed by this sort of "useless" coaching. I usually felt that I was being scolded and accused of being ignorant or incapable of seeing the obvious solution. It was as though the group members were telling me that something was wrong with me because I did not seem to understand what had gone wrong in the situation I was discussing in the first place, and was now being silly or dumb or lacked the moral fortitude to do what needed to be done.

To me, the biggest problem that occurred when I declined to fulfill the leadership role is that the group simply wandered. The sessions consisted of one random, directionless conversation after another. Discussions had neither direction nor depth. I kept hoping that this dynamic would change—that after I had gone to all the trouble of exposing one or more of my fallibilities the group would suddenly become cohesive, serious, and productive. But that never did happen.

From my un-leader era I learned that a group of people who are trying to do what a counseling and therapy group sets out to do needs somebody who will coordinate the effort. The group may well need somebody to specify how progress is to be made. It certainly needs someone who will encourage members to disclose and to talk about what is really bothering them and to respond sensitively and skillfully whenever someone takes the risk of saying what hurts or what the problem is. Somebody in the group needs to have an awareness of the entire group and each person in it, to be alert to what each person is doing and what kind of mood each group member is in. The person performing these functions need not be masterful, necessarily; but rather than merely listening to accounts of member difficulties, he or she must focus on the non-content, structural processes, because patterns invariably emerge relative to who talks to whom, which members seem to be influential, what themes are present but unspoken, which messages are being disregarded or avoided, and the like. Providing an overall perspective and commentary from time to time about these dimensions of the group gives members a word picture of how they are communicating. Without this kind of feedback a group session may be nothing more than a series of individual events, each involving one or two people at a time. The resources of the group as a whole are not realized because either the members are not aware of their potential usefulness to one another or nobody knows how to locate and release the interpersonal energy that is always present.

I learned in only a few trials that I simply cannot be both counselor and client, leader and member, in the same group. I am incapable of being alert, aware, and responsive to others while at the same time thinking about my own troubles or unresolved issues. When I tried to do both I was not very good at either. I finally realized that when group members invited me to "be like a member" they were not asking me to discuss personal problems. They were merely asking me to participate authentically, to be thoughtfully honest in the here and now, rather than to act in an impersonal, objective, stylistic way.

It also became clear to me that although somebody needs to fulfill the management function of the leader initially, eventually—sometimes quite early in the group's existence—the leader must relinquish that function and turn it over to the group. Every leader must accept the reality that at some level none of us knows any more about being alive, being human, coping, and struggling than anyone else. Every person must ultimately rely on his or her own resources to resolve life's dilemmas. Leaders and therapists who attempt to provide answers rather than to enable members to find their own answers are likely to be scorned by the group, sooner or later. To put it another way, group members at first believe they need a leader, and they are correct insofar as the role consists of teaching and demonstrating various facilitative methods. But the leader must realize that managing and teaching are needed by the group only temporarily, that most people quickly outgrow their need for sponsorship, direction, and approval. I learned that my job is to get the group going, to encourage people to disclose, to teach and demonstrate how to attend, listen, and respond. After doing so, however, I must step aside and get out of the way.

Individual Therapy for All

Once I became relatively adept at conducting counseling with individual clients, I viewed my group leadership role as counseling each individual member of the group, thinking it was my job to understand each person's struggles of the moment and to assist group members as actively as possible in resolving those struggles. I believed it was my responsibility to ensure that each member had made some kind of significant improvement by the time of the group's close. Several things went awry, however—one of which is that I got very tired. I also felt frustrated, unsatisfied, and defeated. Slowly, I began to see that the changes I hoped the group members would accomplish were not going to happen simply as a consequence of my direct, personal intervention. I had thought, inaccurately, that a group was basically a collection of individuals and that success in group therapy was a function of the therapist's skill in working with individual members.

I found that when I directed my efforts to individuals, I was able to achieve some success with some members but none at all with others. Similarly, I felt personally involved with some members but not at all involved with other members. Further, I found that I sometimes had to monitor the group's communications when their attention began to shift to someone other than my client of the moment. I did not realize at the time that my overinvolvement in the therapist role and my not understanding the difference between individual and group methods limited the impact I was able to have by inhibiting the members' collective use of their personal resources. I tended to personalize everything, claiming responsibility for successes and failures alike. I was well-intentioned, perhaps, but misguided.

A Technique for Every Occasion

In a somewhat later stage of my development, after I had participated in human relations groups, person-centered groups, and Gestalt therapy groups and had observed countless student-led groups, I aspired to become more comfortable and adept in the use of several types of methods and techniques. I made a conscious effort in some groups to use a variety of strategies, including group-centered, existential, communications, behavioral, psychodynamic, Gestalt, and the like. In retrospect, I realize that my decision to intervene in a particular way was, at times, probably based as much on my interest in hoping to master a particular method as upon a group member's need for my full attention to a problem. For a considerable period I was, for the most part, atheoretical, cloaking this outlook in the robes of eclecticism. In fact, I had concluded that most counseling theory fails both in accounting for client behavior and in instructing the practitioner in deciding how to intervene. Therefore, I chose to devote myself to more practical matters, namely to becoming proficient in the use of various methods, strategies, and techniques. Lacking a conceptual framework, I would judge whether a given intervention had been appropriate on the basis of the group member's immediate response. At the time, I was pleased with this un-complicated, pragmatic view of group work.

I was also quite active in the groups I led during this era. Whenever I had a clear idea of the struggles a member faced, I intervened promptly and directly to assist (I told myself) the member in making contact, heightening awareness, examining logic, exploring alternatives, hearing the perspectives of other members, and so forth. As a result, I sometimes intruded, and my influence sometimes turned the group away from a more appropriate direction it might otherwise have taken.

I learned some valuable lessons from this period, one of which is that I am more confident and more likely to be effective when I make use of a conceptual framework, though not necessarily a comprehensive theory, for thinking about the group and its members. In other words, different methods have different purposes, and a skilled therapist performs according to the properties of the specific group. It finally dawned on me that for each given group some goals, communication patterns, and methods are more appropriate than others. I found that using a particular framework not only did not hinder my performance or limit me methodologically but, in fact, proved useful for helping me connect how I perceived a situation with what I hoped to do about it, what I actually attempted to do, and what subsequently happened. I also noticed that I could conceptualize a group according to one framework while simultaneously using a different framework for an individual member. Eventually, I came to the realization that I required a conceptual framework for everything I attempted and that all of the frameworks I used had to be relatively simple, consisting of only a few variables. I discovered that I cannot control all the influences in a group—or even be aware of all of them. But I must acknowledge that they exist and then develop a way of thinking about the group that permits me to comprehend and assess what I am trying to accomplish.

OTHER SOURCES OF LEARNING

During my career, concurrent with conducting various forms of group work, I have participated as a member in ongoing and weekend encounter groups, human relations training groups, person-centered groups, and training groups for Gestalt therapy. For me, the most valuable result of these adventures was not what I learned about group counseling and therapy, though I did learn a formidable amount; rather, what was most valuable for me was the massive increase I made in my own self-awareness. My rationale for joining these groups was that I wished to learn more about group work. The plain truth, however, was that I was a prime candidate for extensive assessment of my priorities, motives, coping behaviors, relationship patterns, and self-perceptions of all kinds. In addition to receiving many hours of effective therapy, I witnessed the work of several experienced counselors and therapists, some of them brilliant in their wisdom and talent.

From these experiences I learned that people behave in relatively predictable ways in groups and that a group leader's use of nothing more than conventional, basic attending skills is likely to produce desirable effects almost immediately. In addition, I learned a great deal about patterns of group development, the effects of disclosure, disruptive and obstructive behaviors, facilitative versus destructive communication, and the like.

Teaching group courses has also contributed to my learning about group work. During the early years of my interest in group work, I had the motive of wanting to be able to teach these methods and understandings to others. When I actually attempted to teach or demonstrate what I had seen and experienced, I found that I acquired a better understanding of the subject at the same time. Moreover, after teaching others I was able to watch their efforts to perform and observe the effects of their efforts. Thus, I obtained feedback not only on the effects of my teaching but also on the depth of my understanding of the intervention in the first place. A steady and heavy supply of this high-grade feedback contributed immensely to my effectiveness as both practitioner and teacher.

Approximately 15 years passed from the time of my earliest interest in group work until I began to feel relatively confident conceptually and methodologically in this area. During this period in my life I had married, become a father, completed my doctoral work, started a career, and watched my children grow out of childhood. During the same time period, the mental health field was in the process of creating itself, experimenting, and moving sometimes in all directions at once. Throughout these years I was perpetually engaged in the process of becoming a group leader—practicing, learning about, and teaching individual and group counseling.

Kathryn Norsworthy: From Emulation to Authenticity

I chuckled as I read the notes Allan prepared for writing his autobiographical portion of this chapter. "What went wrong" seems to be the theme both of us have identified for our experiences in learning to do group work. The "humanity" of his story and the struggles themselves remind me of how perplexing and confusing situations can later seem obvious or universal.

I am one of those people who cannot claim only one professional identity. I identify both as a clinician and as a counselor educator. Currently, I have a full-time job in a graduate program in counseling and continue to practice my trade—counseling psychology—in the community. Although I came into the profession relatively recently, with my entry into a doctoral program in 1980, I am aware that the field of group therapy has changed a great deal since Allan's early working years. At the same time, I am aware that many of the debates, issues, and challenges that Allan faced in his early years endure today.

BEGINNINGS

My first experience in group counseling was with children. I was hired to serve as the counselor for a group of seven severely emotionally disturbed preadolescent boys. Naive and full of ambition, I initially attempted to help the members express their feelings and talk about their problems. As one might imagine, my goals rapidly became less lofty, and I saw that working toward having all the boys sit in the same room together without causing utter chaos and ruin would probably be a more realistic first step. Quickly, I realized that any therapeutic breakthroughs would depend on my finding out what to do with these extremely challenging children. It was in this context that I began my journey as a counselor and a group worker.

Like Allan, I view the process of development as a group worker as highly connected with one's evolution as a human being. In my case, I was initially drawn to such highly structured theories of counseling as social learning and cognitive behavioral models because I needed the boundaries and well-articulated directions about how to work that they provided.

Over time, I developed a greater sense of security in my ability to do group work, and I began to feel the need to expand personally and professionally. I decided to begin to work with adults. Naturally, my earlier feelings of fear and incompetence returned. I was working with a co-therapist, leading a multifamily group, while completing a graduate course in marriage and family therapy. I both loved and hated this group experience. Week after week I went to work with a sense of dread and a fascination with what could be accomplished by bringing all of these families together for a few hours. But I also felt that I had very little room to "not know." We felt constant pressure from the clients and administration to "make progress" so that the families could reunite and the bills could be paid. This experience occurred 15 years ago, but still today neophyte counselors must face the same pressure, especially with the advent of managed care. Novice therapists are placed in the difficult position of trying to balance economic and therapeutic pressures, while typically working with the most challenging clients in the mental health care system, at a point in their careers at which they have the least amount of knowledge, skill, and experience.

What did I gain from my initial experience with adults in group work? I established that I could survive the experience of 12 to 15 people expressing pain, rage, sadness, joy—the full range of emotions and thoughts. I learned that the clients were more impacted by one another than by us as leaders, yet they appeared to need us for something because they did very poorly when we were not present or when we remained silent for too long. Occasionally, a powerful, almost life-changing moment occurred in the group following an intervention by one of us. Mostly, I concluded from the experience that group counseling was hard work that required perseverance, patience, and trust on the part of the counselor. Trust in what I had not really determined. The words "trust the process" were not yet a part of my counseling framework.

At about this time, my own personal therapy began to hit me like the proverbial "ton of bricks," and I began to see what counseling was really about. Though I intentionally did not analyze the techniques and methods employed by my therapist, I found myself using them almost instinctively with my clients. It seemed to me that as I began to access and liberate aspects of myself, I began to invite my clients to do the same. This discovery represented a pivotal point in my understanding of how therapy works. As I became less threatened by my own feelings, I significantly expanded my therapeutic orientation with clients to include a strong focus on affect and experience.

Finding My Own Voice

Though this shift in my development as a group counselor was exciting, even with this change I continued to maintain a "there and then" focus. In other words, I encouraged clients to bring into the group experiences that had already happened, work through them, and make a plan for how to be different in the future. Of course, this approach can be useful in counseling, and it certainly kept me out of trouble while I did what I had to do in my personal therapy to become capable of having or facilitating an "existential encounter" in the group. Further, at that point in my life, my impression of the role of the group leader was to "do" something—to facilitate, to employ techniques, to direct or question. I did not yet really understand how my presence affected the members of the groups I led.

I remember watching the leaders of groups I attended during those years and paying some attention to who they were. Occasionally, I would feel touched by one of them, aware that I would like to be like that person. Yet I had no sense of the ways in which I changed through my encounters with those group leaders.

When I began teaching group work to others, I saw that students seemed to benefit the most from a highly collaborative process in which they contributed and participated maximally. The classroom became a laboratory in which the students developed and practiced group facilitation skills and techniques. I saw myself in my students—excited, terrified of doing the wrong thing, yet eager to learn and experiment. Watching their tremendous talents as they completed course projects and activities involving group work dramatically affected my own development as a group leader.

For many of us, dramatic personal or professional changes are coupled with serendipitous discoveries of metaphors that describe what has been missing in our life or work. In my case, Buddhist Zen philosophy supplied the missing "voice." Zen teachings emphasize learning through experience rather than through the analytic, intellectual model so deeply embedded in Western teaching philosophy. I felt liberated by the Zen idea of setting aside the goal in favor of "doing for the sake of doing" and by its valuing of "being." All of these qualities are cultivated through the practice of sitting meditation, during which concentration and moment-to-moment awareness are developed. Through my study of Zen and regular meditation practice, I began to approach my life and work differently, to divest to some degree from the achievement and production-oriented value system of academia and mainstream society, and to define my successes somewhat differently. In my group work, "here and now" encounters became an essential part of the counseling process.

Out of this study and practice, I began to recognize the importance and centrality of the experience in the present moment as the vehicle for growth and change. As I continued to return to the present moment over and over again, my clients and students began to do the same. Though I had studied existential psychotherapy and Gestalt theory in the past, they took on new meaning for me. This change in my receptivity toward different frameworks speaks to the issue of readiness in the learning process as well as to the need for relevance of the vehicle or modality through which the learning is delivered.

Concurrent with my study of Zen Buddhism, I awakened to the influences of feminist theory and practice in counseling and psychotherapy. My recognition of social and political factors that impact an individual's sense of control, choice, value, and agency expanded my understanding of how these dynamics can be replayed in the therapy room. I soon began to see how the dominant value systems in society are played out in the group, often leaving little room for those aspects of members that did not "fit in." Studying feminist theory also helped me to find my own voice, to value my own experience as a source of authority, and to invite my clients to do the same. The metaphors of this approach spoke to me at a deep level, articulating what I and my clients knew yet could not articulate.

Feminist theory and Buddhist philosophy in tandem provided me with a model for a way of "being" as a therapist that I had not found before. Perhaps I had not found my path previously due to a lack of readiness and maturity; perhaps I was hindered by our society's dominant value system, which emphasizes "being in control or in charge"—values that are modeled in the classroom and the therapy room. Feminist theory and Zen philosophy offered me a more egalitarian approach to group work, which fit well with my philosophy of counseling and my experience of what is therapeutic and empowering. The point I wish to make is that while it is not important to identify with my particular sources of inspiration, it is important, as a group worker, to find one's "self" in the process of group work, since who we are seems to be all that we have available to us in the final analysis.

FORMAL TRAINING

What I consider to be my formal training in group work began relatively late in my career, during postdoctoral study. Formal course work and systematic supervision at that time provided me with opportunities to articulate my experiences and identify gaps in my learning. I will never forget my first group practicum experience, during which I led a required group for master's students in student personnel. The group was made up of seven individuals who did not want to be in the group, and me. Because I had done a good deal of group work before, I felt pressured to do well, and it was probably in part due to the expectations I had for myself that the experience proved frustrating. To add to my misery, I was required to show videotapes of the group sessions to my supervisor and to my supervision group, something I had required of my own students in almost every skills course I had taught. The terror and humiliation I felt as I showed the tapes had to be as great as that of even the most frightened of my former master's students, but the experience of being observed was pivotal in my growth as a group counselor. It helped me to improve my skills dramatically, and seeing that I would not disintegrate when exposed to others in that way helped me to increase my ego strength. I also discovered that I was a harsher judge of my behavior than were the group members or my individual supervisor.

Other important learnings occurred during that period that also illustrate the process of my "becoming" a group leader. For one, I spent a year doing group therapy with some of the most talented clinicians I have ever known. Sitting with these master practitioners on a daily basis, receiving continuous feedback from co-leaders about my impact on the group, and having supervision specifically oriented toward my experience of the group and its impact on me were invaluable. This kind of supervision, primarily aimed at who I was in my "role" as counselor and how I, as a group leader, could use my own experiences of the group in a powerful way, set the stage for light years of progress. Equally powerful in this experience was being "seen," as the Gestaltists would say, by people I admired and respected. Who I was and what I could do were mirrored back to me in a way that helped me increase my confidence and self-esteem both personally and professionally. I think I learned far more about myself than any of the clients learned about themselves in the groups I led that year.

RECENT MENTORS

Today, in my work as a counselor educator and practitioner, my personal learning process continues. The central theme in my education at this phase of my work as a group leader seems to be risk-taking, learning to have the courage to keep trying something new. I have never been one to allow myself to get too comfortable at any junction. I am seeing that my journey involves stirring things up, then letting the dust settle to see exactly what I know, or can do, before moving on. I have been inspired by a few special guides, whom I have adopted as models, teachers, and friends. These mentors are people who have always been, and continue to be, inquisitive and questioning about our profession and who are active and contributory to the field of group counseling. Fortunately, they also have taken the time to make the efforts to "bring me into the profession." Their efforts have been critically important in my process of growth and of establishing myself as a professional. Their guidance has helped to steer me at times when I have found it hard to see exactly what steps to take, for the possibilities are often so vast. I am grateful to them also for modeling how to "be" and how to care for a junior "partner" who has "latched on," something that I find invaluable now that I am being called on to perform the senior partner role for my own students and beginning colleagues.

CRITICAL REFLECTIONS ON THE GROUP COUNSELING LITERATURE

What became apparent to us from a review of our personal histories is that we became "advanced" group leaders as a result of several sets of circumstances, some serendipitous, others quite deliberate. So far in this chapter we have written personally about the people and experiences that have had an impact on us. From a different point of reference on the topic of advanced group leadership, we now present a brief review of the current professional literature.

Most of the literature addressing group leadership describes the skills and behaviors that are needed to function effectively as a counselor (Corey & Corey, 1992; Gladding, 1995; Kottler, 1994). How these skills are acquired and how one becomes an effective group therapist are typically presented within the context of discussing training models (Anderson, 1982; Pearson, 1985) for students enrolled in circumscribed training programs rather than within the context of discussing the changes counselors undergo over a life span or career. In fact, with the exception of Kottler (1994), rarely does one find efforts to distinguish advanced group counseling in any way.

In the current literature, group leadership has been defined in a variety of ways (Johnson & Johnson, 1991), with the most agreement surrounding the factors involved in leadership (Forsyth, 1990). We have noticed in our own efforts to evolve as group leaders the importance of many of these factors; including identifying goals and directions in the group, facilitating the appropriate use of influence, and learning to motivate group members.

As discussed early in this chapter, scores of different types of groups and leadership styles exist. Leadership style is often dependent on the type of group or the particular demand characteristics at any given point during a group meeting (Kottler, 1994). Hersey and Blanchard (1969) described a model by which group leaders themselves select an orientation based on whether they are task- or people-oriented. In our own experience, our personalities, training, and practice, combined with our developmental phase, have determined our style of leadership. Clearly, leadership style is contextual and ever-changing, a dynamic process of growth for the counselor.

A key factor in grounding the advanced group counselor is adopting a theory or an integrated, yet flexible, system for conceptualizing the functioning of both the group and the leader (Gladding, 1995; Kottler, 1994). Corey and Corey (1992) suggested that without theoretical guidance, it is unlikely that a group leader will be able to help the group progress to the working stage. Kottler (1994) promoted the notion of pragmatism as the underlying philosophy for group workers. According to this philosophy, knowledge about group work is organized and integrated into a system of that which works in specific situations. Theory, experience, and information generated from continued research inform this dynamic system of practice. At the same time, the effective leader can articulate a rationale for each intervention.

These ideas resonate for us personally because, as we stated earlier, we both discovered on our respective paths as group leaders a need for a more clearly articulated system underlying our work. As most authors on this topic specify, one's experiences, gender, personality, and the like seem to impact how one selects a theoretical framework and determines future directions of change. Both of us agree strongly with the emphasis of Yalom (1985) and of Robison, Morran, and Hulse-Killacky (1989) on treating the group as a research problem, with idiographic outcome assessment as a part of each group. By treating the group in this way, the leader remains open to new information while systematically selecting the most promising intervention in the therapeutic moment. Thus, practice is not limited by orthodoxy, nor is it swayed, at the whim of the naive practitioner, by the "fashion" of the times.

It appears that a useful way to distinguish beginning and advanced group leaders is their level of skill development and knowledge about the array of interventions available (Kottler, 1994). It appears that, by definition, the more one knows, the more advanced he or she is.

Yalom (1985), Pearson (1985), Tollerud, Holling, and Dustin (1992), and others have outlined components of training models for group leaders. Most models include didactic presentation, skills practice with feedback from peers and instructor, and modeling of skills by peers and teacher. Yalom (1985) specified that each trainee must participate in a training group experience in which the goals are increasing self-awareness as a participant and potential counselor, gaining an understanding of the impact on clients of group counseling, and cultivating an appreciation for the multiple and complex roles and functions of group leaders. Although there is general agreement in the literature about the value of training groups, significant debate has ensued over several issues, including whether faculty should lead the groups, whether the group should be a counseling group, and to what extent the experience adversely affects the relationships between trainees when they are outside the group.

Yalom (1985) also stressed the value of personal psychotherapy during the training process. He pointed out that although the trainee may get very good feedback from supervisors regarding countertransference, blind spots, and other blocks to effective leadership, "some type of personal psychotherapy is usually necessary for fuller understanding and correction" (p. 531). Our own experiences certainly suggest that Yalom was right.

No model is perfect, but it does seem clear that some fairly sound ones are available for the initial formalized process of training group counselors. The questions remain, however, of what happens after the initial training; how people go on to become adequate, effective, advanced practitioners of group counseling; and what process of development occurs for the evolving group counselor. The literature does not address these vital questions.

CUTTING-EDGE BEHAVIORS

Each of us in the field of group counseling is on our own journey, learning from our successes and failures as well as from the literature available on the topic. We propose that as group counselors become more skilled clinicians, they are likely to engage in cutting-edge behaviors (CEBs). These behaviors may or may not represent original ideas in the field of group work; however, they represent a combination of advanced knowledge, experience, and trust in one's self that is unavailable to the novice group counselor.

We suggest that a CEB has these characteristics:

1. It is new, often an application of a group method to a new or different population.
2. It is unique, an extraordinary response to a situation that has not been made by others.
3. It is successful or shows potential for success in addressing the root cause of a problem.
4. It involves a significant amount of risk, either personal, professional, or economic.

CEBs may represent the counselor's creative solutions to perplexing problems or dilemmas in the group and may go against the conventional, mainstream practice of the time. We believe CEBs represent the true spirit of the scientist-practitioner tradition in action. Thus, CEBs are not typically "taught"; they are sometimes desperate, sometimes deliberate attempts to apply one's best guess as a therapist to a novel situation or to a group experience that has not been going very well. We have noticed that our own CEBs tend to involve recognizing an opportunity to try something new, having the courage to make the attempt, and allowing the experience to teach us what we need to know. What we have learned from these attempts has sometimes been unexpected and has often been something about ourselves. The interventions we have tried have frequently been effective; when, however, they have failed miserably, they have produced painful yet pivotal learning opportunities.

The most satisfying circumstance of our interests in group work has been that throughout our respective careers we have applied group principles, the principles of healthy interpersonal relationships, in every dimension of our professional lives, including routine and developmental faculty projects, social relationships with colleagues, classroom processes, and group counseling. We have learned that being involved and active in our own group contexts is a key to recognizing opportunities for the application of CEBs. We believe that the use of CEBs is a hallmark of a more advanced group leader.

IMPLICATIONS AND CONCLUSIONS

Although we have followed different paths in acquiring advanced group work skills, upon reflection we realize that we have both progressed through the same three relatively distinct but not mutually exclusive stages of development. In the novice stage, we were engaged in didactic and experiential learning about forms of group work, specific methods and techniques, and group leadership styles and were participating as members and clients in individual and group counseling. During an intermediate stage, our emphasis was on skill proficiency. The conspicuous activity was gaining practice in the use of specific methods and techniques. During this stage we became gradually more adept at performing various interventions while making observations about the idiosyncrasies of each. By the end of this stage, we had become comfortable in the leadership role while working with a variety of groups and in using a collection of individual-focus and group-focus strategies. However, we both recall that we were, at that point, functioning in an almost random way at times and that we felt a large, empty space where a conceptual framework should have been. We were unable to explain to our own satisfaction the relationship between such elements as goals, methods, personal-role presence, and communication patterns. Now in an advanced stage of development as group leaders, we have continued to conduct group work, alone and with co-leaders, often with the same populations and formats as before but occasionally in a new setting with individuals whose circumstances are different from those of the clients with whom we had worked previously. We have also attended training events, workshops, and conferences, and we have consulted frequently with colleagues about our work and theirs. Two important learnings have emerged for each of us during this period, one personal and the other conceptual. Each of us has finally arrived at a point at which we have attained a relatively advanced level of knowledge and aware- ness of ourselves as both person and person-as-leader; we can relate authenti- cally to others while also performing necessary leader functions. A hallmark of this stage has been becoming able to describe a conceptual framework for con- ducting and evaluating a group, session-by-session and across its entire exist- ence with respect to objectives, processes, and outcomes.

The experience of examining our own patterns of development has helped us to understand some essential tasks our students face. We think it would be helpful if other practitioners told their stories in their own voices as we have done in this chapter. Such accounts might form a starting point for group coun- seling research to address the qualitative aspects of how individuals evolve as group therapists.

The individual counseling supervision literature offers a blueprint for be- ginning to articulate the developmental process of the group leader (Bernard & Goodyear, 1992; Borders & Leddick, 1987; Stoltenberg & Delworth, 1987). The authors have described counselor characteristics within a progression of devel- opmental stages, articulating the skills most directly associated with each pe- riod. Although more research is needed to validate these theoretical models, many of the ideas may apply to the group counselor's evolution, even though the nature of group leadership can be so different from that of individual therapy.

We are hopeful that the knowledge base in group leadership will continue to expand, particularly in the area of articulating the path of development for the group counselor and the experiences and learnings that lead to advanced skill in this exciting form of counseling. Paradoxically, the final choices and directions will remain in the hands of the individual group worker on the front line or in the classroom, where the only thing that is available is one's self.

REFERENCES

Anderson, W. (1982). A training module for preparing group facilitators. *Journal for Specialists in Group Work, 7,* 119–124.

Bernard, J. M., & Goodyear, R. K. (1992). *Fundamentals of clinical supervision.* Boston: Allyn & Bacon.

Borders, L. D., & Leddick, G. R. (1987). *Handbook of counseling supervision.* Alexandria, VA: American Association for Counseling and Development.

Corey, M. S., & Corey, G. (1992). *Groups: Process and practice.* Pacific Grove, CA: Brooks/Cole.

Forsyth, D. (1990). *Group dynamics* (2nd ed.). Pacific Grove, CA: Brooks/Cole.

Gladding, S. T. (1995). *Group work: A counseling specialty* (2nd ed.). Englewood Cliffs, NJ: Prentice-Hall.

Hersey, P., & Blanchard, K. H. (1969). Life-cycle theory of leadership. *Training and Development Journal, 23,* 26–34.

Johnson, D. W., & Johnson, F. P. (1991). *Joining together* (4th ed.). Englewood Cliffs, NJ: Prentice-Hall.

Kottler, J. A. (1994). *Advanced group leadership.* Pacific Grove, CA: Brooks/Cole.

Pearson, R. E. (1985). A group-based training format for basic skills of small-group leadership. *Journal for Specialists in Group Work, 10,* 150–156.

Robison, F. F., Morran, D. K., & Hulse-Killacky, D. (1989). Single-subject research designs for group counselors studying their own groups. *Journal for Specialists in Group Work, 14,* 93–97.

Stoltenberg, C. D., & Delworth, U. (1987). *Supervising counselors and therapists: A developmental approach.* San Francisco: Jossey-Bass.

Suzuki, S. (1986). *Zen mind, beginner's mind.* New York: Weatherhill.

Tollerud, T. R., Holling, D. W., & Dustin, D. (1992). A model for teaching in group leadership: The pre-group interview application. *Journal for Specialists in Group Work, 17,* 96–104.

Yalom, I. D. (1985). *The theory and practice of group psychotherapy* (3rd ed.). New York: Basic Books.

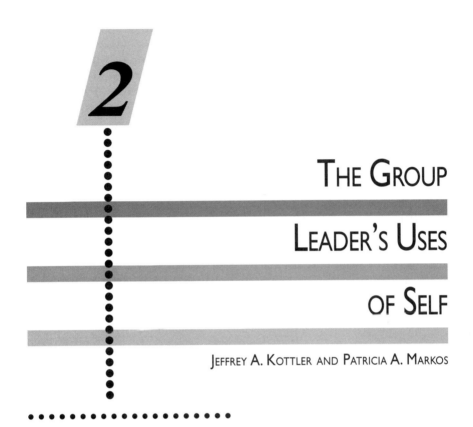

THE GROUP

LEADER'S USES

OF SELF

JEFFREY A. KOTTLER AND PATRICIA A. MARKOS

*G*roup leadership, especially by experienced practitioners, requires an extraordinary amount of synthesis. A thousand things are happening at the same time in a group session, some of them between members, others inside each individual. The leader has to make sense of what is transpiring at any moment and, given this assessment, attempts to intervene in a manner likely to be constructive in accomplishing process and outcome goals.

If one were to listen to the inner workings of a typical group leader's mind, something similar to the following dialogue would likely be heard:

There's something strange going on here, something not quite right. I can feel it, even if I can't figure out what is happening. I wonder if I should check this out or, at the very least, share my uneasiness with the group. Given how safe some members have been acting, they need to see some good ways to take risks in here. I could even demonstrate internally based language as I'm talking, a concept I've been trying to get through to them for some time.

If I want them to be more open, I need to be that way myself. Maybe I could disclose my own caution as a way of letting them know that I'm struggling with similar issues. I could even structure...Wait! What's going on now?

*I sense the mood is changing again. A few members are talking to one an-
other with their eyes. What are they saying? I'll join them with my eyes.*

Contained in this brief excerpt are several ways that the group leader attempts to interpret events occurring in the group and to focus on those elements
that might offer the best opportunities for learning and growth. Using the self
as the means by which to assess inter- and intrapersonal dynamics, process stages,
and systemic forces, the leader attempts to synthesize a large amount of information in the hope of coming to terms with the complexities underlying group
behavior.

WHAT IS THE SELF?

People, including group counselors, are typically leery about this whole business of "self." What is it anyway? People speak of the self as if it were a
single entity rather than a multitude of selves each seeking authentic expression. And what is this self that is purported to distinguish each of us from
one another?

As many definitions of self exist as there are authors writing about the subject. According to Roccatagliata (1986), the ancients believed that the self was
part of the soul, the essence of human experience. Mead (1934), however, viewed
self more as a process emanating from social interaction. Erikson (1963, 1980),
a representative of a more developmental orientation, conceived of the self as
an emerging ego state that is always in a process of evolving.

Some authors have described the use of self in terms of transference (Basescu,
1990) and countertransference (Epstein, 1990), consistent with a psychody-namic
perspective. They believe it is important for group leaders to reflect on the emotional impact they have on others. Not only must they be attentive and caring,
but they must be aware of every aspect of the way in which they present
themselves—the ways in which they dress, furnish their offices, speak, and
interact.

From a systemic orientation, Aponte and Winter (1987) described the use
of self as the internal voice the therapist brings into the session. Based on intimate self-knowledge and self-discipline, the group or family therapist continuously monitors how he or she is reacting personally to everything that is transpiring. The therapist then converts these internal reactions into verbal or nonverbal responses, whether in the form of self-disclosure or immediacy (Shadley,
1987; Watkins, 1990).

Adhering to a more constructionist orientation that takes into consideration
the cultural influences that shape one's notions about the elusive concept of self,
Cushman (1995) believes that the self does not exist in the sense of a universal
subjective experience. Rather, each particular time and place creates a different

self that can be understood only within the context of a person's indigenous cultural beliefs and shared moral understandings.

Each of these theoretical orientations adds a different facet to the puzzle of what the term "self" actually refers to. Even the definition of self in most dictionaries is presented in terms of compound, or hyphenated, words, its very existence dependent on a connection to another word with more substance—self-esteem, self-concept, self-expression, self-direction, self-centered, self-respect, self-deception, self-abuse. But "The Self"? How intangible, ethereal, smoky, and insubstantial.

The self is the total of one's unique awarenesses, perceptions, attitudes, characteristics, and personal reactions to experiences. It is the vantage point by which each of us views the world. It is also the compelling and persuasive voice through which professional communicators seek to influence others. It is the means by which individuals make sense of what they know and understand; it is through the self, as well, that individuals express ideas in a way that other selves can comprehend.

WHERE DOES THE SELF RESIDE?

The principle of "self" is usually thought to represent wholeness, or the integration of all parts of an individual—unconscious and conscious, past, present, and future (Satir, 1987). Yet David and Erickson (1990) distinguished an "ethnic self" that is unique for each person, dependent on his or her cultural identity and ethnic background. The ethnic self, according to these authors, is one facet of the therapist's self, that part that allows the therapist to make contact with each client's ethnicity by being aware of his or her own ethnicity. The same could be said for all other aspects of the self, including gender and a host of other "self" definitions.

Where does the self reside? In the head? In the heart? In the gut? Or, as Cushman (1995) has contended, in one's cultural beliefs? Making the concept even more complex, different parts of the self may pull the individual in different directions at the same time (Haber, 1990), as illustrated in the following excerpt.

The silence in the group seems to have lasted for hours, though when you check your watch you see that only 4 minutes have elapsed. Only 4 minutes? It seems like an eternity.

Your heart whispers that you feel insecure and vulnerable: "Have I done something to offend them? Maybe I wasn't clear enough? I wish I could..."

Your gut interrupts: "Shut up! This isn't your problem anyway; it's theirs. At least that's what you told them—that this is their group. Wait it out. Let them be responsible for their own behavior."

Then, your head-self kicks in: "What does this silence mean for each person here? For me, it might represent doubt, but I notice that a few people seem to be reflecting on things."

Each part of us, the doubts within our hearts, the reassurances within our guts, the reasoning in our heads, comes together in the very definition of self. In fact, when therapists speak of self, they are referring to the synthesis of all these different ways of viewing their role in the world of groups.

In the words of Polster (1995, p. 5), "There is no 'real' self, hidden by surface experience, but rather a community of selves that vie for ascendancy." A multiplicity of selves lives within each one of us. Therapists become acutely aware of the existence of their own selves at choice points in group leadership. Such critical junctures represent not only points at which clinical judgments must be made about which intervention to select but also points at which the therapist must decide which self will be permitted greatest prominence. Consider the following internal dialogue:

I (Jeffrey Kottler) am listening intently to the disclosure of a woman who is talking about the newfound power she feels as a result of the previous group session. She is tearful, emotional, and I can see her state of being is making the man sitting next to me nervous. Sure enough, he interrupts her with a distracting analysis of something that happened the previous week, not something in his life but a tragedy in the national news. Another group member challenges him to talk about his connection to those events, but he continues his intellectual sermon.

I consider my choices at this point, and as I review a dozen possibilities of how I might best intervene, I am aware of a different part of me, a distinct self, that is speaking. It is a "projected self," and it is distorting this incident, blowing my feelings of indignation out of proportion: I am rehearsing a particularly severe censure of this man's behavior in my head. But I also hear a "compassionate self" that is resonating with the man's feelings of being threatened, and I am tempted to reflect back to him his fear and apprehension. In addition, joining the internal dialogue, are a "manipulative self," a "withdrawn, aloof self," a "punitive self," a "worried self," and others I can't even begin to name. Each of them suggests—no, nags with—a different solution.

Although people often speak of these selves as "them," as disjointed parts, all of one's selves are connected internally. In fact, we contend that what makes group leaders most effective is their awareness, ability, and willingness to listen to their various internal selves as the parts of themselves that make contact with every group member and group action. The difficult task is deciding, through intuition, reasoning, experience, reality testing, supervision, and sound clinical judgment, which aspect of one's essential self will be most therapeutic at any given moment of time.

SELF AS INSTRUMENT

The concept of the use of self in therapeutic methods has often been traced to humanistic theorists such as Carl Rogers and Viktor Frankl, but its roots are actually found in the existential philosophy of Martin Buber and Soren Kierkegaard (Baldwin, 1987). More recently, Combs, Avila, and Purkey (1971) emphasized the idea that the self is the therapist's primary instrument of assessment and treatment. As much as therapists may delude themselves into thinking that they are relying on sound scientific principles and objective, reliable methods, much of the time they are "shooting from the hip," reacting to what is going on, improvising according to their whims.

Unlike medical doctors, therapists do not have tools like magnetic resonance or ultrasound equipment that can allow them to see inside people's heads during group sessions to determine why they are behaving in a particular way. Therapists have only their powers of observation, perceptual systems that, although highly trained and disciplined, are subjective. Unlike medical practitioners, therapists have no lasers, scalpels, or medications to use when they want to intervene in groups in a way that will affect changes. Therapists can use only their selves—their voices, personalities, and therapeutic actions—to make a difference. And unlike physicians, therapists cannot measure the impact of their interventions with biopsies, autopsies, and laboratory tests. They can rely only on client self-reports and on what they observe, sense, feel, and hear through the perceptual filters of their selves.

POSITIONING THE SELF FOR THERAPEUTIC LEVERAGE

According to a constructivist perspective such as that proposed by Gergen (1985, 1991) and Watzlawick (1987), there is no "objective" reality in groups. Nothing is objectively knowable, or even describable. Group workers create constructions of reality through the self as part of a system, whether that system involves a family they have joined or a group they are leading (Hoffman, 1988).

There are at least five derivations of the self that can be used as positions from which to initiate therapeutic leverage in groups (Real, 1990). In the *eliciting stance*, the group leader adopts a "one-down" position, using the self as a way to initiate structural changes. As stated by Real (1990, p. 260), "The eliciting therapist is like a little boat steaming along a rocky coastline, trying to gain access to the interior. Suddenly, there is a place where the sheer cliffs part. Turning inward, she follows this river until it forks off into two tributaries; choosing one, she follows it until the next bifurcation, and then the next, and so on, until she finds herself deep inside the mainland."

Consistent with a constructivist approach, the self as elicitor is employed to promote a shift in perception. Keen observation, as well as hunches, lead the therapist in particular directions. By immersing himself or herself in the client's narrative, the therapist elicits deeper and deeper elaborations of meaning until a constructive transformation occurs.

In the *probing stance,* the group leader presents alternative conceptions rather than merely eliciting deeper exploration of those presented by the client. The leader's stance is not one of expert; instead, he or she presents alternatives in an inquisitive, questioning way, using the self to communicate. For instance: "Help me to understand. Is the problem a matter of trusting the others here or of trusting yourself?"

In the *contextualizing stance,* the group leader employs a technique that resembles the "circular questioning" popularized by the Milan Team of family therapy (Boscolo, Cecchin, Hoffman, & Penn, 1987). The self is used as leverage for redirecting focus from the individual actions of one group member to the interactional patterns that connect members together. Speaking to one client, the leader says: "You talked of feeling hesitant to speak up here because you are shy. What happens in the group that leads you to act most shyly?" In other words, the leader helps members explore the interactional context for the behavior. As with the other stances discussed thus far, the leader's self is one of a curious inquirer, nonthreateningly exploring how any one member's behavior is both the circular cause and effect of every other members' behavior.

In the *matching stance,* the leader's self mirrors whatever pattern is currently occurring in the group. Rather than confronting a group dysfunctional behavior that has become entrenched, the leader joins with it. On an individual level, this technique is called empathic listening; on a group dynamic level, the system is altered when the leader resonates with the present patterns. For example, consider a scenario in which a series of arguments between group members has led to a lot of blaming and externalizing: "It's not *my* fault—*you* pushed my button." The leader may mirror the pattern by continuing to externalize what is going on to the point that members adopt an alternative position that is more self-responsible.

Finally, in the *amplifying stance,* the leader uses the self to elicit more of something (e.g., cohesion, intimacy, disclosure) in order to use it as a resource. A group leader might ask members to talk more about a feeling they experienced after something dramatic has just taken place.

Each of the five self stances just described are strategic choices; the leader selects a stance depending on desired outcomes and therapeutic goals. In this perspective, the leader's self is treated not as a stable entity but as a position one takes in order to influence group interactions in a particular way.

GROUP LEADER AS MODEL
OF PERSONAL FUNCTIONING

Thus far, we have described the leader's use of self as a choice, a deliberate position that the leader takes at any moment in time to facilitate a particular outcome. Yet there are also some relatively stable aspects of the leader's self that act in powerful ways to influence group members. By being the kind of person the leader wants his or her clients to be, the leader demonstrates through personal manner and style his or her very being, the embodiment of all that he or she considers most important in daily life (Kottler, 1993, 1994).

Being a model of high personal functioning places the leader in a position of greater power and influence (Beutler, 1983; Frank, 1973). It helps the leader to appear more confident, credible, self-congruent, and genuine (Orlinsky, Grawe, & Parks, 1994). Through the force of his or her personality, in addition to the application of any techniques or interventions, the leader increases his or her chances of impacting others (Dyer & Vriend, 1973; Kottler, 1994).

INTERNAL PROCESS, INTUITION, AND HUNCHES

Therapeutic excellence is based not only on the technical aspects of leadership but also on the personal aspects. Because groups are conducted by people, it is the leader's self that is making contact with others. For this reason Satir and Baldwin (1983), among others, believe that the leader's capacity and ability to monitor his or her internal reactions to what is happening in the group are critical therapeutic tools. Especially during times when groups seem mired in dysfunctional patterns, or members appear to be stuck, it is by relying on the self that the leader is often able to generate hypotheses about what is happening and even hunches about how to break through impasses.

Aponte and Winter (1987, p. 110) described a person-practice model of working with families that applies equally well to groups. According to these authors, the model "focuses primarily on the *bridge* between the therapist's personal life and his actual conduct of treatment. The model strives to enhance the psychotherapist's ability to utilize his own life experiences, personal assets and struggles in behalf of his professional performance."

To do this kind of work, of course, the group leader must be (1) willing and highly motivated to explore personal issues of the self as they are sparked by material in group sessions; (2) open to working on those issues that may interfere with his or her personal and professional effectiveness; and (3) skilled at bringing the self into group sessions in a way that capitalizes positive benefits (such as identification, intimacy, cohesion, and modeling) and minimizes side effects (such as self-indulgence).

This internal process of self can be illustrated in the following personal example:

In leading an ongoing therapy group for counselors, I (Jeffrey Kottler) noticed a pattern of conflict that had emerged between myself and one group member. I felt angry, misunderstood, and even abused by this person, but at the same time I reminded myself that I was the professional and the feelings I was having may be about my own issues. I was not happy with the ways I interacted with this member; even more, I despised the way I thought of her as I mused over the situation. Something was disturbingly familiar about these feelings—I realized that my relationships with several colleagues were conflicted in similar ways.

All of this internal dialogue took place during several minutes of the group session, during which time conversation moved on to another subject. I was jolted back to the present when I noticed everyone looking at me, waiting for me to do something. Unwilling to admit that I had not been following what was happening, so lost had I become in my own internal reverie, I deftly sidestepped the need to make this admission by asking another group member to summarize what he thought was going on. After buying myself a little time, I felt more willing to own my share of the previous conflict and suggest that the group attempt to make sense of what had transpired previously. Following a hunch, I admitted how sidetracked I had become by relating to this member not only how she presented herself but also how I imagined her to be. This vulnerability on my part stimulated similar sharing from her and prompted a breakthrough in the ways we related to each other.

SELF-DISCLOSURE

As the previous example highlights, disclosing one's self can often be a powerful way for a group leader to promote dramatic changes in member behavior, especially with regard to breaking down barriers to intimacy. However, self-disclosure is also one of the most frequently abused leader interventions, and it can create as many problems as solutions.

As Watkins (1990) noted from his review of the literature on the subject, a moderate degree of leader self-disclosure that is not perceived by group members as too personal is often considered helpful, but too much or too little of this type of self-disclosure can be harmful. Several others (Basescu, 1990; Kottler, 1994) have noted that group members can be exploited all too easily by a leader's disclosures that are excessive or designed to meet his or her own needs for attention and sympathy. Yet these authors have also reported a number of clinical examples in which the leader's revelation of personal stories appeared to be more effective therapeutically than was conveying understanding through other means.

Leader sharing has several dimensions, from the pedestrian revelation of age or marital status to the most intimate story. Basically, leader self-disclosure varies according to (1) the amount of information the leader shares; (2) the time spent revealing the information; (3) the intimacy level of what is shared; (4) whether the information shared is primarily positive or negative in nature; and (5) whether the information is congruent or discrepant with the members' experiences (Corey, 1995).

EXPERIENCING SELF

In one of the few articles that have been written about the leader's use of self in groups, Epstein (1990) referred to the dual modes of the "observing self" and the "experiencing self." Whereas the group leader ordinarily thinks of the former as his or her analytic posture, the latter—the self that recognizes coalitions as well as diagnoses member and group issues—often goes unrecognized.

Within any group session, or even part of a session, the leader experiences a whirlwind of internal thoughts, feelings, reflections, and images, many of which have little to do with the therapeutic work that is taking place and everything to do with his or her own issues. Sometimes this experiencing self acts as a distraction, a kind of countertransference that is out of control. At other times, the leader's inner reactions provide clues about the meaning of interactions or about possible courses of action.

When, for example, a group leader feels anger rising in response to another group member's perceived manipulation, this reaction represents both a self-indulgent overreaction and a legitimate response to the testing of boundaries. It is the *experience* of anger that, when bridled and directed properly, can provide valuable information about how others may be reacting to this person under similar circumstances. Epstein (1990, p. 153) described such a reaction: "I am feeling some anger rising now. I feel sandbagged, thinking this is typical of Marie.... I have often felt worked over by her in this way. My anger subsides, however, when I recall the fact that this kind of guilt-mongering is less true of Marie than it used to be."

The "experiencing self" can be used therapeutically in a number of ways. Here are just a few examples:

- *For immediacy:* "I'm aware of feeling manipulated and angry right now."
- *For internal self-monitoring:* "This isn't about me. This is just her way."
- *For cueing members:* "I'm having a strong reaction to what is happening right now. I wonder if anyone else is."
- *For modeling directness:* "I find it hard to hear you when you push me away like this."
- *For demonstrating limit-setting:* "It's not okay to play games in this way. If there's something you want to say, you know how to do it."

In each of these leader interventions, and in others such as projective iden-tification, which is described next, the self is used as the primary means by which the leader senses what is going on and then expresses those reactions to the group so as to initiate change.

PROJECTIVE IDENTIFICATION

Transference and countertransference phenomena come together in the process of projective identification when group members attempt to protect themselves by splitting off unacceptable parts of themselves and projecting them onto the self of the leader (Ogden, 1982). Miller (1990) described several stages in which this sequence unfolds.

In phase one, the client attempts to escape from threatening aspects of his or her self. The client may be feeling discouraged and frustrated, helpless to break out of a dysfunctional pattern of interaction in the group in which he exaggerates passivity in order to be rescued. The client projects these feelings of futility onto the leader, viewing the leader as the one who is incompetent and powerless.

In phase two, the client imposes additional pressure on the leader, uncon-sciously acting as if the projection is, in fact, reality. At this point, the leader's self comes into the picture, for it is likely that the leader is now not only feeling defensive and threatened but is also resonating with the member's helplessness. The selves of the two people, plus those of others in the group, are now intermingled in such a way that it is difficult to unravel who is causing what.

Miller emphasized that to make therapeutic use of projective identifica-tion, the leader must be open to using the self to work through transference and countertransference feelings. Phase three begins with the leader fully experi-encing the client's projections and using his or her feelings of vulnerability and hurt to work through the process. At this point, the leader must recognize the dynamic of what is happening—that it is the client's own sense of powerless-ness that is projected onto him or her. This recognition can occur only through careful self-scrutiny: "Wow, do I feel angry and misunderstood! I'm working as hard as I can here and all I get is grief; the clients are blaming me for things not working. I don't even want to be here.... Wait a minute! What is this all about?"

The leader begins to recognize what is happening: "Maybe this is not so much about me, about my shortcomings, as it is about this client who is feeling hopeless." Once the leader makes this distinction, he or she is in a position to intervene more effectively. The leader is no longer taking things personally. He or she has pulled out from underneath the weight of self-doubt and fear of fail-ure. The leader has disrupted a dysfunctional pattern of interaction by consult-ing the self and thereby reclaiming compassion and empathy.

Of course, the other side of this dimension of projection is the tendency for group leaders to disown the self, and especially those parts they experience as most threatening. Whereas at times group leaders take on responsibilities that are not really their own, at other instances they may be unwilling or unable to recognize their own roles in a struggle. When, for instance, clients do not meet their expectations for improving as quickly as they would like, when clients do not acknowledge sufficient gratitude for their help, when clients cooperate in ways that are different from their expectations, group leaders may very well project their own fears of failure and feelings of ineptitude on the clients (Kottler, 1992).

Therapeutic impasses often occur when group members become trapped in repetitive dysfunctional patterns. The leader, as much as the other group members, is part of this system, often as a result of some neglect, collusion, or enabling behaviors that are part of the self. Haber (1990) cited family of origin issues, cultural and gender biases, and other factors that are signaled by recognizable clues (such as looking at one's watch frequently during a session, finding that one is often leaving the group through lapses of fantasy, having strong emotional reactions, or feeling impatient). Only when group leaders are able to recognize their own contributions to an impasse will they be in a position to make adjustments in their attitudes and reactions and thereby affect different outcomes (Kramer, 1985).

OTHER USES OF SELF

From a study of how family therapists of various orientations made use of the self in their work, Shadley (1987) concluded that female practitioners were far more likely to capitalize on personal, disclosing methods than were male practitioners. In addition, the more years of experience the practitioner had, the more likely he or she employed a self-disclosing style. Not surprisingly, theoretical allegiance was also seen to play a role, in that humanistic-existential proponents relied on the self far more than strategic therapists did. Of course, one could also say that these types of clinicians simply use the self differently, since strategic clinicians make definite use of their intuition when constructing therapeutic tasks.

By analyzing input from diverse practitioners, Shadley found that therapists use the self in several ways, as described in the following list.

- *Creating connections:* By investing his or her self in the group process, the leader seeks to build cohesion and increase attachment among members. The leader might express this personal investment by saying, "I really feel close to all of you right now and am so honored that I can be part of your experience."

- *Encouraging members:* By using the self to challenge, confront, or push for goals, the leader initiates movement. He or she might say, "I am so proud of what you have already been able to accomplish and think you can do so much more."
- *Setting limits:* By deliberately creating distance between his or her self and others in the group, the leader maintains boundaries: "I sense that you want my approval for what you are doing. Perhaps that is something that only you can give yourself."

To these three examples, we would add the following:

- *Self-talk:* The leader models aloud constructive ways of talking to oneself: "It just made me so angry...I mean, I made myself angry over what happened."
- *Personal modeling:* Through personal behavior the leader demonstrates actions he or she believes others would benefit from emulating: "I have also had difficulties getting what I want, but I refuse to give away my power to others."
- *Structured demonstrations:* Leaders often model behaviors they wish other group members would try out: "Let's role-play this confrontation. I might try being more direct, like this..."
- *Transcendent empathy:* The deepest level of interpersonal engagement is one in which the group leader feels what others are experiencing: "It must have felt so humiliating for you to have been treated that way. I could feel myself blushing as I was listening to your story. I wanted to lash out at him, to make him stop."
- *Narratives and metaphors:* Much of what group leaders do is tell therapeutic stories that are intended to help members reframe their experiences: "I know of another group not unlike this one. People argue and disagree a lot there as well, but they think of the arguing as the way they show their love. It is only safe to really disagree with those people you care the most about."
- *Immediacy:* Group leaders may use the self in the present moment to reflect back to group members how they feel as a result of something occurring in the group, thereby providing constructive feedback: "Right now I feel so judged by you it is difficult for me to even hear what you have to say. It would help if you could say that to me differently."
- *Vicarious reinforcement:* Group leaders can increase the likelihood that certain desirable group behaviors will increase if they use the power of the self to reward individuals who are acting appropriately: "Raul, I really like the way you just took responsibility for your own difficulties rather than blaming others."

USES OF THE SELF: AN INTERNATIONAL FLAVOR

A few practitioners from several different regions of the world have described to us how this process of using the self in groups operates for them. We devote the remainder of this chapter to some of these instructive accounts. Our first example comes from a counselor educator in New Zealand who sees risk-taking as the essence of what he attempts to model in his groups. By judiciously and appropriately disclosing private thoughts, fantasies, dreams, and other personal reactions, he promotes a vibrant and invigorating group environment. The following episode illustrates this phenomenon.

The group I was leading had shared a very intense, intimate, and emotional encounter over a period of a weekend. One member, whom I will call Clive, spoke frankly and honestly about the distrust he felt in the group and the racial prejudices that he had experienced in his life. He described in graphic detail the humiliation he had suffered as an adolescent growing up and the abuse he received because he was Maori (the indigenous people of my country). He described further the emptiness and isolation he felt as a high school student and his powerlessness in not being able to alter people's perceptions because of the color of his skin. He shared at such a deep level that most of the other group members were profoundly moved by his disclosure.

As the leader, I felt overwhelmed by what I had just heard. The group was about to end, and I was at a loss over how to bring things to closure. I decided to share aloud my own feelings of paralysis, that I wanted so badly to say or do the right thing but I wasn't sure what to do next. This was a rare thing for me to admit publicly, that I was confused and disoriented, uncertain where to go.

Not surprisingly, a number of group members had their own opinion about how we should best end the session. As more and more people jumped in, the group took responsibility for preparing themselves to finish. In that moment, I felt like I had handed over any power I had to the group to make their own decisions about what they needed to do.

I have never ceased to be amazed at the resourcefulness of group members when they are given the opportunity to lead themselves. It all started with one group member sharing at a deep level, taking a risk to trust others. When I took a risk of my own, by disclosing my feelings of fright, this group came together in a way I could never have anticipated. My use of self was a small and insignificant act but one that reminded me about both the simplicity and complexity of being an effective group leader.

A school counselor and teacher from Australia who specializes in discipline problems among the youth of his country uses his self in a more logical than intuitive way:

I used to be a physics teacher, so I am reluctant to say that anything as soft as inner feelings plays a role in what I do with kids who are showing behavior problems. Rather, I prefer to say that I use my analytic and problem-solving skills, especially those that help me sort out what it is about a child's behavior that is disruptive to others, what is irritating to me, and what is self-destructive for the child.

I know that some of the most creative solutions that I have come up with to circumvent a crisis or resolve a conflict did not come so much from what I have learned before as from how I applied that previous knowledge to this novel situation. I am free to use my self in a number of ways: I will tell kids how I feel as a result of their disruptive behavior; I will share examples from my own life of when I felt bored; most of all, I will try to demonstrate aloud my own process of unraveling what I believe is going on and how I might intervene to change the course of events.

Another story of a group leader's experience with using the self as a catalyst for action was described by an American counselor educator who specializes in the supervision of group leaders:

I don't work on my issues or present problems in groups, but when something strikes me, and I have had an experience similar, or dramatically different, that might broaden or even change the client's perspective, I will share it. Group members have told me over and over again that they like my groups because I am open and willing to share myself with them.

I think the most important thing I can do as a group leader is to bring my self to the sessions. I recall one especially moving episode with a group member with whom I had really been struggling over a long period of time. Other group members had pretty much tuned her out, as she demanded so much and never seemed to get enough. I suppose I am describing a person that we unaffectionately call a "borderline." The label probably fit.

This client was like a sponge for love and attention, yet she drove people away with her neediness. One day she was telling a story—I don't even remember what it was about—that particularly moved me. My eyes filled with tears, even though I noticed others in the group had clearly checked out and closed down. I wasn't far behind them, but something she said hit me. Hard. She stopped her story abruptly, dropped her jaw, and gulped, "You DO understand." I had been mouthing words to the effect that I understood for months, but she couldn't hear them, no doubt because I was insincere. But when she saw my tears, finally she could trust me and the group.

The group leader, by allowing her self to be present in the group, to react spontaneously and emotionally to what was happening, facilitated a breakthrough that broke down barriers to progress.

Another means of using the self in groups was described by a Canadian nurse educator who specializes in group counseling for patients. Because music is an important part of her life, this group leader brings music that is especially meaningful to her into the group as a way of promoting spontaneous risk-taking, something that the New Zealander also mentioned was so important.

I like to start a new group, whether of adolescents or adults, by dimming the lights and playing a piece of music related to revealing oneself. I ask members to pay attention to how they are feeling as they listen to the music. Then I tell a short story about myself, revealing some of the feelings of reluctance to share that I have felt in the past, feelings that I have overcome.

As each group member tells his or her own story, I draw upon my awareness of what he or she is really saying, or not saying. I pay attention to the multiple levels of the stories, the pain that is hidden from view. I try to use what group members are disclosing directly, indirectly, and, at times, metaphorically. This helps me to increase the level of relevance, immediacy, and realness of whatever we are experiencing.

In all of these examples, the use of self that is most crucial is the part that communicates genuine caring and compassion for group members who are without hope. Group leaders' knowledge of group dynamics, processes, and stages is certainly important. Likewise, their techniques and interventions are useful as tools to meet the process goals of the group and the outcome goals of each member. Yet it is through the self that group leaders make contact with their clients, understand their clients' worlds and behavior, make sense of theories, and organize their actions in such a way that they can make the greatest difference.

REFERENCES

Aponte, H. J., & Winter, J. E. (1987). The person and practice of the therapist: Treatment and training. *Journal of Psychotherapy and the Family, 3*(1), 85–111.

Baldwin, D. C., Jr. (1987). Some philosophical and psychological contributions to the use of self in therapy. *Journal of Psychotherapy and the Family, 3*(1), 27–44.

Basescu, S. (1990). Tools of the trade: The use of self in psychotherapy. *Group, 14,* 157–165.

Beutler, L. E. (1983). *Eclectic psychotherapy: A systematic approach.* New York: Pergamon.

Boscolo, L., Cecchin, G., Hoffman, L., & Penn, P. (1987). *Milan systemic family therapy: Conversations in theory and practice.* New York: Basic Books.

Combs, A. W., Avila, D. L., & Purkey, W. W. (1971). *Helping relationships: Basic concepts for the helping professions.* Boston: Allyn & Bacon.

Corey, G. (1995). *Group counseling: Theory and practice.* Pacific Grove, CA: Brooks/Cole.

Cushman, P. (1995). *Constructing the self, constructing America: A cultural history of America.* Reading, MA: Addison-Wesley.

David, A. B., & Erickson, C. A. (1990). Ethnicity and the therapist's use of self. *Family Therapy, 17*(3), 211–216.

Dyer, W. W., & Vriend, J. (1973). *Counseling techniques that work.* Alexandria, VA: American Counseling Association.

Epstein, L. (1990). Some reflections on the therapeutic use of self. *Group, 14*(3), 151–156.

Erikson, E. H. (1963). *Childhood and society.* New York: W. W. Norton.

Erikson, E. H. (1980). *Identity and the life cycle.* New York: W. W. Norton.

Frank, J. D. (1973). *Persuasion and healing.* Baltimore: Johns Hopkins University Press.

Gergen, K. (1985). Social constructionist theory: Context and implications. In K. Gergen & K. Davis (Eds.), *The social construction of the person.* New York: Springer-Verlag.

Gergen, K. (1991). *The saturated self.* New York: Basic Books.

Haber, R. (1990). From handicap to handy capable: Training systemic therapists in use of self. *Family Practice, 29,* 375–384.

Hoffman, L. (1988). A constructivist position for family therapy. *Irish Journal of Psychology, 9,* 110–129.

Kottler, J. A. (1992). *Compassionate therapy: Working with difficult clients.* San Francisco: Jossey-Bass.

Kottler, J. A. (1993). *On being a therapist* (rev. ed.). San Francisco: Jossey-Bass.

Kottler, J. A. (1994). *Advanced group leadership.* Pacific Grove, CA: Brooks/Cole.

Kramer, J. (1985). *Family interfaces: Transgenerational patterns.* New York: Brunner/Mazel.

Mead, G. H. (1934). *Mind, self, and society.* Chicago: University of Chicago Press.

Miller, R. C. (1990). Projection identification and the therapist's use of self. *Journal of Contemporary Psychotherapy, 20*(1), 63–73.

Ogden, T. H. (1982). *Projective identification and therapeutic technique.* New York: Jason Aronson.

Orlinsky, D. E., Grawe, D., & Parks, B. W. (1994). Process and outcome in psychotherapy. In A. Bergin & S. Garfield (Eds.), *Handbook of psychotherapy and behavior change* (4th ed.). New York: Wiley.

Polster, E. (1995). *A population of selves.* San Francisco: Jossey-Bass.

Real, T. (1990). The therapeutic use of self in constructionist/systemic therapy. *Family Process, 29,* 255–272.

Roccatagliata, G. (1986). *A history of ancient psychiatry.* New York: Greenwood.

Satir, V. (1987). The therapist story. In M. Baldwin & V. Satir (Eds.), *The use of self in therapy.* New York: Haworth.

Satir, V., & Baldwin, M. (1983). *Satir step by step.* Palo Alto, CA: Science and Behavioral Books.

Shadley, M. L. (1987). Are all therapists alike? Use of self in family therapy: A multidimensional perspective. *Journal of Psychotherapy and Family, 3*(1), 17–25.

Watkins, C. E., Jr. (1990). The effects of counselor self-disclosure: A research review. *The Counseling Psychologist, 18*(3), 477–500.

Watzlawick, P. (1987). *The language of change: Elements of therapeutic communication.* New York: Basic Books.

White, M., & Epston, D. (1990). *Narrative means to therapeutic ends.* New York: W. W. Norton.

SUGGESTED READINGS

Anderson, B., & Anderson, W. (1989). Counselors' reports of their use of self-disclosure with clients. *Journal of Clinical Psychology, 45,* 302–308.

Anderson, S. C., & Mandell, D. L. (1989). The use of self-disclosure by professional social workers. *Social Casework: The Journal of Contemporary Social Work, 70,* 259–267.

Anscombe, R. (1989). The myth of the true self. *Psychiatry, 52,* 209–217.

Aron, A., Aron, E. N., Tudor, M., & Nelson, G. (1991). Close relationships as including other in the self. *Journal of Personality and Social Psychology, 60,* 241–253.

Bandura, A. (1977). *Social learning theory.* Englewood Cliffs, NJ: Prentice-Hall.

Boyd, R. D. (1990). An approach to facilitating personal transformations in small groups. *Small Group Research, 21,* 522–537.

Brewer, M. B. (1991). The social self: On being the same and different at the same time. *Personal and Social Psychology Bulletin, 17,* 475–482.

Butz, M. R. (1992). The fractal nature of the development of the self. *Psychological Reports, 71,* 1043–1063.

Cox, M., & Theilgaard, A. (1987). *Mutative metaphors in psychotherapy.* London: Tavistock.

Decker, R. J. (1988). *Effective psychotherapy: The silent dialogue.* New York: Hemisphere.

Derlega, V. J., Hendrick, S. S., Winstead, B. A., & Berg, J. H. (1991). *Psychotherapy as a personal relationship.* New York: Guilford.

Dien, D. S. (1983). Big me and little me: A Chinese perspective on self. *Psychiatry, 46,* 281–286.

Ettin, M. F. (1987). Within the group's view: Clarifying dynamics through metaphors and symbolic imagery. *Small Group Behavior, 17,* 407–426.

Giles, J. (1993). The no-self theory: Hume, Buddhism, and personal identity. *Philosophy East and West, 43,* 175–200.

Gladding, S. T. (1991). Counselor self-abuse. *Journal of Mental Health Counseling, 13*(3), 414–419.

Gordon, D. (1978). *Therapeutic metaphors.* Cupertino, CA: Meta Publications.

Guy, J. D. (1987). *The personal life of the psychotherapist.* New York: Wiley.

Hermans, H. J. M., Rijks, T. I., & Kempen, H. J. G. (1993). Imaginal dialogues in the self: Theory and method. *Journal of Personality, 61,* 207–236.

Hinson, J. A., & Swanson, J. L. (1993). Willingness to seek help as a function of self-disclosure and problem severity. *Journal of Counseling and Development, 71*(4), 465–470.

Hollan, D. (1992). Cross-cultural differences in the self. *Journal of Anthropological Research, 48,* 283–300.

Jacobs, T. J. (1991). *The use of the self: Countertransference and communication in the analytic situation.* Madison, CT: International Universities Press.

Kottler, J. A., & Blau, D. (1989). *The imperfect therapist: Learning from failure in therapeutic practice.* San Francisco: Jossey-Bass.

Layton, L. (1992). The self you seek is the self you find: Recent works on the empty, satiated, and/or transformed self. *Psychiatry, 55,* 147–159.

Littlefield, R. S., & Sellnow, T. L. (1987). The use of self-disclosure as a means for reducing stage fright in beginning speakers. *Communication-Education, 36,* 62–64.

McConnaughy, E. A. (1987). The person of the therapist in psychotherapeutic practice. *Psychotherapy, 24,* 303–314.

Merten, D., & Schwartz, G. (1982). Metaphor and self: Symbolic process in everyday life. *American Anthropologist, 84,* 796–810.

Mondale, L. (1985). A humanist use of the self: Driver or driven? *The Humanist, 45,* 31–32.

Ogbonnaya, A. O. (1994). Person as community: An African understanding of the person as an intrapsychic community. *Journal of Black Psychology, 20*(1), 75–87.

Sass, L. A. (1988). The self and its vicissitudes: An "archaeological" study of the psychoanalytic avant-garde. *Social Research, 55,* 551–607.

Scharff, J. (1992). *Projective and introjective identification and the use of the therapist's self.* Northvale, NJ: Jason Aronson.

Sharf, R. S., & Lucas, M. (1993). An assessment of a computerized simulation of counseling skills. *Counselor Education and Supervision, 32*(4), 254–266.

Sherman, E., & Webb, T. A. (1994). The self as process in late-life reminiscence: Spiritual attributes. *Aging and Society, 14,* 255–267.

Smith, M. B. (1994). Selfhood at risk: Postmodern perils and the perils of postmodernism. *American Psychologist, 49,* 405–411.

Tloczynski J. (1993). Is the self essential? Handling reductionism. *Perceptual and Motor Skills, 76,* 723–732.

Usher, C. H., & Borders, L. D. (1993). Practicing counselors' preferences for supervisory style and supervisory emphasis. *Counselor Education and Supervision, 33*(2), 66–79.

3

CULTURALLY RESPONSIVE

GROUP LEADERSHIP:

AN INTEGRATIVE MODEL FOR

EXPERIENCED PRACTITIONERS

JESSE A. BRINSON AND COURTLAND C. LEE

A cursory review of textbooks on the theory and process of group work reveals that many authors often relegate discussion of the multicultural aspects of group work to a brief section in one of the final chapters. This section, when it is included in a textbook, generally provides definitions of key terms associated with cultural diversity, stresses the importance of understanding the worldview of group members, and emphasizes that the leader should be aware of his or her cultural biases. The textbooks, however, generally lack clear-cut direction for facilitating the group process with clients from diverse cultural backgrounds, particularly individuals from racial or ethnic minority backgrounds. Furthermore, rarely, if ever, do the authors address the stages of group development in a culturally diverse context.

The cursory nature of these discussions of cultural diversity in group work suggests that group work with racial minorities is often considered relatively unimportant or that group dynamics with culturally diverse clients are no different than with members of the dominant cultural group. Regardless of the point of view, the small amount of available information points to the need for further research on cultural diversity issues in group work. Chau (1992) would agree. He has suggested that group work with diversity is a new frontier, with only a few lone souls treading on its soil.

As two African-American counselor educators, we have been treading on this soil for a long time. We have each conducted numerous groups with individuals from racial or ethnic minority groups. We have, over the years, written extensively on this topic (Brinson, 1995; Lee, 1982, 1989, 1992) and have wrestled with a number of issues associated with conducting such groups. We believe that any group leader, whether a member of a minority or the majority racial group, would be challenged by these issues.

In this chapter we discuss some of our struggles associated with group work with racial or ethnic minority clients and then present recommendations for enhancing service delivery to these clients through group work. Specifically, we offer a framework for facilitating more culturally responsive consciousness-raising and support groups. We hope that this chapter will expand the skills repertoire of group practitioners and advanced counseling students and will help to empower them in becoming culturally responsive group leaders.

GROUP WORK AND CULTURAL DIVERSITY: PERSONAL CHALLENGES

Collectively, our group work with ethnic minority populations over the years has comprised interventions in a variety of settings, including schools and community agencies. Because we have often been the only minority mental health professionals in a particular setting, the responsibility for providing leadership to address the academic, career, or personal social issues of culturally diverse clients has, explicitly or implicitly, fallen on us. Although it offers significant challenges, group work has proven to be an excellent way to address these issues.

A major challenge concerns the issue of power. Many times our group work has been with individuals who, because of their racial or ethnic status in society, have been marginalized or disempowered in some fashion. For many of these individuals it is a daily struggle to maintain some sense of sanity, or what can be called positive mental health. Their marginal or disempowered status often impacts negatively upon their self-esteem and self-concept. Many of these clients lack what can be called a "therapeutic sense of self," that is, an ability to value who they are and to recognize and accept their unique selves. It is only when people accept themselves and their realities with a sense of pride that tangible therapeutic gains are possible. Such prideful self-awareness contributes significantly to personal empowerment. Thus, a common challenge for the group leader is to promote a group process that will foster a therapeutic sense of self. The following case example illustrates how marginalization can impact upon the self-esteem of minority clients.

As a counselor doing volunteer work for a local community agency, I (Jesse Brinson) was asked to conduct a group with at-risk adolescents. The director of the agency referred 12 black adolescents to me for the first group experience. When I met with the group, I became aware that many of the adolescents had problems with self-image. Many of them made limited eye contact, spoke in inaudible tones, and appeared uncomfortable around others. I decided to conduct an exercise to get some feedback about the participants' self-image. I had each participant look into a box and say something positive about what he or she saw. Within each box was a mirror, so the first thing the participants saw when they opened the box was their face. None of the 12 participants could say anything positive. When I asked one girl to say something positive about her face and eyes, she responded, "My eyes and face aren't pretty; they're black." During the next 30 minutes, the group experience made clear that many of them had internalized a negative self-image.

Whereas this example involved African-Americans, similar examples could be provided for group work with gay and lesbian clients, people with disabilities, racial minorities, and women.

We have found that the challenges associated with power and ethnic minority clients in the group process generally center around the issue of trust. Trust is, of course, a critical ingredient in all groups, but our group experiences have led us to believe that trust can be the most difficult dynamic to foster with racial or ethnic minority group participants, particularly those who are marginalized, disempowered, or have a poor sense of self. People from culturally diverse backgrounds are often conditioned to believe that the same people who can help you can also hurt you (Brinson & Kottler, 1993).

Because trust is so difficult to engender among these clients, we constantly struggle with presenting ourselves to prospective or participating group members in a manner that will model trusting and trustworthy behavior. Although the color of our skin and our cultural realities may resonate in a positive fashion with some ethnic minority group members, those factors, in and of themselves, are not enough to establish the level of trust that will propel a group into the working stage. Like any good leader, we must also be nonbiased and nonjudgmental, communicate unconditional positive regard, be willing to become transparent, and take risks. It is important that group members from culturally diverse backgrounds perceive us as coming from a place that they feel comfortable with and understand, on both a personal and cultural level.

Fostering trust, while challenging for us, may be even more difficult for group facilitators who represent the dominant racial or cultural group. A question often asked of us in workshops on multicultural issues in counseling is: Can a white counselor really counsel an ethnic minority client effectively? We firmly believe that white counselors can be effective with ethnic minority clients in both individual and group interventions. However, any counselor, to be effective with ethnic minority clients in group interventions, must be culturally responsive in his or her approach to the group process.

We developed the guidelines that follow to promote cultural responsiveness in group leaders and to take the concepts of diversity beyond the cursory reviews found in most group-counseling textbooks. The concepts evolved from our own, and others', challenges and experiences in counseling culturally diverse clients in groups.

GUIDELINES FOR FACILITATING CULTURALLY RESPONSIVE CONSCIOUSNESS-RAISING AND SUPPORT GROUPS: AN INTEGRATIVE FRAMEWORK

A number of experts in multicultural counseling have described effective group interventions for culturally diverse client populations (Arredondo, 1991; Dufrene & Coleman, 1992; Fukuyama & Coleman, 1992; Harper, 1984; Lee, 1987, 1989, 1990; McWhirter, McWhirter, & McWhirter, 1988; Rollock, Westman, & Johnson, 1992; Sue & Sue, 1991; Tomine, 1991). Although the specific objectives of these interventions differ, they share a common goal—to raise the cultural consciousness level of group participants and provide them with a degree of social support. Significantly, cultural experts in both psychology and counseling have for years stressed the importance of a healthy racial or cultural consciousness for the optimal psychosocial functioning of ethnic minority individuals (Atkinson, Morten, & Sue, 1989; Clark & Clark, 1947; Cross, 1971; Helms, 1985). At some level, all of the reported interventions stress promoting such consciousness as a part of the group process. The interventions are generally based on a fundamental knowledge of the cultural realities of the participants and their potential for positive psychosocial development. With these interventions, cultural dynamics can be transformed into positive psychotherapeutic experiences.

A review of the interventions reveals that they involve multisession group consciousness-raising experiences that provide a supportive atmosphere through which participants are able to develop attitudes, insights, and skills that can help them meet personal, interpersonal, and environmental challenges. Such an atmosphere can promote empowerment in an often oppressive society. Further, it can help group members examine their options for change within the context of their cultural realities.

The remainder of this section provides direction for conducting a culturally responsive group experience, offering guidelines for facilitating consciousness-raising and support groups for ethnic and racial minority clients. These guidelines provide an operative framework for multicultural group counseling.

PRELUDE TO PRACTICE: IMPORTANT LEADER CHARACTERISTICS

No counselor, regardless of his or her cultural background, should attempt to lead a consciousness-raising or support group with members of diverse client groups unless he or she is perceived as being empathic and sensitive to human diversity. One manner in which group leaders can demonstrate a sensitivity to human diversity is to have an open and *honest* dialogue with group members regarding the views they hold about culturally diverse groups (Locke, 1992). Such dialogue could consist, for example, of a discussion of the roles of childrearing and sociopolitical factors in the shaping of current attitudes toward culturally diverse groups. This level of honest self-disclosure will convey to the group members that the leader has developed the awareness, knowledge, and skills to effectively intervene in the lives of group members from a variety of cultural backgrounds.

A culturally responsive group leader is aware of his or her own cultural values, assumptions, and biases and how these might impact upon the group process. Such awareness should include an acceptance of one's possible limitations in facilitating a group experience with members from a different cultural background. Accepting such limitations might necessitate, for example, co-facilitating a group experience with a member of a specified cultural group.

Culturally responsive group facilitation also suggests that the leader must have a knowledge base from which to operate. The challenge for the leader is to bring to the group process an understanding of and appreciation for the history and cultural experiences of the group members. The leader of a culturally diverse group must take into consideration the collective history of the population as an identified group as well as the individual differences among group participants. As Corey (1995) suggested, part of this knowledge base comes from having an existential perspective with regard to facilitating culturally diverse groups. A core value in such a perspective is an understanding of the group members' phenomenological world, including their cultural background.

A group leader must also be cognizant of cultural conditioning, have respect for certain values and traditions among diverse client groups, and be aware of how those values may play out in the group process. For example, when working with African-Americans in groups, the counselor must bear in mind that group's cultural mode of emotional expressiveness (Pasteur & Toldson, 1982). African-Americans may display their emotions in culturally specific language patterns or by displaying nonverbal behavior in a demonstrative manner. Likewise, for American Indians, the concepts of holism and spirituality may be important factors in the group process (Dufrene & Coleman, 1992). American Indian group members may be reserved in their level of self-disclosure when they are among non-Indians. Similarly, the idea of saving face may be a significant aspect of the process for Asian-American group participants (Leong, 1992). For Hispanic group members, sex-role socialization issues may impact upon the process (Arredondo, 1991; Barón, 1991). Hispanic women tend to be more reserved than Hispanic men.

Finally, the group leader must be able to employ a repertoire of culturally relevant techniques—that is, techniques that are consistent with the clients' life experiences and cultural values. Corey (1995) advocated technical eclecticism as an operative approach in group work across cultures. Such an approach is highlighted by flexibility on the part of the facilitator in using a variety of techniques to adapt group practice to fit the needs and cultural realities of the group members. To develop and implement such techniques, the facilitator not only must have awareness and knowledge related to cultural diversity but also must possess culturally responsive basic counseling skills.

DIRECTIONS FOR GROUP PRACTICE

Counseling professionals working with culturally diverse clients within the same group must be cognizant of the cultural dynamics that may arise. In other words, when members of more than one racial or cultural group are in the same group, the leader should be prepared for the various communication styles, values, and worldviews that are likely to emerge. What follows is a model framework for group intervention experiences designed to raise the cultural consciousness of group members and provide them with academic, career, or personal-social support. The primary goals of such a group experience are to heighten the group participants' cultural awareness and appreciation and to enable them to widen their support network of individuals who share common cultural experiences.

This framework is presented as a starting point for group counseling with ethnic minority clients. It can be adapted for use with youth in educational settings, elementary through higher education, as well as with adults in numerous community mental health venues. The framework can provide the structure for groups devoted to a variety of academic, career, or personal counseling issues.

NUTS AND BOLTS OF THE FRAMEWORK

The model presented here comprises a multisession developmental group experience. It is designed specifically to increase cultural awareness and promote academic, career, or social skills associated with a positive racial or ethnic identity. Six to eight participants would be an ideal size for the group experience. The number of group sessions is issue-dependent.

It is important that consciousness-raising or support groups for ethnic minority clients be approached from a developmental perspective. Given the oppressive environmental challenges that have historically impinged upon the psychosocial development of ethnic minority groups, the group must focus on assisting members in working toward their full potential. Individual and collective empowerment should be a key theme that permeates the group process.

Due to the importance of role modeling and cultural credibility in this type of experience, it is best facilitated by a member of the same ethnic group as the group participants. If this is not feasible, a competent and sensitive individual from the specified group should be sought out to participate in the experience as a co-facilitator.

Key aspects of the different phases of development for this group framework follow.

PREGROUP PHASE

As with any group intervention, careful and systematic planning during the pregroup phase will increase the chances of a successful experience with this model. In addition to attending to the traditional pregroup issues that have been outlined by experts (Corey, 1995; Gladding, 1995), the counselor working with ethnic or racial minority groups must consider a number of culture-specific issues as well.

For example, group entry anxiety can be particularly acute for ethnic minority individuals (Barón, 1991). This increased level of anxiety may be related to general ambiguity concerning counseling, lack of knowledge about counseling, or a general suspicion of counseling as a helping intervention (Fischer & Cohen, 1972; McKinlay, 1973; Neighbors & Jackson, 1984; Van Deusen, 1982; Veroff, Kulka, & Douvan, 1981; Yuen & Tinsley, 1981). The group leader should begin the process of alleviating such anxiety during the pregroup interview. General group goals and objectives should be described in as much detail as possible to reduce the ambiguity of the process. In addition, possible misgivings or concerns clients may have about counseling in general, and group counseling in particular, should be explored within the context of the clients' cultural worldview.

Further, during the pregroup planning phase decisions should be made concerning group composition. In addition to age, gender, education, family status, and socioeconomic status, the group leader may need to consider cultural value orientations and their impact on prescribed interaction patterns. For example, in some cultural contexts it may be inappropriate for men and women to be in the same group. Likewise, it may be culturally inappropriate to place people of different ages together.

Along these lines, careful thought should be given to placing individuals with different levels of ethnic or racial identity in the same group. Because an important aspect of the group experience is its effect on the participants' racial or cultural identity, the group leader should carefully consider what group composition will maximize this variable. A key question is: Will the group process best be enhanced with individuals who are at roughly the same stage of ethnic identity development or with people who are at various stages in this evolutionary process?

ORIENTATION AND EXPLORATION PHASE

The goal of the initial phase of a consciousness-raising or support group is to orient members to the group experience and afford them an opportunity to explore the nature of the group process. During this phase, the members get acquainted, define specific goals, establish ground rules, and articulate expectations. With ethnically or culturally diverse groups, an issue that may need to be considered carefully is whether a ground rule should be set regarding the beginning and ending time for the group session. Because distinct cultural differences concerning perceptions of time exist, it may be necessary to make accommodations for differential time perspectives. Significantly, group members must begin to develop a sense of trust in one another, the facilitator(s), and the process itself.

It is important, therefore, that the facilitator(s) work to create a safe environment and provide structure to further alleviate, as much as possible, entry anxiety. Specifically, this process entails promoting cultural comfort and validation for the group participants. An important aspect may be acknowledging cultural prohibitions against disclosing personal or family problems or against the open expression of feelings. Because the group process is generally predicated on self-disclosure and the expression of feelings, it is important that the facilitator(s) communicate respect for each group member's personal and cultural boundaries with regard to these behaviors. The facilitator(s) should model, respectfully, each member's right to pass or self-disclose in a personal and culturally appropriate manner as the group process unfolds.

During this phase, the facilitator(s) should invite members to begin to tell their story. Westwood and Ishiyama (1990), in discussing the communication process as an intervention for client change, provided practical suggestions for facilitating the storytelling process among culturally diverse group members. First, the facilitator(s) should, as appropriate, encourage group participants to speak their own language when telling their story; they will best illustrate their feelings using their own words and expressions. Second, if necessary, the facilitator(s) should encourage alternate modes of communication—that is, modes other than verbal exchange—to increase members' comfort and involvement. These alternate modes may include, for example, acting, drawing, singing, or dancing. Third, the facilitator(s) should acknowledge nonverbal expressions as part of the storytelling process. However, because such expressions are often culturally based, it is important to check in with group participants to ensure that their nonverbal communication is being accurately interpreted.

The leader(s) should model support and acknowledgment of each person's story, considering each story as a gift that the participant gives to the group. Doing so is important because in many cultures gift-giving is a ritual that is a significant aspect of interpersonal relationships (Sue & Zane, 1987).

After the stories have been shared with the group, the leader should assist the group in exploring common cultural experiences embedded in the presentations. Acknowledging common experiences will help to underscore the universality of those experiences and will help to build a foundation for group trust and cohesion.

A number of authors have suggested that the key to success at this phase of a consciousness-raising or support group for ethnic minorities is the development, by the group leader and group members, of behavioral, goal-oriented, prescriptive, and structured activities (Arredondo, 1991; Barón, 1991; Herrera & Sanchez, 1980; Jordan, 1991; Lee, 1987, 1990; Sue & Sue, 1991). Such an approach allows group members to develop criteria by which to monitor their progress and reduces the ambiguity of the group process. As this phase progresses, a reduction in ambiguity should be accompanied by a rise in the level of trust among group members.

COHESIVENESS AND PRODUCTIVITY PHASE

In this phase of the group experience, the group explores significant member issues in depth and develops action plans for personal empowerment. Significantly, in ethnic or racial minority groups, issues are addressed that will help raise levels of cultural consciousness and individual members are offered direction in dealing with specific cultural challenges.

Once an ethnic minority consciousness-raising or support group enters this working phase, its development follows some core themes that typically revolve around social, cultural, and historical influences on psychosocial development or problem etiology. The leader should provide opportunities for members to explore cultural value orientations and how these may contribute to personal issues or challenges. Specifically, members should be encouraged to examine how cultural dynamics such as kinship influences, sex-role socialization practices, religious and spiritual influences, and immigration experiences contribute to the etiology of personal and interpersonal challenges and issues.

In addition, the group participants should be encouraged to consider how the same cultural dynamics may contribute to resiliency and optimal mental health. They should consider ways in which they can use their cultural value orientations to effectively address or cope with academic, career, or personal-social challenges.

As needed, group members should be encouraged to discuss issues surrounding their acculturation status and level or stage of ethnic identity development.

They should have the opportunity to explore feelings associated with maintaining a sense of belonging and identification with their ethnic group while at the same time attempting to adapt or conform to the attitudes, lifestyles, and behaviors of the dominant cultural group. The facilitator(s) should encourage members to share with one another strategies and techniques for maintaining a balance between maintaining ethnic identity and acculturation.

The leader(s) should also invite members to disclose feelings related to oppression, encouraging them to explore incidents of racism in their lives. Such explorations should be conducted within the context of societal oppression and healthy ethnic identity development.

As members explore the dynamics of racism and oppression in their lives, it is crucial that the facilitator(s) prevent the group from becoming stuck at a place characterized by anger and blaming members of the majority group. The group members must move beyond anger and blame to personal empowerment. They must work to help one another channel their anger into developing the skills and capacity for gaining responsible control over their lives—control that they can use to support the empowerment of others.

During this phase of the group experience, the facilitator(s) might consider integrating culturally traditional and therapeutic practices to promote group interaction. Jordan (1991), Lee (1992), and Toldson and Pasteur (1975), for example, provided direction for integrating African and African-American expressiveness into group work with black clients. They described using selected African and African-American art forms, specifically music, poetry, literature, folklore, and graphic expression, as therapeutic aids in the group process. Similarly, Sage (1991) offered a model for incorporating American Indian craft work, which is traditionally done in communal settings, into group counseling.

Integrating cultural traditions, often ignored or considered deviant in counseling, into the group process helps to transform those traditions into positive therapeutic experiences. Further, such validation of cultural traditions during the group experience can help to increase the group's trust, cohesion, and productivity as well as decrease group members' resistance to the process.

CONSOLIDATION AND TERMINATION PHASE

As with any group experience, the final phase in consciousness-raising or support groups for ethnic or racial minorities is concerned with helping members put what has occurred during the group experience into meaningful perspective and bringing the group to an end. During this phase members assist one another in transferring insights and behaviors acquired in the group to their lives on the outside.

The facilitator(s) should assist the group with the following termination tasks. First, they should invite members to reflect on their cultural value orientations and the cultural factors associated with their presenting issues or challenges and ask members to share with the group any new insights they have gained related to their cultural consciousness as a result of the experience.

Second, the facilitator(s) should promote the development of concrete action plans. As part of the action planning process participants should be encouraged to assist one another in formulating goals and future objectives. Because a significant part of the empowerment process inherent in consciousness-raising is the realization that personal development is contingent upon group development (McWhirter, 1994), group members should be encouraged to consider how their action plans will help to empower family, community, or other kinship groups.

Third, the facilitator(s) should invite the group members to share affirmative personal and cultural statements with the group that reflect how they perceive themselves at the personal, racial or ethnic, and universal-human level.

The final group activity should consist of some type of celebration of self and culture. Innovative examples include a celebratory group meal featuring foods representative of the culture and a rites of passage ceremony in which group participants, along with members of their families and community, mark their passage from the group experience to the real world armed with new attitudes and skills. Such celebrations provide more than conceptual and emotional closure to the group experience. They also help participants culminate the process of increasing their cultural awareness and enhance the sense of kinship and support that has developed among the group members during the experience.

Conclusion

Throughout this chapter we have stressed that effective group leadership requires that the leaders be psychologically healthy individuals who manifest the core conditions of effective helping. Before leading a consciousness-raising or support group with ethnic or racial minority members, counselors must confront their beliefs and values about culturally diverse individuals and examine how their prior learning may impact upon the group counseling process. Although culturally diverse group work may be difficult for some leaders, we believe that it is not solely within the province of those who choose to specialize in working with culturally diverse groups. From our perspective, all group leaders have a professional responsibility to understand the cultural dynamics that make service delivery with racial or ethnic minorities different from most traditional models of group work.

The model described here is presented as a starting point for group counseling with ethnic minorities. With modifications, the basic framework can be used to explore a variety of academic, career, and personal issues with ethnic minority clients in a group setting. In all such groups, promoting a sense of self in a cultural context should serve as the basis for group intervention. This aspect of the group process is especially crucial, for members of cultural minorities often get little cultural validation in the majority society.

The group leader's competencies in facilitating such a group experience can result from a mixture of different elements. Although some can be acquired from an advanced understanding of group leadership and process, the ultimate success of consciousness-raising or support groups for ethnic minorities is dependent on the leader's appreciation of diverse worldviews. Although the theoretical basis for the group process may come from traditional approaches to group counseling and psychotherapy, the awareness and support emerge from the validation and affirmation of cultural value orientations among group members. It is important, therefore, for culturally responsive facilitators to be able to integrate the helping dynamics of traditional group procedures with cultural value orientations in the group process.

REFERENCES

Arredondo, P. (1991). Counseling Latinas. In C. C. Lee & B. L. Richardson (Eds.), *Multicultural issues in counseling: New approaches to diversity* (pp. 143–156). Alexandria, VA: American Counseling Association.

Atkinson, D. R., Morten, G., & Sue, D. W. (1989). A minority identity development model. In D. R. Atkinson, G. Morten, & D. W. Sue (Eds.), *Counseling American minorities: A cross cultural perspective* (pp. 35–52). Dubuque, IA: William C. Brown.

Barón, A. (1991). Counseling Chicano college students. In C. C. Lee & B. L. Richardson (Eds.), *Multicultural issues in counseling: New approaches to diversity* (pp. 171–184). Alexandria, VA: American Counseling Association.

Brinson, J. A. (1995). Group work with black adolescent substance users. *Journal of Child and Adolescent Substance Abuse, 4*(2), 49–59.

Brinson, J. A., & Kottler, J. (1993). Cross cultural mentoring in counselor education: Implications for retaining minority faculty. *Counselor Education and Supervision, 32*(4), 241–253.

Chau, K. L. (1992). Needs assessment for group work with people of color: A conceptual formulation. *Social Work with Groups, 15*(2), 53–66.

Clark, K. B., & Clark, M. P. (1947). Racial identification and preference in Negro children. In T. M. Newcomb & E. L. Hartley (Eds.), *Readings in socio-psychology* (pp. 169–178). New York: Holt, Rinehart and Winston.

Corey, G. (1995). *Theory and practice of group counseling* (4th ed.). Pacific Grove, CA: Brooks/Cole.

Cross, W. E. (1971). The Negro-to-black conversion experience: Towards a psychology of black liberation. *Black World, 20,* 13–27.

Dufrene, P. M., & Coleman, V. D. (1992). Counseling Native Americans: Guidelines for group process. *Journal for Specialists in Group Work, 17,* 229–234.

Fischer, E. H. & Cohen, S. L. (1972). Demographic correlates of attitude toward seeking professional psychological help. *Journal of Consulting and Clinical Psychology, 39,* 70–74.

Fukuyama, M. A., & Coleman, N. C. (1992). A model for bicultural assertion training with Asian-Pacific American college students: A pilot study. *Journal for Specialists in Group Work, 17,* 210–217.

Gladding, S. T. (1995). *Group work: A counseling specialty* (2nd ed.). Englewood Cliffs, NJ: Prentice-Hall.

Harper, F. D. (1984). Group strategies with black alcoholics. *Journal for Specialists in Group Work, 9,* 38–43.

Helms, J. E. (1985). Cultural identity in the treatment process. In P. B. Pedersen (Ed.), *Handbook of cross-cultural counseling and therapy* (pp. 239–245). Westport, CT: Greenwood.

Herrera, A. E., & Sanchez, V. C. (1980). Prescriptive group psychotherapy: A successful application in the treatment of low income Spanish-speaking clients. *Psychotherapy: Theory, Research, and Practice, 17,* 67–174.

Jordan, J. M. (1991). Counseling African American women: Sister-friends. In C. C. Lee & B. L. Richardson (Eds.), *Multicultural issues in counseling: New approaches to diversity* (pp. 51–63). Alexandria, VA: American Counseling Association.

Lee, C. C. (1982). Black support group: Outreach to the alienated black college student. *Journal of College Personnel, 23,* 217–223.

Lee, C. C. (1987). Black manhood training: Group counseling for male blacks in grades 7–12. *Journal for Specialists in Group Work, 12,* 18–25.

Lee, C. C. (1989). Counseling the black adolescent: Critical roles and functions for counseling professionals. In R. L. Jones (Ed.), *Black adolescents* (pp. 293–308). Berkeley, CA: Cobb & Henry.

Lee, C. C. (1990). Black male development: Counseling the native son. In D. Moore & F. Leafgren (Eds.), *Problem solving strategies and interventions for men in conflict* (pp. 125–137). Alexandria, VA: American Counseling Association.

Lee, C. C. (1992). *Empowering young black males.* Greensboro, NC: ERIC/CASS.

Leong, F. T. L. (1992). Guidelines for minimizing premature termination among Asian American clients in group counseling. *Journal for Specialists in Group Work, 17,* 218–228.

Locke, D. C. (1992). *Increasing multicultural understanding: A comprehensive model.* New York: Sage.

McKinlay, J. (1973). Social networks, lay consultation and help-seeking behavior. *Social Forces, 51,* 275–292.

McWhirter, B. T., McWhirter, E. H., & McWhirter, J. J. (1988). Groups in Latin America: *Comunidades eclesial de base* as mutual support groups. *Journal for Specialists in Group Work, 13,* 70–76.

McWhirter, E. H. (1994). *Counseling for empowerment.* Alexandria, VA: American Counseling Association.

Neighbors, H. W., & Jackson, J. S. (1984). The use of informal and formal help: Four patterns of illness behavior in the black community. *American Journal of Community Psychology, 12,* 629–644.

Pasteur, A. B., & Toldson, I. L. (1982). *Roots of soul: The psychology of black expressiveness.* Garden City, NY: Anchor Press/Doubleday.

Rollock, D. A., Westman, J. S., & Johnson, C. (1992). A black student support group on a predominately white university campus: Issues for counselors and therapists. *Journal for Specialists in Group Work, 17,* 243–252.

Sage, G. P. (1991). Counseling American Indian adults. In C. C. Lee & B. L. Richardson (Eds.), *Multicultural issues in counseling: New approaches to diversity* (pp. 23–36). Alexandria, VA: American Counseling Association.

Sue, D., & Sue, D. W. (1991). Counseling strategies for Chinese Americans. In C. C. Lee & B. L. Richardson (Eds.), *Multicultural issues in counseling: New approaches to diversity* (pp. 79–90). Alexandria, VA: American Counseling Association.

Sue, S., & Zane, N. (1987). The role of culture and cultural techniques in psychotherapy. *American Psychologist, 42,* 37–45.

Toldson, I. L., & Pasteur, A. B. (1975). Developmental stages of black self-discovery: Implications for using black art forms in group interaction. *Journal of Negro Education, 44,* 130–138.

Tomine, S. I. (1991). Counseling Japanese Americans: From internment to reparation. In C. C. Lee & B. L. Richardson (Eds.), *Multicultural issues in counseling: New approaches to diversity* (pp. 91–105). Alexandria, VA: American Counseling Association.

Van Deusen, J. (1982). Health/mental health studies of Indochinese refugees: A critical overview. *Medical Anthropology, 6,* 213–252.

Veroff, J., Kulka, R., & Douvan, E. (1981). *Mental health in America: Patterns of help seeking from 1957 to 1976.* New York: Basic Books.

Westwood, M. J., & Ishiyama, F. I. (1990). The communication process as a critical intervention for client change in cross-cultural counseling. *Journal of Multicultural Counseling and Development, 18,* 163–171.

Yuen, R. K., & Tinsley, H. E. A. (1981). International and American students' expectancies about counseling. *Journal of Counseling Psychology, 28,* 66–69.

4

ROUND PEGS IN

SQUARE HOLES

ARTHUR M. HORNE AND LINDA F. CAMPBELL

*W*e began our careers in counseling from a teaching and school counselor orientation. From the beginning, we were convinced that our job was not to fit the round student into the square hole of the school but to find ways to get the education process to work more smoothly for all concerned. Early on, it became clear to both of us that the students we found most interesting and appealing to work with were the ones who were most likely to be in the school counselor's office—that is, those who were continually in trouble at school (the truants, the bullies, the loudmouths who refused to comply with the rules) and those who presented other ways of being difficult (including whiners, slackers, and anxious, withdrawn, or narcissistic students). These were the students who elicited tremendous anger from teachers and administrators and, in general, made life less enjoyable for their fellow students and families.

As the years have gone by, we have noticed repeatedly that the difficult students are the ones who catch our interest and our energy. Like many others in the field of counseling who have jobs similar to ours, we are intrigued by the deviant, the different, the malcontents, and the maladjusted. While we want our families and friends to be in the adjusted sector of society, we are challenged, excited, and piqued by those who are different, and we enjoy the opportunity of earning our livelihood by working with those people most others do not want to work with, and for this we are grateful!

We have pinpointed several reasons for why the acting-out person has always piqued our interest. First, people have a reason for acting out, for defying the system that seems to work so well for most others. America itself became what it is as a result of people who acted out, people who defied authority and challenged that the system should be explained. While those who act out cause us anguish as we attempt to mold them to our methods, we have an admiration for the idea of independence and autonomy fought for and won. They are the ones who used their creativity to frustrate an unnatural system, who rebelled against institutions unnatural to much of human development. We laud their independence, autonomy, and antiestablishmentarianism, but at the same time we recognize the importance of facilitating the healthy demonstration and enactment of their independence rather than the "in your face" or manipulative, subversive, controlling approach so many people take.

Second, we are certain that people who act out are asking to be heard, to be counted in the system that so often denies them recognition and participation. They use the means they have to gain recognition, and while they push away acceptance, their acting out is a message of wanting to be counted and accepted, just on their terms. From working with clients ranging from elementary-aged children to chronologically mature adults, often in institutionalized settings such as group homes, state juvenile schools, and state and federal prisons, as well as in community mental health centers and private practice, we have become aware that much of their acting-out behavior is a function of a failure to find ways of being accepted and appreciated.

Third, the difficult group members are the ones who most specifically need our help. A common problem in the field of counseling is that most counselors want to work with the easiest clients. The upper-middle-income person who presents with a clearly defined problem and needs assistance in adjusting a life out of balance, who is motivated to change and is cooperative in his or her efforts, is the client many counselors wish for. Yet such clients are also the least likely to need counselors' help; they are the people who can find direction through reading, discussions with friends, or minimal contact with therapeutic services. It is the most difficult clients, the ones least likely to change on their own and the ones who often need the most powerful interventions, who are most likely to benefit from counseling. One private practitioner commented to us that he works only with highly motivated people who have a high probability to change and said that he referred difficult and oppositional clients to social workers and psychiatrists. That way, he believed, he was developing a reputation for being very effective and powerful. However, he was also missing out on the enjoyment of helping those most in need of counseling services.

The struggle we have experienced in working with difficult clients derives from two major paradoxes. First, we believe we can offer these clients services that will make their lives better, happier, and more functional. We are convinced that we can use our skills to facilitate their moving through life with less pain and more pleasure and to help them be more at harmony with the world. But people act out because they have not been provided the experiences that would enable them to support the position we take; we are seen as part of the system, not part of the solution. Second, in thinking that what we have to offer may lead to more enjoyable and satisfactory lives for our clients, we recognize that we are demanding an acceptance of our worldview. But we have seen sufficient evidence in our lives to let us know that the world we have created may not be the best for those with whom we work. We often wonder if their acting out is not a way of telling us that what we offer is too restricted and too confining.

DIFFICULT CLIENTS AND DIFFICULT THERAPISTS

That someone is being difficult is a judgment by a person in a position of authority about another person's failure to meet expectations (Kottler, 1992). Some have said that there are no difficult clients, only difficult therapists. The "functional" truth most likely speaks to the need to recognize that the therapist and client bring to therapy two lifetimes of experiences, some of which are shared, many of which are not. The therapeutic alliance built between the client and therapist or among the collective members of a group is unique. It will not be duplicated in any other therapeutic relationship. Thus, the therapist's perspective on who and what is "difficult" is as important as his or her knowledge of the conventionally recognized characteristics of difficult clients.

How a difficult group member is identified by the leader is as much a function of the perception of the leader as it is a function of the behavior of the member. All of the following may play a part in why a therapist may find a client difficult to relate to: (a) a lack of flexibility on the part of the therapist; (b) the stylistic way in which the therapist works; (c) the theoretical framework or interpersonal patterns through which the therapist interprets behavior; and (d) the way in which the therapist defines resistance (Kottler, 1992).

Working with difficult members in groups has been a central focus of the group literature from the earliest writings on group work. This focus is understandable given the appeal of acting-out members to therapists. Therapy or counseling groups are most frequently composed of members who have problems, who do not function as well as they or someone else would like. When a group of problematic people meet in a room for a period of time, one can anticipate that there will be challenges and frustrations for the group leader.

Difficult group members present in a variety of styles and have been described by authors in the group field as having a wide range of characteristics. In the modern group counseling literature, one of the first people to describe characteristics of and interventions for difficult group members was Merle Ohlsen (1970), who devoted a complete chapter of his book *Group Counseling* to group members who present difficulties for leaders and fellow group members. He identified the following types of difficult members: the resister, the advice-giver, the dependent, the submissive or other-controlled, the silent or withdrawn, the anxious, the griever, the scapegoat, the socializer, the acting-out, the hostile, and the monopolist. In his discussion of these difficult group members, Ohlsen provided descriptions of each category including the dynamics of the behavior and recommendations for group leaders on how to best address it.

Most authors writing about group counseling have included detailed descriptions of difficult clients. Some have done so very directly (e.g., Jacobs, Harvill, & Masson, 1994); others have described the characteristics of difficult group members and recommended interventions as part of discussions of age-groups, settings, or types of group interventions (e.g., Gladding, 1991). Ohlsen, Horne, and Lawe (1988) did both, including a chapter on difficult clients but also describing interventions for such clients throughout their book in discussions of age level, settings, and problem areas.

One of the most thorough discussions of difficult group members and interventions for group leaders to use was presented by Yalom (1995). He described the most problematic clients as monopolistic, silent, boring, help-rejecting, complaining, psychotic, characterologically difficult, and borderline. He did not include acting-out, aggressive, or hostile group members in his discussion. His presentation focused on group members more likely to be encountered in psychiatric or private-practice settings than in institutional settings such as schools or juvenile justice systems, and included descriptions of clients experiencing severe emotional disturbance. It is interesting to note that in the 1995 edition of his book he placed more emphasis on psychotic, characterologically difficult, and borderline patients than he did in earlier editions.

Jeffrey Kottler (1994b) also provided a description of difficult group members in which he identified the following categories: those who are argumentative, impatient, inarticulate, unduly literal or concrete, significantly divorced from reality, empty inside and unable to access internal states, despondent and expressing hopelessness, those who feel entitled to special privilege, those who have chronic, uncontrollable diseases that impair interpersonal functioning, those who have hidden agendas, those who ignore appropriate boundaries, those who refuse to accept responsibility for their plight and blame others, and those with little impulse control. All therapists have certain expectations for group members and their behaviors; for example, they should be respectful of others, cooperative, responsive, grateful for help, and follow through on their commitments. According to Kottler, the more a client deviates from the therapist's prescribed roles and expectations, the more likely that person will be perceived as a difficult client.

In the literature, difficult clients have often been identified in primarily two categories: the chronically mentally ill and those with personality disorders (Altshul, 1977). Those who are characterologically difficult often present with the following features: ongoing dread of re-creating past experiences in the present;

failure to develop a stable view of the self in relation to a stable view of others; a reliance on primitive defenses; no internal integration of affect; no sense of reliability in others; oscillation in self-esteem from grandiose entitlement to worthlessness; expression of rage in self-destructive acts; and fear of engagement expressed as persecution, abandonment, exploitation, or lack of trust (Leszcz, 1989). This population requires a very specific therapeutic focus and represents a defined and important category of difficulty in treatment. The working base from which we draw our understanding of difficult clients and issues is thus quite broad. In this chapter we focus on "acting-out" members of groups. Significant components of working with acting-out clients are reviewed, and means by which group leaders may organize therapeutic systems of intervention around the behavioral dynamics of acting-out behaviors are offered. One of the dynamics of acting-out behavior is resistance, the focus of the next section.

RESISTANCE

Theoretical perspectives on the function of resistance range from it being an obstacle in the therapeutic enterprise (i.e., psychoanalytic and behavioral perspectives) to it being an active but neutral phenomenon (i.e., social learning and cognitive-behavioral perspectives) to it being a healthy and self-protective process (i.e., humanistic and existential perspectives). From our viewpoint, the most useful approach for working with acting-out clients derives from the humanistic and existential perspectives. Human beings exhibit resistance to change because the preservation of basic life-support functions is a powerful priority and the maintenance of systemic integrity is a fundamental imperative. The continuity of experience, the preservation of a sense of self, the perpetuation of values, and the maintenance of a sense of power are critical to the core ordering processes of human beings. Resistance to change is not, therefore, an expression of pathology but a reflection of basic self-organizing processes operating in the service of the need to feel safe, secure, and viable. Such an explanation of resistance encourages patience, compassion, and a healthy respect for individual differences in the pacing of change. Clients' ambivalent feelings about change may be viewed as powerful allies to be worked with rather than against in the course of therapy. Helping individuals to differentiate their self-caring intentions from self-destructive actions can be an important element in therapeutic progress (Mahoney, 1991).

Otani (1989) developed a means by which therapists may conceptualize the way in which clients exhibit resistance. Its therapeutic usefulness is, of course, dependent on the therapist's operating theory of how and why people change. The four classifications of resistance Otani described are the following:

1. *Withholding communication:* being silent, rambling, making minimal responses

2. *Restricting content:* intellectualizing, making small talk, asking rhetorical questions
3. *Being manipulative:* discounting, externalizing, forgetting
4. *Violating rules:* missing appointments, delaying payment, making improper requests, displaying inappropriate behaviors

Consideration of these classifications, in conjunction with the therapist's diagnostic impressions, the treatment plan, and the perceived function of resistance, may be useful in helping the therapist decide how to respond to a specific behavioral pattern.

Resistant Adolescents

Many profiles of difficult members in groups appear in the literature. From them, it is clear that the dynamics of acting-out behaviors, although found in a number of populations, have most often been seen as a part of the behavioral pattern of adolescents. Because adolescents are a group that is of growing interest and importance in group work, significant findings in the area of adolescents and resistance are presented here.

McHolland (1985) offered the following theoretical and therapeutic model for working with this population. Adolescent resistance, according to McHolland, can be seen in two contexts: the developmental issues of adolescence and the social context in which the resistance arises and is maintained. The resistant behavior must be considered in terms of the system it serves; that is, the individual psychological system of the adolescent or the adolescent's family, peer, religious, or therapeutic system. Often, the behavior serves a protective function for more than one system simultaneously. When working with adolescents individually, the therapist may find these following eight guidelines presented by McHolland valuable in deactivating resistance:

1. Start by eliciting basic information. Do not ask why the adolescent is in therapy or what the problem is.
2. Avoid silences. Contrary to the therapeutic effect silence may have in work with other clinical populations, adolescents often feel intimidated or overpowered by a therapist's silence.
3. Allow the adolescent to talk without interrupting, advising, or judging.
4. Employ self-disclosure if it can be offered in a way that can promote trust and reduce the mystique of counseling. It is important to be aware of boundary issues and not become chummy.
5. Employ either direct or indirect identification of the client's problems, depending on the adolescent. The direct method of identifying issues is, of course, the most efficient and straightforward. If the adolescent is unresponsive, then indirect exploration may be effective, such as by asking, "What hassles are you having?" "What are you not getting that you want?"

6. Assess the level of functioning of the client cognitively and affectively. Can the client talk? Can he or she understand verbal communication? Does the client like to talk? Is the client depressed, anxious, introspective?
7. Avoid making the adolescent feel like he or she is being forced into a corner over the issue of problem identification. The therapist's pursuit of a problem may put the therapist in the same category with the parents.
8. Avoid taking sides with the adolescent or the parents.

Intervention should be based on the type of resistance the adolescent presents. Silence, for example, is common in many types of adolescent resistance; how the therapist responds to silence should depend on whether it is coming from an apathetic or shy adolescent and whether the adolescent is being seen alone or in a group. Four principles can assist the therapist in deciding how best to deactivate resistance:

1. Determine which system the resistance serves. The individual, family, peers, or therapist and client, among others, may maintain the system. The therapist can proceed effectively only when he or she understands the function the resistance serves.
2. Recognize the positive, protective function of resistance. Understand who it protects and how it is positive.
3. Go with the resistance, not against it. Put a positive label or interpretation on the adolescent's resistance whenever possible.
4. Assess how the systems in which the adolescent lives will respond to change. Be aware of the effect of the adolescent's change on others. Will the environmental systems allow change? Can they (i.e., the family, peers) be helped to permit change?

These principles can be particularly powerful in the group setting. A skilled group leader may introduce and facilitate these functions by reinforcing positive group interaction and focusing on the dynamics that deactivate resistance.

THERAPEUTIC USE OF ANGER

Researchers who have explored the presence of therapist anger in the therapeutic setting have consistently reported that counselors are generally unclear about when, how, under what conditions, and with which clients the expression of anger will be therapeutic. However, it is more often with difficult clients than with some other client populations that therapists find themselves dealing with anger toward the client. Good judgment on how to deal with anger is particularly important with acting-out clients because of the inherent power struggles, transferential issues, and resistance that come into play when working with this group.

Cahill (1981) suggested that by allowing anger into therapy, therapists teach clients to commit to relationships, to tolerate intense feelings, to think clearly when angry, and to confront others with their perceptions and feelings before becoming too angry to listen. Many individuals have never experienced healthy, successfully ending confrontations. Both in therapy and outside, anger is typically one of the most feared emotions. From our own experience in taking psychosocial histories of clients on intake, we have found that if a set of feelings were not allowed in the family, those feelings most assuredly were in the anger range rather than in depression, anxiety, or other negative clusters.

Therapists who are able to incorporate anger into therapy, either their own or their clients', assist the clients to normalize the anger and to feel successful in expressing anger without dire repercussions. For expressing anger, Alschuler and Alschuler (1984) suggested that therapists use "I statements" that include a description of their feelings, a nonjudgmental identification of the unacceptable behavior, and a description of the specific effects of the behavior on them. A nonblaming, rational description will increase the chances that the client will be open to change.

Weiner (1979) indicated that expressing anger toward clients is useful but should occur only when a client's self-esteem is strong and the therapeutic relationship is solid enough for the client to understand that the therapist's anger is not a reflection of the client's worth. Fong and Cox (1983) cautioned that the client behaviors therapists find irritating often represent tests by the client of the boundaries of the counseling relationship and of the therapist's trustworthiness, particularly in the early stages of the relationship. Also discussing therapist anger, Johnson (1971) suggested that the therapist's authentic expression of anger followed by a reaffirmation of the warmth he or she feels toward the client as a person may be an effective means of increasing the impact of counseling on the client.

Manipulation

Hamilton, Decker, and Rumbaut (1986) defined manipulation as the "deliberate influence or control over the behavior of others to one's own advantage by using charm, persuasion, seduction, deceit, guilt, induction, or coercion." Almost by definition, acting-out clients are often in the process of manipulation. Group therapists must be able to monitor the dynamic and to intervene when the dynamic is not detected or addressed by group members. Murphy and Guze (1960) described some of the forms of manipulation as the following: making unreasonable demands, controlling the conditions of therapy, soliciting promises, demanding special attention, being self-deprecating, expressing dissatisfaction, and threatening self-destructive behavior. Interventions for manipulation can be as simple and straightforward as making overt what is covert. The challenge is in identifying the manipulation during the group session rather than later and in being able to understand the purpose and desired outcome of the manipulation.

Whether a manipulative client can benefit from group work depends on how dysfunctional the client is and on the particular style of control the client favors (Kottler, 1994a). Because manipulative clients thrive in an environment of tension, conflict, hostility, and chaos, it is important for leaders to rely on confrontation rather than on interpretation as the preferred intervention (Friedman, 1989). It is also important that group leaders set firm boundaries, employ structure, not make exceptions, and limit their self-disclosure (Sklar, 1988). Further, the limit-setting should be therapeutic, not punitive, and not be triggered by the therapist's own frustration and impatience (Kottler, 1994a).

FAMILY RELATIONSHIPS—SOURCES OF SABOTAGE

Although group therapy with difficult clients does not naturally accommodate consultation with families, the therapist may find it necessary to consult with family members if the problem behaviors exhibited by a group member are a function of a family system. In such instances, Stanton and Todd (1981) recommended identifying the family members most capable of sabotaging or encouraging the client's progress and developing communication with them. Anderson and Stewart (1983) suggested the following guidelines for promoting the therapeutic welfare of the difficult client when family consultation is called for: (a) create communication with the person in the family who holds the power; (b) realize that all families resist change by members who hold significant roles in the family; (c) accept the family's view of the problem; (d) do not ask a family member to help in a way in which he or she is not ready; (e) take the road of least resistance and avoid power struggles; and (f) relabel resistance as helpful and view negative responses as feedback. Implementing these suggestions may take finesse because, after all, the group member is the client, not the family. However, when a client is entrenched or enmeshed in a family, the probability of successful change is low without an intervention or shift in the system at the family level.

GROUP COHESION

Group cohesion is a profoundly important dynamic of healthy and therapeutically successful groups and can play a particularly important function in groups that include acting-out members. Its function is parallel to that of the therapeutic alliance in individual psychotherapy. Group members who are dealing with higher levels of dysfunction may be able to make little distinction between transference and therapeutic alliance and may have very minimal abilities in self-observation (Leszcz, 1989). Groups are usually much more supportive of individuals who are perceived as trying but unable to make desired changes than of clients who seem able but unwilling to use the group process productively. Hence, group therapy for difficult clients provides two particularly therapeutic benefits: the means for acquiring empathy, and the means to experience loss without abandonment (Leszcz, 1989).

The absence of empathic capacity resulting from the deprivation of healthy emotional relationships early in life can leave an individual with interpersonal deficits and the inability to connect with others in any but superficial ways. Such individuals often develop dysfunctional means of relating, such as acting out. These same individuals often experience emotional or physical abandonment and rejection. The power of the group for such individuals is that it has the potential for providing corrective relational experiences as well as experience with the termination of relationships without abandonment. The group session is often the first opportunity in which the member can experience loss that does not end in all or nothing, in feeling rejected and worthless. The group session can allow the client to experience, in a healthy manner, feelings such as sadness and can promote self-integration (Leszcz, 1989).

LESSONS FROM THE FIELD

We have each had extensive experience working with groups; combined, our experiences equal nearly 50 years of group work. In that time we have had the opportunity to work with group members representing the full range of difficulties described in the literature. Although all of the members of our groups have presented interesting challenges and, at times, frustrating and aggravating learning opportunities, we have probably grown the most in our understanding of difficult group members through our many years of working with oppositional-defiant, conduct-disordered, resistant, and behavior-disordered clients. Whereas all difficult clients may be seen as acting out (even the silent, withdrawn group member is acting out resistance to participation and change), the more aggressive and emotionally acting-out member has been the most captivating for us. The following discussion is based upon our experiences and observations.

Our approach to group work is one we call "Setting Up for Success." The approach makes sense to us; we fail to understand why anyone would do the opposite, that is, set oneself up for failure. Yet many therapists do. We have worked with students in practicum who set themselves up for failure from the beginning and then are amazed when their groups do not work. The steps in setting up for success are elementary and commonly known, but we repeat them here as a reminder. Even experienced group facilitators and leaders need to have an occasional review and a clear understanding of the steps for success.

The initial step in working with acting-out group members is to have a clear understanding of why a particular group is being developed. Why this group?

Why these group members? Why this setting, this model, this size, this leader? Writers in the group field have indicated that an understanding of the territory can best come from the use of road maps, and the guides have ranged from Ohlsen's (1970) brief review of how to establish a need for, and then set up, a group to Morganett's (1990) outline of steps for establishing successful groups. Counselors who do not want to work with difficult group members should design and develop groups that take into account their preferences. Counselors who do not like defiant adolescents should not offer to run a group made up of any young people a school principal would like to see grow through counseling—the group will have defiant youth in it.

The level of structure the counselor selects for a group will influence the types of behaviors the clients will demonstrate. The more highly structured the group, the less likely the members will act out. Classroom teaching is an example of a highly structured group. Conversely, groups with no structure, those that are without theme or direction, are most likely to elicit acting-out behaviors as members attempt to establish expectations and limits. Of the four models of group work described by Conyne, Wilson, Kline, Morran, & Ward (1993)—task, psychoeducational, counseling, and psychotherapy—counseling and psychotherapy groups are more likely than the others to have the range of client problems described by Ohlsen (1970), Gladding (1991), Kottler (1994a and b), and Yalom (1995). Although many group members who present with problem behaviors respond well to structure, as is the case with anxious members, too much structure evokes a rapid demonstration of problem behaviors for others, as may be the case with hostile group members.

In addition to defining the purpose and structure of the group, the therapist must be able to solicit referrals that are appropriate and relevant to the group. Many beginning group counselors are so eager to have a sufficient number of people to form a group that they will accept any referrals available. Such a course of action is inadvisable. It is important that counselors define the purpose of their groups, the themes that will exist in their work, and the types of participants being sought. The counselor should establish with referral sources clear expectations of the clients they anticipate working with—and those they do not plan to include in their groups—not only to facilitate establishing the group but, even more important, to establish clear communication between themselves and their referral sources. For example, counselors who let teachers know they are *not* offering a group to all students but only to students addressing conflicts with their parents help ensure that they form the group they want. Conversely, counselors who accept all referrals limit their ability to provide the services needed by the participants or expected by the referral sources. The latter may stop making referrals if they deem their recommendations irrelevant.

Once the purpose of a group has been defined and established and referrals have been made, the next step in setting up for success comes into play: Screen, screen, screen. In the rush to initiate a group, many leaders do not take the time to interview potential group members, which is usually a major error. Although it is not always necessary to interview group members, doing so can save considerable effort later, particularly for less experienced counselors. Hilkey, Wilhelm, and Horne (1982) found that, for experienced counselors (those with 5 or more postdoctoral years of leading groups), conducting intake interviews and providing a structuring exercise to orient group members did not have much impact on how well groups functioned, but for inexperienced counselors (those with a master's degree and less than 1 year of group experience), groups developed much better when intake interviews and structuring were done than when they were not. Experienced group leaders may be able to compensate during the group sessions for less preparation, but inexperienced group leaders should not take shortcuts. It is always easier to identify difficult clients in an intake interview and decide to exclude them from the group or prepare in advance for how to address their problem behavior when it develops in the group than it is to not do screening and be unprepared.

There are limitations to the preliminary screening of members for groups, however. Kottler (1994a) made the point that whereas screening is important and should always be done, for several reasons it does not manage all the problems that can develop. First, many of the people counselors work with are adept at making good initial impressions. They may present themselves at the intake in socially appropriate ways, appearing affable, encouraging, and enthusiastic. Often, the difficulties do not develop until later in the group process when the leader begins to challenge, confront, or attempt to facilitate change.

Second, counselors, ourselves included, are typically not the best at identifying and diagnosing who will be a problem in a group. Counselors' diagnostic skills often fail to help them identify people who may bring challenges to the group setting. Although they may have "gut feelings" that a person is not right for a group, they may not be able to come up with concrete and definitive reasons for why this is so. A childhood rhyme illustrates this situation: "I do not like thee, Dr. Fell. Why this is I cannot tell. But this I know and know quite well, I do not like thee, Dr. Fell." Counselors, in general, do not like to be exclusionary or to refuse services to those in need, and so they often ignore their gut feelings and admit members to their groups even when they sense that something is wrong. Only later, when the "something wrong" becomes clear, do they realize they are working with a problematic group member.

Third, it is not possible to know the dynamics of a group until after the group has begun. Often, members will do very well in the initial stages of group work but will begin to develop problematic behaviors as they move toward working on intense personal concerns in the group setting. Some difficult clients, such as the monopolizer, begin to cause problems early on; other problem behaviors do not become evident until later. Yalom (1995) described one group member, Rhoda, who functioned well in the group until the 45th meeting, at which time she experienced a psychotic episode. This behavior problem would not have been evident during the intake process.

Fourth, even when problem clients are identified in intake, the counselor may decide to include them in the group, for they are frequently the people most in need of group work. Upon identifying a problem client, it is important for the counselor to review a basic question all counselors need to raise and continue raising throughout their careers: What is my need to be a counselor? That is, why do I want to be a counselor? All counselors should answer this question early in training and continue to answer it over time. (It is hoped that the answer will change as counselors progress through the developmental stages of being a counselor.) Counselors who do not want to work with difficult group members need to clarify in their own minds why they want to work in a field that addresses the needs of people who are distressed and disturbed and will, therefore, be problematic. We do not mean to suggest that all counselors have to work with all clients, but if counselors are not intrigued by difficult clients, if they do not have caring and understanding for those most in need, then they may be in need of career guidance. Counselors cannot expect that model people—those who are growing, fulfilled, actualized, effective problem solvers, and socially adept—will make up the bulk of their practice. They must anticipate working with people who may be receiving their help involuntarily (such as drug and alcohol abusers, spouse or partner abusers, aggressive and violent court-referred adolescents and adults, and disruptive students). Many of these people will not be cooperative or comfortable in counseling, for therapists represent the "system" as much as any other member of the established institutions that are requiring them to conform.

We offer counselors the following recommendations for working with acting-out group members should such individuals be in their groups.

• **Demonstrate Care and Understanding.** It is important that the acting-out group member experience a relationship of caring and respect with the counselor, one that shows understanding and appreciation for the events in the client's life that resulted in the situation as it exists. Developing such a relationship generally will not, of course, resolve the problem, but it will lay a groundwork that says, "I care." Counselors often have difficulty providing such an experience because they are human and get angry or hurt just as others do. Often the acting-out member will push the counselor to see how far the counselor can or will go before "losing it" and turning against the member. This "testing of limits" is a common occurrence for acting-out group members and should be expected. When it happens, counselors must take the time to turn inward and evaluate what is happening within themselves, what they are experiencing. They must remember that the purpose of the counseling is to help the client. Only after this self-reflection will they be able to figure out what response will be most helpful at the time. It may be a reflection, such as, "Joachim, when you lash out like this you seem to be wanting to push all of us away from you, as though we may be getting too close to you. What is happening here?" Or it may be an interpretation, such as, "Julio, your anger now is out of bounds for what we are doing. Could it be that we have reminded you of other events, other people who have hurt you, and that you are letting us know you don't want to be hurt again?" Or it may be a structuring statement, such as, "Jacob, you need to recall that we have two rules—work on your stuff and help others with theirs. What you are doing is not helping others, because they are getting angry and pulling away from you. Is it helping you? If so, help me to see how. If it isn't helping you, let's move on to something else that may be helpful."

• **Use Interpretations and Reflections Cautiously.** Interpretations and reflections have both benefits and disadvantages, and group leaders need to stay attuned to the potential impact such comments may have. Interpretations are powerful and have the potential of helping group members become cognizant of issues that may not be in their awareness. At times, interpretations may lead to a member having an "aha" experience and making connections between previously unconnected conditions, which can be a powerful and impactive experience. However, interpretations, particularly within the group setting, also have the potential for being problematic. They may imply that the group leader knows more about what is happening in the member's life than the member does; they may lead to dependent behavior on the part of the group member as he or she turns to the leader to provide answers and explanations; and they may lead to intellectualization, with the group member analyzing the meaning of the group leader's comments. In addition, interpretation in group work may be seen as threatening, particularly for difficult clients ("The leader knows more about me than I know about myself" or "I'll show you, you smart-aleck counselor..."). And, because many group members model the behavior of the leader, they may use interpretations, whether accurate and relevant or not, as a means of avoiding dealing with issues that are more relevant for the here-and-now work of the group or as a way of focusing on individual unresolved conflict, something that may be more relevant to individual counseling than to group work. Of course, if work on unresolved conflict is a goal the group leader has set, interpretations will facilitate the process.

The following scenario illustrates both the positive and negative sides of using interpretation in group work.

In one of our recent group sessions, a female high school student was acting belligerently to the counselor and hostile toward other members of the group. Because she had, the week before, talked about how conservative and judgmental her parents were and how they just did not understand the changing times, the counselor asked, "Carrie, are you angry with the group this week because you want to be loved by your parents but aren't able to find a way to bring this about? Are you hurting the group members because you want to punish your parents?" Carrie responded: "These people [the group] are just jerks and tight-asses. They can't even forgive someone if they make stupid mistakes." The counselor leaned forward and asked, "Carrie, what is the mistake you have made? Is it about sex?" At that point Carrie turned pale, began to cry, and said she was pregnant and did not know how to tell her parents. The impact of the counselor's use of interpretation and reflection was dramatic, the issue was relevant, and the progress was rapid. But the counselor's use of interpretation also had a negative side. When the counselor initiated a discussion about the experience with the group, members indicated fear of the counselor ("She knows what we're thinking"; "She knows us better than we do"), concern that they may be in the "hot seat" the next week, and a sense of inadequacy because they did not have the understanding the counselor did and so felt inferior to her.

• **Set and Adhere to Limits on What Is Allowed and What Is Not.** For the most part, limits should have been explained to potential group members during the overview presentation of the group as well as during the intake interview, when potential members were told more detail about the group, and during the first group session, when the ground rules for the group were being agreed upon by the members. Counselors must know what limits they feel comfortable with and what limits are reasonable for other members of the group, and they must make certain that everyone's safety and security are assured. No group member can be allowed to hurt another member. Counselors must be fully aware of the resources available to them within the group setting as well as referral opportunities.

At times, particularly when members are acting out, it may be appropriate for the group to negotiate limits. The benefits of such negotiation can be seen in the following scenario.

Recently one group member in a men's issues group was very nonparticipatory, stayed aloof from the group, and did not share. When queried about what he was experiencing and why he was withdrawn and distant from the group, he explained that he valued the group but that the issue he was dealing with was uncontrollable anger. He explained that he was afraid to participate because if his anger were ever allowed to come out, he might hurt someone in the group. The group members agreed that they wanted him to be a more active member. They commented that they had interpreted his behavior as resistance and perhaps a voyeuristic position but that they now better understood it. They invited him to become more active and encouraged him to express his anger within the group. A contract was developed that he would be able to be in touch with his anger in the group and that, should he begin to lose control, the other members would take action to restrain him. Thus, all six group members would be responsible for his and their safety. With this level of permission, he began describing his anger and his efforts to control himself in the group, and in the process he found he was able to stay in control, the first time he had experi-

enced that sensation in years. It was because the group confronted his nonparticipatory behavior and then negotiated the acceptance of his anger that progress was made. The group had established the limits.

• **Know When to Challenge, Know When to Yield.** One of the clinical skills that is fundamental to being an effective therapist when working with acting-out clients is having a sense of when it is beneficial to challenge a behavior and when such a challenge will only escalate the situation. Consider the following scenario:

In the first session of a recent group of adolescents in a youth detention center, one of the members, Lenny, kept talking about how violent he was and how much he enjoyed hurting people. He dominated the group with descriptions of violent acts that he had apparently committed before being adjudicated and did not allow others time to talk. During the second session, the counselor challenged Lenny as to the veracity of his stories, indicating that if he had really done all that he said he had done, Lenny would not be in a youth detention center but would instead be at the state boot camp for dangerous offenders. At that point, the others in the group began laughing at Lenny and calling him a liar and braggart. Lenny became very angry and stormed out of the room. Later, when the counselor talked to Lenny and asked what had happened, he indicated he had been "dissed" in front of everybody. He had "lost face" and been shamed by being called a liar in the group. He refused to attend the group anymore. The counselor wished he had refrained from making the comments he did and had instead used the group process to help address Lenny's comments in a more constructive manner or talked with Lenny individually, outside of the group, to see if the pattern could have been changed without a direct confrontation in the group. This situation was one in which a direct challenge was not beneficial.

An alternative approach to direct challenge that may be effective during confrontational times is to refer back to the structure of the group and the commitment the confrontational member had earlier made to the group: to work on personal issues and to assist other group members as they work on their issues. This approach was found useful in a recent group.

During one group session, Constance was very angry about being betrayed by her boyfriend, who had decided he wanted to end their relationship. She lost control of herself in the group setting as she described him leaving, and she began yelling, screaming, and crying. As she did so, one of the other members told her to calm down, pull back, and not be so upset about the situation. At that point, Constance yelled out, "Don't tell me what to do, you bitch! You can't keep a man either. You would sleep with anyone that would look at you twice!" The other group member, Shari, was shocked and pulled back, her eyes tearing up. The counselor said, "Constance, we know you are hurt and that you are angry, and we want you to be in touch with those feelings. But did what you just said to

Shari help you with your hurt and anger? Did it help the other group members with their issues?" Constance responded defensively, saying that Shari's comments were not helpful and that she had a right to say what she said to Shari. The counselor followed up with, "I understand that what Shari said did not help you, and we need to look at ways we can be most helpful, but did your response help either the group or you?" The counselor stayed with the theme for a few minutes, after which Constance told the group she was sorry, acknowledging that what she had said did not help her or the group. The group's response was to pull closer to her, and the members asked her to tell them what would be helpful for her. This situation provides an example of the benefits of referring back to the group members' commitment to the group and of staying with the situation rather than distancing oneself from it.

• **Use Humor.** When acting-out clients know that the counselor appreciates them, sincerely cares about them, and has set limits and consequences, they will respond well to humor. One way to use humor is to move to a "one-down" position. Here, the counselor uses humor to defuse a tense moment, and laughter is used to lighten up the interaction. Consider this recent group experience:

In a mixed-gender group being run through the juvenile court, one of the male members began describing how he enjoyed beating up people, particularly teachers. One of the other males in the group began mocking the first male and indicated that the stories he was telling were exaggerations. Very quickly, conflict escalated between the two males, and they stood up, facing each other, looking as though they were going to fight. The counselor turned to one of the female group members, who was looking scared and unsure about what was happening. The counselor said, "It's a guy thing, Theresa. You probably wouldn't understand." At that point, the females of the group broke out laughing, then the other males began laughing, and finally the two males who were standing began laughing too. They tapped each other on the shoulder, gave a "high five," and sat down grinning.

• **Use Paradox and Reframing.** Another effective technique with clients who are acting out is to use paradox. The counselor can take advantage of his or her verbal fluency to present situations that are paradoxical to the client. Often, this technique will defuse acting-out behavior, as occurred in the following scenario.

In a recent juvenile court group composed of all males, one of the members loudly stated several times that he hated the counselor. The counselor, Andy, realized that the group member wanted him to argue back and throw him out of the group. Instead, Andy whispered something to another group member, who then laughed. The angry member asked what had been said, and the laughing group member told him, "Andy said that you are lying, that actually you like him a lot and that your yelling about not liking him is just a cover-up to hide how much you really enjoy being with him." The angry member yelled that he did not like the counselor and did not see how the leader could say such a stupid thing. The counselor explained, calmly and with a smile, that he knew the group member liked him because attendance in the group was required only when a group member really messed up on the outside, that when someone did well outside the group he not only did not have to attend the group but even got special opportunities, such as candy and extra time playing pool. Obviously, the counselor said, anyone who attended must like the counselor a lot to mess up outside the group and give up time playing pool to get to be with the group. At that, the whole group laughed and teased the angry member. After a minute of glowering at the counselor, he, too, broke out laughing, saying he would hate the counselor the rest of his life, and just to show how much, he would change his behavior and from now on play pool instead of coming to the group. Despite his words, he remained a member of the group and began showing positive changes both in the group and outside.

Paradox is one means of reframing a situation, but reframing can be done in other ways as well, as is illustrated by the following:

A group was proposed for acting-out adolescents living in a group home. The social worker said the adolescents would hate the group, would not participate, and would all act out. The counselor explained that he just wanted to have the adolescents meet with him one time as nonvoluntary group members and that he would worry about any behavioral acting-out once the adolescents got to the session.

The group session was held away from the group home, in a university counseling practicum center. The adolescents were brought to the center by social workers, who walked them to the door. As the adolescents entered the room, the counselor gave them each a dollar bill and asked them to sit down. They all sat down, looking somewhat confused and not certain of what was happening. When the group began, the counselor explained that each time the adolescents came to the group they would be given one dollar. If they talked in a useful, constructive way during the group, they would get a second dollar as they left; but if they acted up, they would not get the additional dollar. The counselor also told them that pizza and drinks would be delivered halfway through each session, and that all participants would be invited to participate in the party. The group members were initially surprised, shocked, and caught off guard by the approach, but they expressed appreciation and thanks for being included. As the weeks went by and the group progressed, the members told the leader that he did not have to continue giving them the two dollars to participate but that they were glad that he did. They said that each time they returned to the group home, other kids would tease them for having gone to counseling. Because they received the money, they could respond, "You're the stupid ones. All you did was sit here watching the stupid TV, but we went out, got two dollars, and had pizza and drinks while you didn't get anything. You're right, we go to counseling, because we get something out of it and all you get is more stupid watching TV." The group came to be known as the "two bucks and a pizza" group, and the participants never did any serious acting out.

• • •

All people want to live healthy and satisfying lives. But due to traumatic life experiences, circumstances that get in the way of learning life's tasks, or the development of self-defeating behaviors, many people need help in doing so. It is important to remember that the difficult behaviors people present in group work are not a function of purposeful goals set to frustrate group leaders and fellow group members. The people who participate in groups want to live more satisfying lives. In our experience, those group members who demonstrate problem characteristics are seeking help in making changes but, when faced with the expectation of change, retreat to the safety of past behavior, even if that behavior has not been conducive to a happy life. We work under the assumption that all members of our groups want help with their issues and do want to change. Any other position, we feel, is contrary to all we know about facilitating change. Sadly, counselors often "blame the victim," attributing malice to clients when they do not act as expected.

A core condition for counselors is that they accept the pain of the group member as real, that they realize that acting out is less the result of a desire to resist change and more a resistance to that which is unknown and threatening. When group members act out in the group, they are retreating to known behavior patterns because that is what is safe for them. At times, counselors need to reach out and ask them, "What can we do now to make it safe for you to risk being different, to risk trying to relate to the group in a different way? Can you help the group understand ways to help you now?" Regardless of the form the acting-out or resistant behavior takes, the behavior is a message to counselors to examine the group structure and dynamics occurring in the present and see what they need to do as leaders to restructure the group to meet the member's needs. The counselor would have already demonstrated, early in the intake and initial sessions of the group, ways in which he or she cares, supports, and understands the member. Now, when the leader begins to see the acting out, the noncompliance, the resistance, it is essential that he or she use the supportive relationship already developed to encourage the member to reach out and risk change.

APPLICATIONS TO GROUP LEADERSHIP

Group leadership is a combination of art and skill. The art develops more fully as the leader's skills become greater. All leaders encounter acting-out group members, and they need to know the skills for managing the behavior of such members; the art develops as the leaders attend to their own impact as they work with members of the group. Many group leaders try to make group members fit their expectations; it is much more important for the leader to be pliable enough to bend with the needs of each member. A major cognitive shift must occur within the leader, where he or she moves toward an appreciation of what the acting out is saying, toward seeing the behavior as information and a call for help more than as an act of defiance and belligerence. Until leaders can accept that the acting-out person is truly requesting help, but in a manner that is non-constructive, he or she will not be facilitative. We believe that more leaders need to learn to act out themselves, but so often the counselor is too uptight to relax and enjoy the group. As long as the group leader is afraid of being made to look silly, a group member in an interaction may have control over the leader; it is not until the leader is confident enough to risk looking nonauthoritative that the process of mending acting-out members can occur.

The leader has the potential for levels of therapeutic influence far beyond those attributable to skill, expertise, and designated role in the group. All counselors wear intrapersonal templates constructed from their life experiences. Therein lies the coding for their uniqueness as well as their mutuality. As therapists, they learn to think about such concepts and strive to understand themselves in this framework. They then have the choice to use what they understand simply to process therapy or to go even further—to use themselves as instruments of therapeutic change. Many means exist by which group leaders may use the power of their being to effect fundamental change. The remainder of this section addresses two of those means.

CONTROL: THE FORGOTTEN FACTOR IN THE HIERARCHY OF NEEDS

We find it curious that the role of control or power in the therapeutic process and in interpersonal dynamics is usually clustered with the concepts of manipulation, passive-aggression, entitlement, borderline tendencies, and other behaviors that generally describe dysfunctional means of engagement. A different way to characterize the function of control is through a sociological survival perspective. All day, every day, everyone is in pursuit of maintaining or improving the quality of their lives and others' lives. People do this through attempts to impact the aspects of their environment that they expect to impact them. Their attempts to control their lives range from decisions about where to live, go to school, and work to negotiations with spouses about what purchases to make, what bills to pay, and who gets to control the television remote control.

It is useful to differentiate the need to control the quality of one's life from the maladaptive need to control others. Individuals or groups who engage in control in order to dominate others and enhance a power base (e.g., political, religious, financial) threaten the personal and collective freedom of others. In our opinion, this use of control is the most maladaptive.

Understanding control as an organizing principle of behavior can facilitate the therapist's understanding of acting-out individuals. Everyone wants to be safe, to be accepted (preferably loved), and to belong. No one wants to be rejected, abandoned, have conditional status, or be defective. Acting-out individuals are often developmentally delayed in the pursuit of these life conditions, which were likely denied them as young children. Their core operating premises are often the following: (a) Because they are painfully experienced with abandonment and rejection, they are determined to make sure that if they are destined for that road they travel it on their terms, so that they never again have to experience a new kind of rejection and subsequent pain. The toxic known is better than the potentially nontoxic unknown. (b) They fear that safety, acceptance, and belonging are not in the cards for them and that allowing themselves to believe they may experience such things is too good to be true and would set them up for a type of failure that they are unfamiliar with and thereby cannot prescribe and control.

How can the group leader who adopts this perspective use the function of control to create a therapeutic environment that would promote change? The first task is three factors: First, how does the control component play out in the psychosocial history of the group member? Often, behaviors that are maladaptive to the group are reinforced in the family or community. The member may have been assigned this role in the family or peer group and be expected to stay in this role, or the member's parent may be modeling acting-out behavior.

Second, how does reinforcement for acting-out behavior play out in the group? It is unlikely that positive reinforcement will be a factor, but members displaying acting-out behavior are looking for the absence of unpredictable negative consequences.

Third, given the form and content of the acting-out behavior, what consequence does the acting-out member seem to be most guarded against? Which relational issues absorb the most energy and resistance?

Understanding these fundamental constructs of the acting-out member is essential, but the journey begins with the therapist turning inward, asking him- or herself, Am I willing to step up to the plate? Accepting the role of therapist with this population carries a number of implications:

1. The leader must realize that the acting-out individual has often relied on that behavior as a means of control for so long that the behavior has become part of his or her self-identity. The group leader must set the group tone and provide the safety needed for the acting-out member to begin to give up this primary identity, perhaps even before developing a new, healthier identity.

2. The leader must be consistent and dependable, characteristics that the parents of the acting-out member probably do not have. It is critical that the individual, in opening him- or herself up to a high level of vulnerability, not be abandoned or rejected again. We do not mean that the therapist should allow loose boundaries or be available endlessly, but rather that the group leader be willing to engage with intensity, if needed, and with unconditionality.

3. The leader must facilitate group and member interaction to encourage the development of new, adaptive ways of organizing the need for control of self and of the environment as it impacts the self.

4. The leader must be willing to be the most important "other" to the acting-out member, providing validation, approval, and permission to change and to be.

BEYOND COUNTERTRANSFERENCE

Therapists understand quite well the vigilance they must keep to prevent contamination of their therapeutic alliances by the unwitting intrusion of their own dynamic issues. Even after they accurately and effectively employ checks and balances, they are still individuals who bring a lifetime of unique perceptual experiences to the therapeutic relationship, and they are still transferential figures for members dealing with maladaptive family structures.

It is important that therapists allow great affective latitude for group members who are working through parental issues through them and who are making, with them, that supportive, caring connection missed long ago—even though with that dynamic will likely go the client's anger at the actual parent for failure to parent as needed. Therapists must have tolerance and patience for this process, knowing that it may include being railed against and being perceived negatively.

It is equally important that therapists own their individuality and interpersonal styles. They will not like every client equally. They will differentially value characteristics of clients. Their perceptions of the difficulty level of clients will have less to do with their clients' diagnostic classification than with their clients' interpersonal styles, personality characteristics, manner of presenting issues, conversational patterns, and other idiosyncratic qualities. When a client does not complement the therapist on any of these variables, it is easier for the therapist to disown these dynamics and label the client with clinical descriptors than to use these factors to enhance the effectiveness of the therapy.

Group therapists speak of the group as a microcosm in which the members re-create their families or the social networks they maintain outside the group. Yet group therapists, although generally circumspect and deliberate in their roles and participation in the group, still bring their cumulative life experiences and individuality to the table. They must own that even though their roles are tailored to the purposes of group leadership, the groups they lead are microcosms for them, too.

The challenge is great for achieving this delicate balance: Group therapists must stand as transferential figures, knowing the potential hostility, anger, hatred, despair, and hopelessness in their clients in order for their healing process to occur, yet at the same time they must engage and involve who they are personally in the process in a way that is safe for them.

In doing group work, therapists must always remember that the power of the group is enormous and that the social influence of the group carries tremendous authority in the lives of the members. Often therapists assume they are responsible for all that happens in a group to effect change, but in doing so, they may overlook the power of the group. Most of the discussion in this chapter has been on the role of the leader to confront, challenge, or cajole, but the leader must always remember that the dynamics of the group are the very reason the work is being done in a group rather than an individual format.

REFERENCES

Alschuler, C. F., & Alschuler, A. S. (1984). Developing healthy responses to anger: The counselor's role. *Journal of Counseling & Development, 63*, 26–29.

Altshul, J. A. (1977). The so-called boring patient. *American Journal of Psychotherapy, 31*, 533–545.

Anderson, C. M., & Stewart, S. (1983). *Mastering resistance: A practical guide to family therapy.* New York: Guilford.

Cahill, A. J. (1981). Aggression revisited: The value of anger in therapy and other close relationships. In S. C. Feinstein & L. G. Looney (Eds.), *Adolescent psychiatry: Developmental and clinical studies, Vol. 9* (pp. 539–549). Chicago: University of Chicago Press.

Conyne, R. K., Wilson, F. R., Kline, W. B., Morran, D. K., & Ward, D. E. (1993). Training group workers: Implications of the new ASGW training standards for training and practice. *Journal for Specialty in Group Work, 18*, 11–23.

Fong, M. L., & Cox, B. G. (1983). Trust as an underlying dynamic in the counseling process: How clients test trust. *Personnel and Guidance Journal, 62*, 163–166.

Friedman, W. H. (1989). *Practical group therapy.* San Francisco: Jossey-Bass.

Gladding, S. T. (1991). *Group work: A counseling specialty.* New York: Merrill.

Hamilton, J. D., Decker, N., & Rumbaut, R. D. (1986). The manipulative patient. *American Journal of Psychotherapy, 60*(2), 189–200.

Hilkey, J. H., Wilhelm, C., & Horne, A. (1982). Comparative effectiveness of videotape pretraining versus no pretraining on selected process and outcome variables in group therapy. *Psychological Reports, 50*, 1151–1159.

Jacobs, E. E., Harvill, R. L., & Masson, R. L. (1994). *Group counseling: Strategies and skills* (2nd ed.). Pacific Grove, CA: Brooks/Cole.

Johnson, D. W. (1971). Effects of the order of expressing warmth and anger on the actor and listener. *Journal of Counseling Psychology, 18*, 571–578.

Kottler, J. (1992). *Compassionate therapy.* San Francisco: Jossey-Bass.

Kottler, J. (1994a). *Advanced group leadership.* Pacific Grove, CA: Brooks/Cole.

Kottler, J. (1994b). Working with difficult group members. *Journal for Specialists in Group Work, 19*, 3–10.

Leszcz, M. (1989). Group psychotherapy of the characterologically difficult client. *International Journal of Group Psychotherapy, 39*(3), 311–334.

Mahoney, M. J. (1991). *Human change processes: The scientific foundations of psychotherapy.* New York: Basic Books.

McHolland, J. D. (1985). Strategies for dealing with resistant adolescents. *Adolescence, 20,* 348–368.

Morganett, R. S. (1990). *Skills for living: Group counseling activities for young adolescents.* Champaign, IL: Research Press.

Murphy, G. E. & Guze, S. B. (1960). Setting limits: The management of the manipulative patient. *American Journal of Psychotherapy, 14,* 30–47.

Ohlsen, M. M. (1970). *Group counseling.* New York: Holt, Rinehart, and Winston.

Ohlsen, M. M., Horne, A. M., & Lawe, C. (1988). *Group counseling* (3rd ed.). New York: Holt, Rinehart, and Winston.

Otani, A. (1989). Client resistance in counseling: Its theoretical rationale and taxonomic classification. *Journal of Counseling and Development, 67,* 458–461.

Sklar, H. (1988). The impact of the therapeutic environment. *Journal of Contemporary Psychotherapy, 18,* 107–123.

Stanton, M. D. & Todd, T. C. (1981). Engaging resistant families in treatment. *Family Process, 20*(3), 261–293.

Weiner, M. D. (1979). *Therapist disclosure: The use of self in psychotherapy.* Boston: Butterworth.

Yalom, I. D. (1995). *The theory and practice of group psychotherapy* (4th ed.). New York: Basic Books.

5

THE CREATIVE ARTS

IN GROUPS

SAMUEL T. GLADDING

*I*t was a cold, raw day in New Haven, Connecticut, and I was in the midst of a group that seemed to be frozen. We had gathered with hope a few weeks earlier for the purpose of support and growth. However, no one had really opened up in the group sessions, and the level of trust in the group was about as low as the outside temperature. I was a student and not the formal leader, but I was interested in seeing the group succeed; therefore, I spoke up and shared my perceptions. Just for the fun of it, I said: "I think we should now all stand up and practice moving away from each other." At first, fellow group members were reluctant to stand or move, but with urging and a touch of humor I got them on their feet and we began a "move away dance" that became enjoyable, invigorating, and therapeutic in warming us up to one another and creating an atmosphere of openness within the group. At the time, I did not realize that creativity or the creative arts, such as movement, were not standard procedures for facilitating group development; however, I now know theoretically and practically both the power and potential the creative arts can play in group work.

The creative arts, sometimes referred to as the expressive arts, are visual, auditory, kinesthetic, and written art forms. Humans have used them since antiquity as a means of relating to one another on verbal and nonverbal levels. Within the creative arts, perceptions and emotions are displayed directly and indirectly in paintings, drawings, music, dance, movement, drama, and literature. At times, artistic meaning is shown in pure art forms, such as in dance or

81

works of fiction. On other occasions, art mediums are combined, such as when lyrics are added to music or dramatic techniques are integrated with movement.

As therapeutic tools and healing devices, the creative arts have a long history in the service of humanity. The ancient Greeks, Egyptians, Romans, and Hebrews used drama, music, poetry, and dance to both treat and prevent mental distress (Gladding, 1992). For instance, the Greeks emphasized the power of music and drama in healing, and the Greek god Apollo was the god of both music and medicine (Gorelick, 1987). Likewise, in the late stages of the Renaissance, the English meditation poets, such as Robert Southwell and George Herbert, stressed the power of poetry as a way toward achieving wholeness and health. A similar focus on the power of the arts in promoting mental health can be seen in the moral therapy movement of the 19th century, where selected art forms, such as painting and music, were introduced as a vital part of the treatment of mental patients in rural retreat settings (Fleshman & Fryrear, 1981).

In more recent times, the arts and creative artistic activities have been incorporated into various forms of counseling, including group counseling (Jacobs, 1992). For instance, group leaders have found that in beginning a group, poetry of a nondidactic nature, such as works by Langston Hughes and Lawrence Ferlinghetti, can serve as a catalyst in promoting group interaction and member identity (Lessner, 1974). Likewise, in bringing closure to a group at the termination stage, group leaders have found it useful to encourage members to engage in artistic exercises, such as drawing logos that represent their lives or bringing in music that symbolizes through its lyrics or melody who they are (Wenz & McWhirter, 1990). In short, a wide variety of creative and artistic procedures have been successfully employed in groups in a variety of ways and for a number of reasons.

This chapter reviews the rationale for, and advantages of, using the creative arts in groups, examines how creative art forms may be employed at specific stages in groups, and discusses the limitations that can accompany this group therapy approach. A brief conclusions and implications section ends the chapter. Just as it takes painters years of applying knowledge, skill, and sensitivity to canvas to achieve works of art, so it takes counselors time, dedication, and insight to use the creative arts properly and productively in counseling groups.

RATIONALE AND ADVANTAGES OF USING THE CREATIVE ARTS IN GROUPS

There are a number of reasons for using the creative arts in group settings, and there are many advantages to doing so. The following discussion is not exhaustive, but it covers most of the main points related to the positive aspects of employing the creative arts in groups.

1. The creative arts promote insight, self-awareness, and identity (Arieti, 1976; May, 1975). In most forms of group counseling, members are seeking to become aware of how they function in comparison to others and who they are in the context of the group. The creative arts can heighten various aspects of identity, awareness, and insightfulness by giving those within the group a chance to interact with others in novel ways. For instance, if group members are requested to informally and silently move about at the beginning of each group session in a way that is representative of their feelings, such as happiness or sadness, members have the opportunity to sense more deeply how their behaviors connect with their emotions and to identify with others in the group who may act in ways similar to themselves. Through this use of the creative arts, group members learn something about themselves and others.

2. The creative arts energize and inspire (Lerner, 1994; Masserman, 1986). The creative arts are active processes. They require participants to not only imagine possibilities but act on them as well. It is virtually impossible to be passive and be artistic or creative. Therefore, when therapists use the creative arts in groups, they get members moving and interacting. The group members will feel more invigorated and some, if not all, will be emotionally stimulated by the creative art that is produced or shared in the group.

When discussing the creative arts, people have often said that they have the power to move. In the area of group therapy, music, drawing, movement, or writing may, through its power to move, touch a group member or members and ultimately alter the way the group as a whole functions. For instance, a John Philip Sousa march played at the beginning of an open group in a mental hospital may strike a chord in depressed group members and get one or more of them tapping their feet or physically swaying to the sound of the music's beat. This movement may lead to other actions, such as talking about the music, and thereby help the group as a whole function better. In addition a change in one or more members of a group may lead to others trying new behaviors. The result of using music or other creative art forms within the group, then, is greater than it appears on the surface. At all levels, group members are helped when they actively participate in creative experiences in the group. The group functions better, also.

3. The creative arts are multicultural—that is, they are universal in nature and are utilized by all cultures. A major criticism of groups and counseling in the 1990s is that they are too bound up in an ethnocentric view of helping and are not open enough to a multicultural perspective (D'Andrea, 1995). The creative arts, individually and collectively, are immune to such criticism because the arts and creativity are worldwide phenomena and know no bounds in regard to ethnicity, culture, gender, or other barriers that separate people from one another. Drawings can be found on cave walls and in art galleries; likewise, music, literature, drama, poetry, dance, and movement are universal in nature and

have been utilized to integrate, celebrate, and heal throughout history (Fleshman & Fryrear, 1981).

4. The creative arts communicate messages on multiple levels, including the affective and nonverbal. One of the difficulties experienced in many groups is that members pay too much attention to content and thereby miss subtle and overt messages that are being sent on another level (Okun, 1992). The creative arts help to overcome this drawback of missed communication because they are process-oriented, multifaceted, and often concrete in nature. For instance, a group member may show feelings through the rhythm and fluidity of his or her body movement (Benshoff & Armeniox, 1995). Such a "dance," whether structured or not, conveys meaning on a physical, intellectual, emotional, and even spiritual level (Fisher, 1989). Thus, the creative arts in a group are like the onion metaphor that Carl Sandburg used to describe life. They operate on many levels. As they are peeled back and displayed, they reveal the essence of individuals. Sometimes an appropriate response to such a discovery is to cry. At other times, it is simply to become more aware or to even rejoice.

5. The creative arts are engaging and nonthreatening, promote playfulness, and encourage the consideration of options. When group members do not feel threatened and are willing to play either symbolically or literally, they are likely to be creative and engaging with one another (Koestler, 1964). They are also likely to be cooperative and feel like they can risk making changes. As Waters (1992) stated: "Play lubriates the process of change" (p. 40).

An example of how the creative arts can be playfully utilized in a group is the playing of the game "Adverbs." In this game, which is used to illustrate to group members that they have choices in how they treat others, a group member is asked to leave the room. After he or she has left, the group decides on an adverb that will describe how they will respond whenever the group member asks them to do a task, such as speak or interact. Thus, they might speak "frantically" or "soothingly" to others. The use of "Adverbs" makes a point, but it does so in a way that is fun and engaging. Other creative art forms do the same.

6. The creative arts tap into people's affective nature and encourage the release or acknowledgment of emotions. Men in societies such as that of the United States have traditionally been hesitant to acknowledge their feelings, let alone display them. Yet, in groups that utilize the arts as a part of their helping process, such as the mythopoetic approach of Robert Bly (1990), the power of people's affect surfaces, and the group as a whole, as well as individuals, are enriched. Talking about emotions is not the same as owning or enacting them. The creative arts are a major means through which the ownership of feelings and actions occurs in groups.

An activity that can help people broach their emotions is journal writing. Kay Adams (1993) described a number of techniques involving various forms of writing that counselors can use to help group members become empowered in expressing themselves. Examples are such experiences as the 5-minute writing sprint, where group members write in a fast and fluid motion, and exercises that require writing from selectively prepared sentence stems while thinking of oneself as something different, such as a house or an animal. The result of these exercises is the surfacing of emotions. The impact of the exercises then spreads to the lives of people individually and collectively.

USES OF THE CREATIVE ARTS IN DIFFERENT STAGES OF GROUPS

The creative arts can have a powerful effect when used at appropriate stages in a group's development. For the most potency, group leaders should use a variety of methods that tap into a number of creative art forms. In many cases, creative art forms such as music and poetry or drama and movement are combined.

BEGINNING STAGE OF A GROUP

During the beginning stage of a group, sometimes known as the forming stage, group members tests boundaries and deal with anxieties they have about being members of a group (Tuckman & Jensen, 1977). The creative arts can be used to diffuse tension and promote trust and tolerance at this stage. Some useful creative arts exercises follow.

1. Reading a Poem. As noted, the reading of a nondidactic poem by the group leader at the opening of the first group session is one way of helping group members open up to one another in an imaginative and a creative way (Lessner, 1974). The idea behind this activity is that group members enter a group with images of who they are and what they represent. By relaxing and listening to a nondidactic poem, they can become more fluid and creative in identifying who they are and on what issues they wish to work.

A poem that has been used successfully in this manner is "In Golden Gate Park" by Lawrence Ferlinghetti. In this piece, a number of images, including trees, grass, grapes, orange peels, baskets, hats, and flutes, come up as descriptors of a Sunday outing in the park by a husband and wife. Group members, upon hearing the poem, have responded with statements that connect their own lives to the images in the poem, such as "I'm the flute that nobody plays" and "I want to be in harmony with others, and that's why I joined this group." Regardless of the image they select, group members gain a better understanding of who they are through this experience, plus they gain insight into their fellow group members.

2. Decorating One's Bag. The idea behind the creative act of decorating and displaying bags is that almost everyone claims to have a bag of some type in life. People commonly use the word "bag" to indicate their main interests. For example, a teenage athlete might say; "Basketball is my bag." This concept of a bag is readily understood in most environments, especially among young people.

The exercise of decorating and displaying one's bag requires group members to cut pictures that represent themselves out of newspapers and magazines. They then paste or tape these pictures, along with other representative symbols, such as cotton balls (for soft spots) and string (for linkage), on the outside of the bag. Also as part of the exercise they put loose pictures and symbols they are not yet ready to share in the bag. After constructing their bags, group members introduce themselves to one another by describing themselves in regard to the pictures and symbols on the outside of their bags. As the group develops, members are free to, and even encouraged to, reach inside their bags and bring out materials they wish to self-disclose. The idea of this creative arts exercise is to help group members make covert parts of their life more overt as time and desire allow. By doing so, group members are freed to live their lives more freely and openly (Luft, 1970).

3. Making Sounds. Among the most primitive and universal of the creative arts is making sound. In ancient cultures, drums were often used to help prepare people for rituals ranging from marriage to funerals. The same is true today, although the sounds are now more sophisticated. When combined in certain rhythmic ways, sounds become music that reflects different aspects of life and emotional experiences.

In groups, sounds can be used to reflect the mood of the group as a whole or of an individual within the group (Bowman, 1987). Group members typically are instructed to hum or drum, by themselves or collectively, to reflect a basic feeling they are having in the present. The idea is that such an experience will help all involved gauge the mood or feeling of the person(s) making the sounds. Upon hearing the sounds, the leader attempts to provide an appropriate channel for expression of the feeling. For instance, in a group in which members feel a lot of resentment about being forced to attend, the leader may encourage members to sound off about what it is like being in the group, to vent their frustration early in the group process. The members may then be helped to envision how they would like their lives to go through either humming or drumming how they would like to hear their future.

4. Drawing and Explaining Lines of Feelings. A favorite television show of the 1960s was "What's My Line?" The show was popular because of the unusual nature of its guests' vocations and because of the play on words of its title. The lines-of-feelings exercise used in group therapy has as its premise that everyone has an emotional line or lines in life. To begin this experience, members of the group are asked to draw, using only lines, their feelings as they are occurring in the present. The leader explains that both the shape and the colors of the lines in their drawings should match the emotion being depicted. For instance, jagged red lines might indicate anger, and smooth, flowing pastel-colored lines might indicate peacefulness.

After completing their drawings, members introduce themselves to the group by name and by showing their drawings. They explain their lines both as they are drawn and as they hope the lines will become. A strength of this exercise is that it can also be used at the end of the group, and a comparison between lines in the early and later drawings can be made. Whether the exercise is used only at the beginning of a group or at the beginning and end, group members seem to remember others, as well as themselves, through the lines that are drawn and explained.

5. Drawing Stepping Stones. The idea behind the stepping stones exercise is that life is a journey and that people's paths are filled with marker events through which they define themselves. Sometimes people overlook significant events in life because they do not fit in with their perceptions of who they are and where they have been. In the stepping stones exercise, group members address previous acts of denial. The members are asked to draw significant times or events in their lives as stones and to write, under each stone, some descriptive words about what happened and its impact. Group members then introduce themselves to the group by talking about their journeys in life and the stones they have stepped on in the process. Group members often discover previously forgotten stones or uncover different aspects of remembered stones during the exercise.

A variation of the exercise is a road map experience. Group members are requested to draw the valleys and peaks of their lives. Then, referring to their maps, they tell the group about their lives. To have the group session end on a positive note, members are asked to plan future beneficial paths and discuss some ways they can follow a positive plan.

6. Walking. The idea behind this exercise is to help group members become more aware of their bodies and how they are either in or out of rhythm with others (Fisher, 1989). The exercise can take several forms, but usually it begins by having group members move "in place" through a number of different environments. Some of the settings in which members walk are familiar, such as a grassy field. Other scenarios exist more in the imagination, such as crossing hot burning sands, wading through peanut butter, or plowing through a room full of marshmallows.

In the walking exercise, group members may be asked to alter the speed of their steps from normal to double time or slow motion. The idea is that people's awareness increases when they change their steps to travel either faster or slower. By changing pace, group members get a better feel for how they move and have the potential to move. From the exercise comes reflection as well as new opportunities to try out different behaviors in the safety of the group. Another benefit is the enjoyment, both real and imagined, of traveling in new or unusual imaginary worlds.

Storming or Conflict Stage of a Group

Before the group settles down to work, members must deal with any covert or overt conflicts they have with themselves or with other group members. Resolving these intrapersonal and interpersonal differences and difficulties is essential if the group and its members are not to become mired in bickering, psychological putdowns, and other destructive behaviors. The following are some creative arts exercises that can be used to help members make needed transitions during this stage in the group and to help the group as a whole move on to more productive behavior.

1. Home Spot. One of the most creative movement experiences a leader can offer a group in conflict is called "Home Spot." In this experience, members of the group huddle up like a football team before the quarterback calls a play. With arms around one another's shoulders, the members look around the room and find a spot where they would like the group to go (that is, their "home"). Without telling the group what direction they are to take, each person tries to move the group in the direction he or she considers "home." Within seconds, physical and psychological tension erupts in most groups as members position themselves for power and attempt to push others toward their selected destination.

Group leaders who use this exercise need to be careful to warn members ahead of time not to be too forceful. They also should stop the movement of the group once the conflict has been demonstrated (usually within less than a minute). After the members have experienced the tension among themselves in this exercise, the group leader can sit down with them and discuss how that tension mimics what is happening in the group at the present time. Ways of resolving impasses may be brought up and explored. Where applicable, resolutions that are suggested can be immediately applied to the group.

2. Cartoons. Humor is an artistic and creative means of expression that is too seldom used in groups. Cartoons that point out the absurdity of a situation in a visual and funny way can help loosen group members up psychologically. Group members may be asked to bring in a cartoon that represents where they think the group is or to draw a cartoon depicting the group in its present impasse stage. A member may, for example, draw a counselor with a light bulb in his or her hand and a ballooned thought over the counselor's head that reads, "It only takes one counselor to change a light bulb, but the light bulb really has to want to change." Beneath the cartoon could be the caption: "The enlightened thought of a novice counselor after having met a resistant group member."

While the experience of using humor in the group may work quite well and may help members and leaders laugh at themselves, it can backfire if members or leaders are scapegoated. Thus, the leader of a group who assigns a cartoon exercise must emphasize the importance of not singling members out for ridicule and must intercede if a member does draw a cartoon in such a manner (Dunn, 1992).

3. Human Robot. A symbol in modern times of both efficiency and progress is the robot. In factories, robots perform work in a mechanical and an efficient way. However, they perform the work in a cold, repetitive manner—something humans do not find flattering.

In the "Human Robot" movement experience, the group leader instructs group members to form pairs and silently act, within their dyads, in a mechanical and repetitive way for about a minute. The members of each dyad are then to discuss with each other what the experience was like, after which members bring their thoughts into the group as a whole. Finally, the original pairs interact again, but this time they are free to be spontaneous, and the same types of discussions are held. The group leader follows up by calling the group members' attention to the differences in their perceptions following the two movement experiences. Members are asked to reflect about whether they really listen to others in the group or whether they are treating them as human robots.

4. Draw It All Better. Drawing is a graphic way of illustrating a situation. "Draw It All Better" is an artistic means of visually representing situations and empowering group members to change them for the good (Mills & Crowley, 1986). The experience begins with the leader instructing group members to draw a particular situation (such as the group in conflict). After they have completed their drawings, members are asked to draw the group as if it were all better. In this visual representation, the members may be sitting closer to one another or interacting in a productive manner, whereas in the first picture the members may be drawn geographically separated and acting with hostility. Group members are then asked to draw a picture of a connecting strategy that can be used to help develop picture 1 into picture 2. This third picture might show anything from pleasant or calming words to positive or neutral actions of members to one another.

After completing the third drawing, the group members share their impressions of who they are, how they are functioning, how they would like to function, and how they could change. As part of this discussion, each member presents his or her drawings to the group, and the other members are asked to respond and give feedback to the group as a whole. When particularly good strategies for change are suggested, group members are asked to role play the ideas and discuss whether such actions would be helpful.

5. Cope Opera. A Broadway play in the 1970s was entitled "Don't Bother Me, 'Cause I Can't Cope." Although most members of groups do not have that mind-set, they and the groups they are in often become bogged down because members are unsure of what to do and when to do it. Thus, conflict arises. The "Cope Opera" exercise is a way of dramatically addressing issues about which members and the group as a whole are unsure or unsettled.

To complete a cope opera, each group member writes down the situation he or she most dreads facing in the group or most fears dealing with as a group. The descriptions are then placed in a pile in the middle of the group. The leader selects one of the descriptions and has the group members enact it either on a verbal level or a nonverbal level (i.e., imagery). Then the group as a whole examines what arose in each member's mind during the time of coping. If needed, particular styles of addressing feared situations are role-played so that dramatic and effective ways of overcoming mental, behavioral, or interpersonal difficulties are achieved.

6. Clay Bridges. The medium of clay is seldom used in groups, but activities with clay have potential as a way of helping, especially in the storming stage of development. One way clay can be constructively employed is as a means of closing the distances between group members. In activities with this purpose, the group works together on a project employing clay. The idea is that when people in a group work cooperatively rather than competitively, they accomplish more individually and collectively (Sherif, 1936).

Clay projects vary, but one that has symbolic, as well as therapeutic, benefits is bridge building. In this activity, group members work together to construct a bridge from a design that they mutually agree upon. On the bridge they place clay shapes that represent who they are, such as a clay flute for someone who likes music or a clay book for someone who likes to read. After the bridge is constructed, members talk about the process of working together as well as the shapes they have put on the bridge to represent themselves (Menninger Clinic, 1986). The activity helps group members better understand one another and increases empathy.

NORMING OR PERFORMING STAGE OF GROUPS

The tasks of norming and performing involve creating an atmosphere in which inclusion is stressed and teamwork is promoted. In such an environment, the group as a whole or its members individually can work on issues that are of the highest priority. Such a focus enables the accomplishment of goals on all levels. Some useful activities follow.

1. Therapeutic Fairy Tales. Writing a therapeutic fairy tale is an exercise that helps group members project themselves into another time dimension and see themselves interacting positively in the predicaments of their lives. In this creative and artistic experience, group members are asked to pretend the following in regard to their story:

a. The scene is in a place and time far from the here and now
b. Within this setting they have a problem or predicament
c. They are able to solve their difficulty in a positive and pleasing manner, even if the solution may seem outlandish (Hoskins, 1985)

Because life is a time-bound experience and because people allow their defenses to grow with time, group members are given only 6 to 10 minutes to complete this activity. Then group members read their tales aloud on a voluntary basis and explain how the tales relate to what they want to work on in the group.

2. Rational Songs. This activity was created by Albert Ellis (1981) and is an artistic extension of rational emotive behavior therapy (REBT). Basically, the group members sing songs composed of rational lyrics set to tunes that are a part of the public domain, such as "Dixie" and "Jingle Bells." By singing the songs, group members gain a sense of who they are and the folly of human nature. They also learn to better understand themselves and human nature. For example, singing the line "I cannot have all of my wishes filled—Whine! Whine! Whine! Whine!" to the tune "We Are Poor Little Lambs That Have Gone Astray" helps group members become aware of how they react—and interact with others—when they do not get what they want.

A variation of the activity is creative song writing, where group members write descriptive lyrics that depict their situation to familiar tunes. Thus, to the tune of "I've Been Working on the Railroad," a group member, frustrated with always being in the background at work, might write:

I've been working for the company
All the live-long days.
And I'll be working for the company
Until my dying day.
Can't you see the clock a ticking
Rise up so early in the morn,
Can't you feel the inward pressure
Now's the time to blow your own horn!

After the songs are sung, the group members discuss the thoughts and actions included in the lyrics. Furthermore, they explore how the composed work can have a positive impact on the composer.

3. Fast Forward. American society is steeped in technology, from computers to videocameras. "Fast Forward" is an imagery experience based on the idea that time travel, at least in one's mind, is possible. In this exercise, group members are asked to see themselves in the future, usually in a time period 3 to 5 years from the present. They are to imagine themselves being successful in whatever way they might wish. After giving them time to bask in their success, the leader asks them to work their way back from the future to the present, noticing the steps they took to reach the success they just experienced.

The group members are then instructed to chart the steps necessary to obtain success. Finally, they are encouraged to notice how they might achieve reaching the future milestones, especially in connection with the group as a whole. Thus, fast forward is a cooperative exercise of learning to see and work toward the possible with others.

4. Writing the Wrongs. "Writing the Wrongs" is a writing method geared toward resolving past wrongs. Although this creative activity can be used in work or task groups, it is more commonly utilized in group counseling and group psychotherapy. In the activity, group members are asked to recall a situation in their lives, which is still unresolved, where they were slighted or hurt by someone. They then write down what they would like to say to that person now to help to make the matter right. For instance, if Bill had been insulted by Megan in front of his peers and did nothing but walk away, he might write her a letter telling her of his hurt related to the situation. In the letter, he could tell her how he wishes she had acted or how he wanted to act. After writing about what could or should have been, Bill then writes Megan another note saying that although he cannot change what was, he can change his thoughts and feelings in regard to the situation by forgiving Megan and himself for acting in such wrongful or hurtful ways. It is not necessary for Bill to mail the letters or even for Megan to change. Simply by writing the notes, Bill would have given himself choices and freedom that would otherwise be covered up with, or blocked by, anger.

5. Mailbox. In the creative experience known as "Mailbox," the group members use a camera to gain a new perspective on a familiar object and on life. The group members are instructed to go out and take a roll of pictures showing a mailbox from as many angles as possible. The power and productivity of the experience come when group members explain what they have shot and then see and listen to other group members explain their pictures. It soon becomes obvious that a familiar object can be seen in a multitude of ways. Likewise, problems the group may be dealing with can be viewed from more than one perspective. If group members are at their creative best, they will challenge one another after this experience to view situations from more than one perspective. In their discussions, they may realize that they would benefit from modifying or changing completely something they had decided to do. Just as photography can help group members gain a new perspective on a familiar subject, envisioning problematic areas from the cameras of the mind can be useful in overcoming psychological barriers to change that may be embedded in an individual or a group.

6. Acting As If. The concept of "Acting As If" can be found in several forms in the Adlerian, Gestalt, and Brief Therapy literature (Gladding, 1996). "Acting As If" is a dramatic technique in which group members behave as if the goals of the group have been reached either individually or collectively. From such acting, group members can see what impact resolving present problems or tasks would have on them individually in the context of the group. They can also apply the process to the group to find out how the group would differ if the troublesome areas in it were eliminated or modified.

ADJOURNING OR MOURNING STAGE OF THE GROUP

As a group nears its end, members need to finish the tasks begun earlier and say good-bye to other group members in an appropriate way. Creative arts activities in this stage can help group members complete the work begun in the group and put closure on the group process. The activities revolve around termination and loss issues.

1. Collaborative Poem. In this activity, members of the group are asked at the group's conclusion to each write a line about what the group meant to them or to write about some experience in the group that they remember (Chase, 1989). Thus, Carla might write, "I gained insight into myself and others," and Ralph might write, "I realized anew the power of people together." Once the lines are written, the leader collects them and with the help of group members combines the words into a "poem" that includes each member's most vivid impressions. The leader often contributes the opening and closing lines to the poem, but sometimes that is not necessary. If possible, group members each copy the poem to take with them.

A completed collaborative poem from a growth group in which each member contributed a sentence beginning with "I" and the leader wrote the opening and closing lines might look like the following.

The Growth Group

As a part of the group that was:
I gained insight into myself and others
I realized anew the power of people together
I was aware of new thoughts and differences
I grew in unexpected ways
I gained feelings of confidence and care
I realized I was a person of worth and substance
Now I am moving on!

2. Booklets. To conclude a group with a booklets activity, the leader must plan ahead and have members prepare for this ending from the beginning of the group. The activity takes time to complete, just like writing a book. To facilitate the process, the leader gives each group member an inexpensive booklet during the first session and explains its purpose. The booklets can be bought commercially or the leader can make them. For instance, the leader might say: "In the booklets you now have before you, I want you to write or draw at the conclusion of each session ideas, thoughts, memories, impressions, pictures, or symbols that represent the group experience of the day to you. There is no right or wrong way to do this. You will have an opportunity to share some of these writings or drawings with the group as a whole during its concluding session. I will give you about 5 minutes at the end of each group session to work in your booklet."

The group leader would then entertain questions about the booklets and the process of completing them.

Two questions that often arise during this activity center on how to make sure the booklets are present at each group session and the issue of confidentiality. It has been my experience that if the group leader collects the booklets and keeps them in a safe location between sessions, the logistics issue is solved. Similarly, if the group leader implies that the material in the booklets is confidential unless the group members indicate otherwise, the group seems to run more smoothly and ethical issues are less likely to arise.

3. Logos. This creative arts exercise, devised by Wenz and McWhirter (1990), involves inviting group members to draw logos (i.e., symbolic drawings) that represent their lives at the end of a group experience. For instance, Elaine might see herself as a flower blooming, while Mike might represent himself as the wind blowing through the trees. Drawings of this nature can be enriched by the addition of words to describe them. The group may be instructed to combine their logos into a group collage. In a variation of this exercise, the group can decide as a whole on a common logo, such as a symbol of the sun, that they can jointly create. Wearing the logo will not only identify them as members of their particular group but will also remind them of the group experience.

4. The Group as Music. Groups develop according to the rhythmic ebb and flow of their members in interaction with one another. Capturing this rhythmic growth is often difficult. However, one way to record the group's growth is to have members represent the group experience over time in sound.

In this activity, the leader invites members to recall how the group began and how it flowed through its various sessions. Members can tap on their knees, clap with their hands, or hum the sounds they feel represent the group during its lifetime. It is useful to start the exercise with a go-round, so that each person has an opportunity to reflect and contribute to the final symphony the group as a whole produces. Disagreements may arise about the sound of the group over time. On such occasions, the group leader can encourage the group to reach consensus or have the group construct different ways that group members perceived the group developing. In both cases, all group members get "air time."

At the end of this experience, group members musically express what termination sounds like for them collectively. The members will likely need some time to formulate a meaningful delivery for this part of the music of the group. Lyrical representation of how the group was experienced may be added if members so desire, but because most groups are primarily verbal, it is best if this creative ending can be kept on the nonverbal, or sound, level.

5. Contrasts. The idea behind the creative experience of "Contrasts" is to help group members see how they have grown and how the group has developed as a result of the group experience. In this primarily visual exercise, members are asked either to draw a representative symbol of themselves each week before and after the group experience or to draw a symbolic picture of themselves before the group starts and then another picture of themselves as the group is concluding. In either case, the group members compare their before and after pictures, looking for similarities and differences that resulted from their participation in the group. When differences are noticeable and positive, group members may be especially eager to share. Regardless, the point of this experience is to get group members to reflect on who they are alone and together. A variation of this exercise is to have group members at the concluding session make masks to represent the contrasts in who they were and who they now are.

6. Pat on the Back. Another creative arts experience that is useful at the conclusion of a group is the good-bye "pat on the back" experience. This artistic and expressive endeavor has two forms. In one, group members applaud one another and shake hands as each talks and acts out what he or she has accomplished in the group. For example, Dana might show the group how he is now more assertive through role-playing a situation with Mickey. Just as in a stage production members of the group reinforce Dana through applause for acting in a particular way.

The second form of this experience is to have members each trace their hand or draw a representative hand on a sheet of paper, cut it out, tape it on their back and have other group members sign the hand with positive comments about them. In this version of the activity each group member has a permanent record of what fellow group members wrote and can thereby remember the group in a more concrete format than would otherwise be possible.

DISADVANTAGES AND LIMITATIONS OF USING THE CREATIVE ARTS IN GROUPS

Although creative arts activities can be beneficial to groups in various stages of development, some disadvantages and limitations may arise. These drawbacks have to do with the way the creative arts are employed, the backgrounds of people in different groups, and the nature of the creative arts themselves.

1. The creative arts may be used inappropriately and become "gimmicky." The creative arts, if applied in a whimsical way, can be "distracting at best and dangerous at worst" (Kottler, 1993, p. 252). One of the problems with some approaches to counseling and with some counselors is that the approaches become unbalanced if counselors present activities without adequate reflection about their purposefulness or without allowing time for processing. Fritz Perls (1969), for instance, has been criticized by some leaders in group work because he often did not explain the nature and purposes of the experiences and exercises he had his group members complete. Groups that try to operate without a theoretical model or a major rationale are seldom successful. Typically, practitioners in such groups fall into the trap of concentrating on being active at the expense of working enough with group members to allow them to evaluate what they are learning about themselves and others (Patterson, 1986).

2. The creative arts may not be helpful to group members who are artists. According to Fleshman and Fryrear (1981, p. 6), "For artists, the use of the arts in therapy may be counterproductive." The reason for this negative phenomenon is that artists support themselves through creative expression, hence, if they are asked to represent themselves in creative and artistic ways, they may feel they are having to work. This barrier can be overcome somewhat if artists are asked to relate in creative arts ways that are the antithesis of, or at least quite different from, how they earn their living. For example, a writer may be requested to express thoughts and feelings through mime or music.

3. Creative arts activities may be resisted by group members who have had negative experiences with the arts. Such a reaction may be especially strong for group members who have, in the past, been "turned off" by the creative arts, either in a direct or in an indirect manner. For instance, the group member who has had a stern, rigid, and constantly scolding piano teacher may harbor painful memories about the experience and not be cooperative in exploring creative aspects of him- or herself or others. Likewise, if group members are limited physically or have a mental block about being able to be expressive in a creative and artistic way, they may refuse to become involved in aspects of the group where creative art forms are utilized.

4. The creative arts may not be useful for group members who are emotionally labile. Four main feelings have been recognized as primary in human experiences—anger, sadness, joy, and fear (Meier, 1989). These emotions, if expressed in appropriate or ritualistic ways (such as those surrounding a funeral), can be therapeutic and healthy. When released in a group, these emotions may be especially useful because of the feedback members receive about both the content of their feelings and how they express them. However, if a group member is emotionally labile, he or she may not benefit from this type of feedback. Instead, the individual in the group may simply persist in expressing the emotion and may become especially charged if an artistic component is introduced into the group as a way of exploring feelings. The reason, as pointed out earlier, is that creative art forms work on many levels, and people in the group who are labile may tap into repressed memories and materials when working in this way. The result is a triggering of new or recharged affect and the disruption of progress in the group as well as in the person.

5. The creative arts may become too much of an emphasis or take up too much time, leaving too little time for processing people-related material. Although an overemphasis on artistic procedures is relatively rare, it is not uncommon in groups with undereducated leaders and underprepared members. In such groups, this type of occurrence usually takes one of two forms. In the first, the leader introduces an experience that takes up most of the time scheduled for a group session. If a mask-making activity, for example, takes 40 minutes of the group's allotted 1-hour time frame, there will not be adequate time left to process the experience. Saving the processing until the next group session may work, but such a delay may result in group members becoming frustrated or beginning to rationalize. The second way in which an overemphasis on the creative arts typically occurs is when one activity follows another in a group with little or no connection between the artistic focus and learning at either a personal or a group level. The developmental process so necessary for the group's health does not occur.

6. **The creative arts may lead group members to concentrate in an introspective manner and become too self-occupied.** Although no procedure is guaranteed to lead members to focus outwardly as well as inwardly, creative arts activities have the potential to lead some introverted members of a group to concentrate on themselves more than anything else. In doing art, individuals have to focus their attention and talents in one main direction, which may cause them to have difficulty translating what they have learned from the art experience to who they are in the group setting. Additionally, people may become preoccupied with the finished product they have created. In both cases, the emphasis shifts from the person as a part of the group to the person as apart from the group, and the result is a nonproductive group experience.

CONCLUSION AND IMPLICATIONS

In this chapter, a number of creative arts activities that can be utilized in group settings were examined. As was pointed out, there are both advantages and disadvantages to using the creative arts in groups. Leaders who choose to employ the creative arts in their groups must understand group dynamics and the developmental stages of groups, as well as the strengths and weaknesses of specific art forms. Leaders should also be aware of what creative art experiences have been shown to work best at each stage of a group.

Mastering even this much knowledge requires a continuous commitment. However, even more is required. In addition to knowing about the nature of groups and different art forms, leaders of groups who use the creative arts must be skilled in facilitating the group members' processing of the experiences in a collective and productive fashion. Too often the creative arts are not used to their fullest potential—they are simply tried and not discussed afterward. Group leaders should strive for the group to not only experience the creative arts activities, but to take part in fruitful interactions after the activities are completed. Such a process involves the leader being aware of what was learned in the activity and how that learning can impact individual group members and the group as a whole both now and in the future. Creative arts activities are both collaborative and individual experiences.

Creative arts activities are not for every group leader or group. The purpose and makeup of some groups require a more prosaic approach. However, when creative arts activities are appropriate for and fully employed in a group, they can add richness to the group experience. Such activities can lead members to act in new ways or see themselves and others from a different perspective, adding freshness and vitality to their lives. It is this type of awareness of what the creative arts can do that most likely guided ancient civilizations in their use of the creative arts in the mental health realm. And it is the same awareness that can guide present-day group leaders in their quest to help and heal.

REFERENCES

Adams, K. (1993). *The way of the journal.* Lutherville, MD: Sidran Press.

Arieti, S. (1976). *Creativity: The magic synthesis.* New York: Basic Books.

Benshoff, J., & Armeniox, L. (1995, February). Movement therapy. Presentation made at annual conventions of the North Carolina Counseling Association, Raleigh, NC.

Bly, R. (1990). *Iron John: A book about men.* Reading, MA: Addison-Wesley.

Bowman, R. P. (1987). Approaches to counseling children through music. *Elementary School Guidance & Counseling, 21,* 284–291.

Chase, K. (1989). About collaborative poetry writing. *Journal of Poetry Therapy, 3,* 97–105.

D'Andrea, M. (1995, February). Revising ACA's ethical standards for a multicultural society. *Counseling Today,* 30.

Dunn, J. R. (Speaker). (1992). *Health psychology and laughter: Making sense of humor* [audiocassette]. Jackson, MS: Humor & Health Letter.

Ellis, A. (1981). The use of rational songs in psychotherapy. *Voices, 16,* 29–36.

Fisher, P. P. (1989). *Creative movement for older adults.* New York: Human Sciences Press.

Fleshman, B., & Fryrear, J. L. (1981). *The arts in therapy.* Chicago: Nelson-Hall.

Gladding, S. T. (1992). *Counseling as an art: The creative arts in counseling.* Alexandria, VA: American Counseling Association.

Gladding, S. T. (1996). *Counseling: A comprehensive profession* (3rd ed.). Englewood Cliffs, NJ: Prentice-Hall.

Gorelick, K. (1987). Greek tragedy and ancient healing: Poems as theater and Asclepian Temple in miniature. *Journal of Poetry Therapy, 1,* 38–43.

Hoskins, M. (1985, April). *Therapeutic fairy tales.* Paper presented at the annual meeting of the National Association of Poetry Therapy, Chicago, IL.

Jacobs, E. (1992). *Creative counseling techniques: An illustrated guide.* Odessa, FL: Psychological Assessment Resources.

Koestler, A. (1964). *The act of creation.* New York: Dell.

Kottler, J. A. (1993). *On being a therapist* (rev. ed.). San Francisco: Jossey-Bass.

Lerner, A. (1994). *Poetry in the therapeutic experience.* St. Louis: MMB.

Lessner, J. W. (1974). The poem as a catalyst in group work. *Personnel and Guidance Journal, 53,* 33–38.

Luft, J. (1970). *Group process: An introduction to group dynamics.* Palo Alto, CA: National Press Books.

Masserman, J. H. (1986). Poetry as music. *Arts in Psychotherapy, 13,* 61–67.

May, R. (1975). *The courage to create.* New York: W. W. Norton.

Meier, S. T. (1989). *The elements of counseling.* Pacific Grove, CA: Brooks/Cole.

Menninger Clinic. (Producer). (1986). *Art therapy: The healing vision* [videotape]. Topeka, KS: Menninger Video Productions.

Mills, J. C., & Crowley, R. J. (1986). *Therapeutic metaphors for children and the child within.* New York: Brunner/Mazel.

Okun, B. (1992). *Effective helping* (4th ed.). Pacific Grove, CA: Brooks/Cole.

Patterson, C. H. (1986, April). *Gimmicks in groups.* Paper presented at the annual convention of the American Counseling Association, Los Angeles.

Perls, F. (1969). *Gestalt therapy verbatim.* Moab, UT: Real People Press.

Sherif, M. (1936). *The psychology of group norms.* New York: Harper.

Tuckman, B. W., & Jensen, M. A. (1977). Stages of small group development revisited. *Group and Organizational Studies, 2,* 419–427.

Waters, D. (1992, September/October). Therapy as an excellent adventure. *Family Therapy Networker,* 38–45.

Wenz, K., & McWhirter, J. J. (1990). Enhancing the group experience: Creative writing exercises. *Journal for the Specialists in Group Work, 15,* 37–42.

THE TAO OF

GROUP WORK

HOLLY FORESTER-MILLER AND CHARLES F. GRESSARD

*I*n this age of accountability, empiricism, outcome measures, and treatment planning, what has often been lost along the way is the attention to process. It is not that the former concepts are not important. They certainly are, as are the other ideas and concepts presented in this book. However, if one loses touch with the process, one loses touch with the foundation on which all of these other concepts are based. Whereas skeptics might scoff at the notion that the Tao can provide something of use to group practitioners, many aspects of what we present in this chapter will seem quite familiar to experienced group leaders.

The Tao te Ching is the second most translated book in the world. This Chinese classic is based on the teachings of the 6th century b.c. Chinese philosopher and spiritual leader Lao Tse. Legend has it that Lao Tse wrote the Tao at the request of the people. They asked him to share his knowledge about life and especially about the ways of an effective ruler or leader. The Tao, which means "the way," is the product of this request. The Tao te Ching describes a way of life and how humans can work and interact effectively with one another and the world in which they live.

In this chapter, we apply this ancient wisdom to the group process. We have found that problems in group leadership can often be resolved by turning to the Tao te Ching for guidance. We have attempted to explain how some of the basic concepts of the Tao apply to group leadership issues. This task, however, was often difficult because the Tao cannot be easily expressed in words.

The Tao itself is full of paradoxes, and it presents a major paradox for group workers. Group leaders often want specific, concrete ideas about what to do. The Tao explains that to be an effective leader one needs to learn to "not do" and to "do without doing." The focus of the Tao is on "being" rather than "doing." We discuss in this chapter how these concepts have helped us to become more effective leaders.

The Tao te Ching is meant to be interpreted by each person individually, and each person is to use it to find his or her own "way." Through our explanations of the Tao and by sharing how it has helped us to resolve some of our own issues and challenges in group leadership, we hope to help other group leaders in finding their own way and enhancing their leadership skills. We first discuss our own difficulties in learning to be present and learning to trust the process of group work. Next, we explore what others have said regarding the Tao and counseling. Then we discuss how we feel the Tao applies to various issues and challenges in group work. Finally, we offer examples, exercises, and techniques that we hope will assist others in understanding and applying the Tao to their work in groups.

ISSUES AND CHALLENGES

The two major challenges we confronted in applying leadership concepts from the Tao to our group work were learning to be present and learning to trust the process. Other issues also arose as we learned to apply these two concepts, some of which we will discuss in the section entitled "Applying the Tao." However, once we learned to be present and started trusting the process, our effectiveness as group leaders was greatly enhanced.

LEARNING TO BE PRESENT

The key, we have found, to following the Tao as a group leader is learning to be present. One needs to be aware of the here and now dynamics of the group and of the process. Only with this awareness can a group leader effectively focus on the broader picture and not get caught in the details.

What I (Holly Forester-Miller) have learned to do is to take it all in. I keep my eyes moving around the group, and I observe and listen. I have stopped worrying about what I will say or do; I just trust that the necessary response will be there when I need it to be. As I listen and observe, I allow a picture to develop in my head. Then I respond to that picture, sometimes to provide clarification. I often share the picture, whether realistic or a metaphor, and ask the group members if it fits. Doing so often allows one or more members to reframe an issue.

A woman (Mary) in a personal growth group I was leading was discussing how she had been having some health problems and felt that they related to two decisions she had to make and had been putting off. She went on to describe the difficulty of making a decision regarding such important matters at this point in her life. She described the impact this dilemma seemed to be having on her blood pressure, headaches, and her digestive tract. Another woman (Ann) mentioned how she understood the difficulty of making important decisions, as she was also struggling with one.

The picture that came to me was of a person struggling between knowing what to do and actually doing it. So I shared the picture in my head with the group. "As I listen to you both I get this sense that you each really know at some level what it is you want to do but that you are struggling with actually doing it rather than with the decision of what to do. Does this fit for you?"

Mary thought for a few moments and said, "As I stop and think about it, down deep I do know what I need to do and want to do. But I keep rethinking it because I am scared. I keep looking for an easier answer. I just hadn't realized that was what I was doing." So we talked about the messages her body was giving her and what gets in her way and stops her from doing what she feels she needs and wants to do. Mary went on to say how she feels like a pressure cooker. So I asked her, "How can you release some of the steam?" After contemplating that for a while, she said that this group has helped her realize that over time she had let go of her resource people and that she needs to build her support network again before she takes action on her tough decisions.

Ann wasn't sure if the picture I presented fit for her. She really didn't know what to do. Interestingly, a few weeks later, Ann indicated that she realized she really did know what she needed to do and realized that at some level she had known for a long time. Ann then went ahead with plans to take action.

For some people, this example may seem vague. But in actuality, the description provided here is as concrete as the discussion was in group. Neither I nor the other group members knew exactly what the decisions were that these women were exploring. We could have explored the details of the situations and the decisions to be made, but that did not seem to be the most important thing. Had we gone in that direction, we could have gotten lost in details and missed the bigger picture—the importance of listening to one's inner voice and paying attention to the messages our bodies give us.

*When I find myself **trying** to focus, I lose focus. When I think about how to reply, I cannot listen and observe and thus cannot effectively reply. I have also found that the more I try to direct the group, the more the group travels away from its path. So I have learned from the Tao to allow myself just to be present and to take it all in.*

Learning to Trust the Process

One common issue for group leaders is wanting to know just the right technique to use or steps to follow to ensure a successful group. Sometimes leaders follow models or theories that have a series of concrete, tangible steps because they know they can follow them easily, even though they may not necessarily believe in the approach or its underlying assumptions. When we first started leading groups, we kept looking for the answers. We wanted someone to tell us what to do, to give us some easy steps to follow. We struggled with using set exercises and planning what we would do in group prior to each meeting. But something was missing. In one sense our groups seemed to work, for people came and participated. But the groups did not seem lively or energizing.

We needed to learn to trust the process: to allow the group to develop and grow with our occasional facilitation rather than our interference.

One of the group leadership issues I (Charles Gressard) have had particular trouble with is trusting the process of the group. Allowing events to run their course and trusting that the group mind knows what it is doing appear to be difficult for my ego to accept. Sometimes it has taken a reading of the Tao to get me back on track, trusting the process, in groups I have led. One group I remember particularly well was a substance abuse aftercare group I was leading at an out-patient treatment program. The group members tended to avoid dealing with emotional content by sticking only to issues that felt comfortable, such as discussion about some of the steps of Alcoholics Anonymous, or by focusing on what other members were doing wrong in their recovery program. Because I had a limited number of weeks with each member and because I felt pushed to see the group accomplishing something, I spent much of my energy during the sessions fretting about how to change the course of the group and how to manage some of the more controlling members. I tried every technique I knew, but I only grew more frustrated and the group continued to flounder.

As is typical for me, it took a reading of the Tao te Ching to remind me of what I needed to do. The leader, as the Tao te Ching explains, needs to trust the group and lead more by not doing than by doing. I needed to be in the group but not take responsibility for it. I could lead best by allowing the process to unfold rather than by being the visible director. As soon as I began to trust the process, the group responded beautifully. Group members confronted the controllers and began to bring out the pain that needed to be expressed. In addition, I found myself making facilitative responses with little or no effort, and I became a part of the process rather than a directing hindrance.

One of the challenges in learning to trust the process is to learn to facilitate experiments or experiential activities in the group at the moment they need to happen based on what is taking place in the group. Doing so enhances the group process, whereas introducing preplanned exercises and techniques usually takes away from the energy and momentum of the group. As stated in the Tao, "The wise leader's ability does not rest on techniques or gimmicks or set exercises. The method of awareness-of-process applies to all people and all situations" (Heider, 1986, p. 53). As Holly Forester-Miller illustrates, even experienced group leaders have to be reminded of this.

Trusting the process was definitely an issue for me when I first started leading groups for clients with eating disorders. I had just graduated from my doctoral program and was working as a counselor at a college counseling center. I really did not know much about eating disorders, but I was unofficially designated the "eating disorder specialist" and the school sent me to several seminars and workshops.

I found myself being a very different leader in these groups than in some of the other groups I led. I would leave each group session thinking about what we could do the next week to address some of the issues that had been raised in the group that day. Then I would plan exercises or discussion questions to use in the next group. Although the participants always did the exercises, they never quite worked. The experiences always seemed contrived or forced. Although I did not realize it, the group members had moved on from the previous week but I was continually pulling them back and slowing down, if not stopping, the group process.

In thinking about why these groups felt so different from others that I had led, I realized that I was allowing my lack of confidence around eating disorder issues to interfere with my group leadership skills. I was constantly looking to the literature and the experts to "tell me" what to do in group. So, I actually was unable to do anything at the moment. Before I would respond to something happening in the group, I would go home and check the literature to be sure I didn't do anything wrong or was using the best technique.

Ironically, my concern with being a good group leader hindered me from being a good group leader. Once I relaxed and started treating the members as people rather than disorders that I was still learning about, I was able to start trusting the group, the group process, and myself. Only then was I able to be a group facilitator rather than simply the "eating disorder specialist." It was then that I started to facilitate experiential activities in the group as issues arose.

The Tao te Ching addresses these two challenges to group work—learning to be present and learning to trust the process—very clearly. The Tao stresses practicing simplicity, cultivating the ability to see the way things must naturally resolve themselves, and the importance of the "way of noninterference" (Wing, 1986).

At times, people have asked us, "What do you do if the process is broken or doesn't work?" According to the Tao, the process cannot be broken. It always works if one allows things to follow their natural course and facilitates that course rather than direct it. That is the "way of noninterference." So, if it feels as though the process is not working, one should stop and look at how he or she might be getting in the way.

THE TAO, COUNSELING THEORY, AND THE LITERATURE

Very little has been written that directly discusses the Tao and group work. However, several theorists have addressed the concepts of "being present," "trusting inner nature," and "*wu wei*" (doing without doing) especially as they apply to individual counseling. Their work is discussed in this section.

Evidence exists that Carl Rogers was directly influenced by Lao Tse's writings. Dreher (1990, 185–186) reported that Rogers kept the following Taoist quote in his wallet as a daily reminder of his role as a counselor and as a peace negotiator: "When Tao master leads and the work is accomplished, the People say, 'We did it ourselves.' " Indeed, Rogers's work, on the whole, is congruent with the Tao te Ching.

Most of Rogers's writing describes the importance of being in touch with one's true self and not pushing the process. By valuing the client and allowing clients to get in touch with their own healing process, Rogers demonstrated that the process was more important than the counselor and that counselors should not allow their own egos to get in the way. Rogers trusted the client, valued intuition, encouraged counselors to acknowledge problems when they emerged, and stressed the importance of allowing the process of counseling to emerge on its own. Also in line with Taoist thought, Rogers felt that the source of many personal problems is subtle coercion (conditional positive regard) and not allowing one's true self to emerge.

From his writings, it is clear that Carl Rogers was truly a modern Taoist. The congruence of his beliefs with the philosophy of the Tao te Ching is clear in the following quotes from his book, *Carl Rogers on Encounter Groups* (1970):

> I usually have no specific goal for a particular group and sincerely want it to develop its own directions. There are times when, because of some personal bias or anxiety, I *have* had a specific goal for a group. When this has happened, either the group has carefully defeated that aim or has spent enough time dealing with me so that I have truly regretted having a specific goal in mind. (p. 45)

> I believe that the way I serve as facilitator has significance in the life of the group, but that the group process is much more important than my statements or behavior, and will take place if I do not get in the way of it. I certainly feel responsible *to* the participants, but not *for* them. (p. 46)

Milton Erickson, too, appears to have worked from a belief system congruent with Taoist thought. The psychotherapeutic techniques he employed followed many of the same premises as those of Carl Rogers and are in sync with the key concepts of the Tao te Ching. Gordon and Meyers-Anderson (as cited in O'Hanlon,

1987) recounted the following story, which Erickson reportedly told to define what he believed to be the essence of therapy:

When he was a young man, Erickson said, he was with some friends when they found an unfamiliar horse grazing in a field. He told his friends he was going to take the horse back to its owner. They asked him how he could do that when he did not know who the owner was. He said that the horse knew. So off he went, riding the horse bareback to the road. Then, as the horse turned onto the road, he let the horse lead the way. Whenever the horse started to stray off the road, he just guided it back onto the path. He let the horse turn where it chose, directing it only to keep them on the road. When they turned into the farm where the horse resided, the farmer asked him how he knew where the horse belonged. Milton replied, "I didn't know...the horse knew. All I did was keep his attention on the road." Erickson summarized the story by saying, "I think that's the way you do psychotherapy" (p. 9).

Though he did not use these words, Erickson was addressing a concept referred to in the Tao as "*wu wei*," or "doing without doing." One needs to provide the environment for growth to occur and then allow it to happen without interfering. As Holt and Steingard (1990) indicated, "The Tao te Ching is saying, in effect, that the reason so many leaders fail is that they try to do too much" (p. 255).

A notion that was at the core of Erickson's approach to psychotherapy was that of helping the client to find the answer within. He believed that all people have the answers and abilities that they need—their "inner nature," so to speak—but that for a variety of reasons people at times lose touch with those answers and abilities. According to Erickson, the goal of therapists is to help their clients utilize the competencies that exist within them at both a psychological and a physiological level. Therapists must help their clients access and trust their own inner nature.

As Hoff (1982) pointed out, people go astray by not following their own inner nature. In *The Tao of Pooh* he wrote the following:

As we have likely recognized by now, no two snowflakes, trees, or animals are alike. No two *people* are the same, either. Everything has its own Inner Nature. Unlike other forms of life though, people are easily led away from what's right for them, because people have Brain, and Brain can be fooled. Inner Nature, when relied on, cannot be fooled. But many people do not look at it or listen to it, and consequently do not understand themselves very much. Having little understanding of themselves, they have little respect for themselves, and are therefore easily influenced by others. (p. 57)

According to Taoist thinking, people go astray because they ignore the nature of things and their own inner nature. It is in accordance with the nature of things that humans will have some pain and suffering in their lives. To attempt to avoid pain, or to attempt to eliminate pain before accepting it, is impossible.

Doing so will only cause more pain or greater difficulties. The role of the counselor then, whether in group or individual work, is to help people get back in touch with their own inner nature. In group work, counselors must help people to get in touch with their own inner nature, while simultaneously experiencing the group and the ways in which they may allow themselves to be influenced by others.

In discussing applications of the Tao to counseling Knoblauch (1985) wrote, "A Taoist counselor helps clients move from rational thinking and toward their own intuitive logic" (p. 55). We would rephrase his word: "A Taoist counselor helps a client move toward trusting his or her own inner nature."

When theorists talk of intuitive logic, they imply that one must think about, or work at, intuition, rather than just letting it be—*wu wei*—or allowing things to happen without working at them. When counselors try too hard to make something happen they get in the way of it being able to happen. To allow things to happen, or to "do without doing," counselors must trust their own inner nature and that of their clients.

Heider (1986) would agree. He contended that counselors need to approach leadership without being attached to the outcomes and with the patience to allow group members to discover and learn without "telling" them or taking credit for their learning. An effective leader, Heider wrote, remains "unbiased, clear, and down-to-earth" (p. 19).

APPLYING THE TAO

TRUSTING INNER NATURE

As discussed earlier counselors must not only help clients get back in touch with their inner nature, they must also learn to trust their own inner nature. If counselors are not in touch with, or do not trust their own inner nature, they cannot possibly help their clients to get in touch with theirs. In the following example, Forester-Miller describes the importance of being in touch with one's inner nature in group work.

In the story I related earlier in this chapter, I talked about not being effective with my eating disorder groups because I forgot to trust the process and, as part of that, was looking to others to tell me what to do. In looking to others for the answer, I was ignoring my own inner nature. I was trying to implement the answers of others, and they didn't fit; it was the proverbial round peg in the square hole. I could not succeed as a good group leader for two reasons. First, I was trying too hard, and "trying" always implies failure. Second, I was not being me and was not in touch with my own inner nature. I was looking to someone else for the answer rather than looking inside myself.

We believe that the counselor who understands the group process and has basic leadership skills can lead most groups simply by trusting his or her own inner nature and the process. But the skills and knowledge do have to be learned and internalized first, before they can be drawn upon.

QUALITIES OF LEADERSHIP

The success of a group often reflects the ability and skills of its leader. Although some groups can succeed on their own, the personality and actions of the leader will have a significant effect on the outcome of any group. Numerous books have been written about the characteristics of the group leader, but the Tao te Ching provides further enlightenment. Guidance for group leaders can be found in many of its chapters. They describe, for example, how the "master," or leader, can influence the energy flow and the growth of those he or she leads. The Tao te Ching gives a clear indication that the most effective group leader is one who views leadership from a humble perspective and who leads by respecting the inherent wisdom and potential of the group members.

Group leaders often fall into the trap of feeling that they must explain to their clients their intentions, interpretations, and goals and that their clients cannot grow without the benefit of their explicitly stated wisdom. The Tao indicates that perhaps their wisdom and knowledge would be better communicated by what they do not say. Much of the time leaders would be better off, to borrow words from the Tao, settling their own dust and softening their own glare than spouting their wisdom to their clients. Leaders' periods of silence are often more powerful than their periods of verbal expression. As the Tao explains, "Those who know do not speak. Those who speak do not know" (Wing, 1986, chap. 56).

The focus of the group is best centered on the members and not the leader. From the perspective of the Tao te Ching, ideal group leaders are those who say the least and who trust the process and their clients to get the job done. After all, what is the ultimate goal? For the group members to think the leader is a wonderful counselor and that they grew as a result of the leader's efforts? Or for the group members to feel that they grew as a result of their own efforts? Only leaders who are striving to meet their own ego needs would feel the need to be loved and credited for the growth of the group. The Tao states:

The Master doesn't talk, he acts.
When his work is done,
the people say, "Amazing:
we did it, all by ourselves!"
(Mitchell, 1988, Chap. 17)

The Paradox of Process

Too often counselors rely on first-order change techniques. They attempt to coerce, persuade, and advise, and assume that their clients will behave and change in a rational manner. A few theorists, however, have shown that nonlinear methods often lead to more profound and lasting change. One such method is the use of paradox, a technique advocated by Alfred Adler, Viktor Frankl, Paul Watzlawick, Milton Erickson, and Jay Haley, among others.

The Tao te Ching speaks to the importance of paradox, and thus to the importance of finding nonlinear solutions, in the process of dealing with life's problems.

> Yield and overcome;
> Bend and be straight;
> Empty and be full;
> Wear out and be new;
> Have little and gain;
> Have much and be confused.
> (Feng & English, 1972, chap. 22)

By allowing a problem to expand, by accepting and entering the problem rather than avoiding or solving it, the problem transforms.

Paradox is especially useful in approaches to group resistance. If a leader attempts to confront any type of resistance directly, the group will likely continue resisting and perhaps resist even more strongly. A lesson may be learned from the Tao: To get rid of something, allow it to flourish; to straighten something, first allow it to be crooked. By allowing, and perhaps encouraging, the resistance, it will often "magically" disappear.

Once in a substance abuse recovery group I was leading, I (Charles Gressard) was faced with the resistance of clients to attending 12-step groups. Although attendance was part of the clients' contracts, several of the members had stopped attending meetings or were showing up only once every 2 weeks. This situation is typical, but frustrating, for substance abuse counselors. Typically, the more the counselor pushes, the more the clients resist. After several weeks of pushing, I realized that I was only creating more resistance by trying to convince the members to attend more meetings. After considering the options and consulting the Tao te Ching, I decided to encourage the resistance to grow by accepting it and focusing on it.

*In the next session, I announced that I was tired of fighting 12-step group attendance and that the rest of the session would be devoted to listing and discussing all of the reasons not to attend meetings. After I allowed the group members to vent their frustrations and accepted their anger, the group eventually came around to discussing reasons why they **should** attend the* *meetings. I have found that this response often occurs when I remember that groups do not always grow in a linear fashion and act accordingly. Sometimes it is necessary to not only accept resistance but prescribe it before growth can occur.*

Physical science validates the nonlinear way of things. Chaos theory, for example, has allowed scientists to take a new look at complex systems. The way of the Tao seems consistent with these ideas.

NOT GETTING ATTACHED TO OUTCOME

Group leaders sometimes err in becoming too invested in the outcome of the members' decisions and the results of the group. Heider (1986) interpreted the Tao as indicating that people do their best work when they forget their own point of view.

Ironically, counselors are taught to be invested in the outcome. Ultimately, the grades they earn are dependent on how well they do working with their clients. Thus, they often try too hard and take it personally if their clients do not change or do not make the "right" decision. They become overly invested in the outcome because they want things to look good for their supervisors. Later, however, they learn that to be effective counselors, they need to learn to let go of what they were taught and to not be attached to the outcome. They need to help their clients to find their own answers and not direct them to the counselor's answers.

TAO AND THE GROUP MIND

The concept of the group mind was developed to help explain the cohesion, or sense of identity, that exists in a group beyond the minds or egos of the individual members. At times, it seems that the group has a mind of its own and that the group counselor can relate to this group mind almost as though it were its own entity. Just like the individuals in the group, the group mind develops and changes as the group continues. Most group counselors have experienced times when the group seems to create a system wherein the whole becomes more than the sum of the parts.

The Tao would indicate that the group mind is a result of the combined energy flowing from and among the group members. Lying in the background and seemingly acting in a subtle fashion, this invisible link between the members has a power far beyond the power of the single ego.

The wise counselor is one who learns to work with this energy, realizing that it is far more powerful than the individual counselor. Although the group mind cannot be seen or touched, it exists as a potent factor when any group of people come together with some common purpose. Group counselors need to understand and respect this energy.

COUNSELING FROM THE VOID

Another difficulty for a group leader may be the tendency to clutter the mind with thoughts that interfere with grasping the subtle energy in the group and allowing intuitive solutions to emerge. Thoughts about diagnosing, advising, or directing, about the most helpful response, about fears of failure, and about what will be happening after the group, as well as other personal matters, distract from the leader's comprehension of the energy flow in the group. To sense the energy, the Tao encourages simplification. Counselors often make the mistake of making group counseling, and their lives, too complex. According to the Tao te Ching, there is power in simplicity. When mental processes are concerned, the Tao te Ching advises that less is more.

HOPEFUL HINTS

In this section we present ideas, perspectives, and exercises that we hope will aid counselors in further exploring the Tao and the concepts we have been discussing.

WORKING WITH THE ENERGY OF THE TAO

As in many areas of counseling, that which is obvious is often difficult to learn and use wisely. Although many chapters in the Tao te Ching address the use of the energy of the Tao, it often remains elusive. The energy of the Tao is not something that can be grasped or used in a direct manner.

Fortunately, the Tao te Ching offers some suggestions on how to use this elusive energy. One way is to focus on experience rather than on talk and intellectual understanding. The more people are in touch with their experiencing of life, the more they learn.

The Tao suggests that it is important to keep things simple. When people keep both their inner and outer life simple, they can more readily tap into the energy of the Tao. It appears that the more complicated people's lives become, the less they are able to use this potent form of energy in their work and personal lives. Too many distractions may get in the way of their sensing and using the energy.

The Tao te Ching also indicates that people need to stay centered and not get too caught up in themselves and their pride if they are to be in touch with and be able to use the energy of the Tao. Staying centered means allowing one's energy to flow freely. That energy, according to the Tao, flows around the body in a vertical, circular fashion from one's center, which is metaphorically located around the internal area of the belly button. When counselors become overinvested in what is happening within a group or allow their pride to get in the way, they lose their sense of being centered.

In our own experience, we have found that staying centered can be difficult at times, but that when we do allow ourselves to stay centered, it is well worth it. Our intuition becomes sharper, the workings of the group mind become clearer to us, and the group becomes more effective.

I (Holly Forester-Miller) have developed several methods and sets of cues that I can use in my personal and professional life to help me return to being centered. The simplest technique, and the one I use most often in my group leadership role, involves keeping a polished stone in my pocket. When I recognize that I feel off balance or distracted, I can return to being centered simply by fingering the stone in my pocket. This simple and unobtrusive act allows me to feel grounded and return to center. An important part of this technique is first recognizing that I am off balance or distracted. I think each of us can learn to recognize the cues that our body gives us that our energy is not flowing freely.

LEARNING TO RESPOND CREATIVELY

To be able to respond creatively, the counselor needs to be fully present within the group, to trust his or her own inner nature and training, and to know that the appropriate responses will be there if he or she lets them. Creative responding often has to do with responding to a metaphor or picture and building on it. Whenever a counselor responds in a group setting, he or she can do so in one of two ways: (a) responding to the individual within the context of the group, or (b) responding to the group as a whole. Both ways are useful, though one is often more beneficial than the other in a given situation.

The following exercise is one that I (Holly Forester-Miller) use with my group counseling students to help them develop confidence in their abilities to respond in these ways. In the exercise, I present several scenarios and encourage my students to picture each of them and then see what responses come to mind. Following is an example of a scenario with my response addressed to the group as a whole as a result of an individual member's comment.

One group counseling member, Tom, was talking about all the issues in his life and how he felt like he was always carrying such a burden. Many of the other group members were nodding as though they could relate to Tom's experience. I chose to respond to the group as a whole. The picture that came to my mind was one of Tom carrying a huge bundle. I decided it might be helpful for Tom and the other members to see what their own burdens might look and feel like to them.

I asked Tom and the group if they were willing to do a little visualization exercise around the issue of burdens. They agreed, so I asked them to close their eyes and allow themselves to look inward and see what their own personal bur-

den looks like. I asked them what shape it was, what color it was, and how they were carrying it. After giving them a few moments to visualize, I asked them what they could do to shift the burden, to make it easier to carry, perhaps by carrying it differently, or to lighten the load in some way.

The responses from the group members were wonderful. Tom divided his burden into two and put half on each shoulder instead of all on one. And I could physically see him shift positions and sit in a more balanced way. Other members chose to describe their burdens and were amazed at how easily they were able to make changes that made life a bit easier. One woman described her burden as a ball and chain that she had to drag around. She realized that she had been letting her burden drag behind her and stuff was catching on it, so she was dragging more than was necessary. So she cleared away all the extra stuff and picked the ball up so she wouldn't have to carry any more extra burdens.

Before I read the scenario aloud, I instruct the students to close their eyes or look down at the floor (so they have no distractions) as they listen. The goal is for them to allow a picture to evolve in their mind and then form a response to the whole picture rather than the details.

We next conduct the same exercise with the following scenario: Imagine you are the group leader for a small women's therapy group. It is highly cohesive and the women have been sharing at a very deep emotional level. The members have regularly been using imagery and metaphor in the group.

One woman has been a very active member but has difficulty with sharing on an emotional level. Being able to be in touch with her emotions and recognize what they are as they are happening is one of her therapeutic goals. She can talk about things after they happen but has difficulty talking about or even recognizing what they are at the time.

One day in group she asked for group time and wanted support from the group as she looked inside herself at the source of her emotional pain. She closed her eyes and began looking inside to see where all the pain was coming from. She had been talking about how scary this would be for her but thought it was necessary. She described herself as going down into her emotions and then said, "I can't go any further; it's like there is a brick wall in front of me preventing me from going any further."

After reading the scenario aloud, I ask my students how they would respond in a way that addresses the individual within the context of the group and how they would respond in a way that addresses the group as a whole.

We encourage all counselors to conduct this type of exercise many times with each scenario, sometimes focusing on the individual, and sometimes on the group as a whole. In my classes, we have come up with as many as 100 viable responses for just one scenario. Counselors can gain additional practice by transferring client comments onto audiotape and then playing them back; in that way, they can be fully present when listening to them.

CONCLUSIONS

When writing this chapter, we were well aware that the Tao that can be written is not the true Tao. As Hartz (1993, p. 9) wrote, "Taoists say that the Tao that can be expressed in words is not the real or 'eternal' Tao. Masters and writers can help to point the way, but each person must find his or her own Tao." It is in this spirit that we embarked on this endeavor.

We hope that we have helped point the way for others to find their Tao. We encourage those who are interested, as they learn and grow with the Tao, to open themselves to different interpretations, seeing how all the pieces fit together. Each interpretation will have something to offer.

There are many versions of the Tao te Ching. We have cited several to provide a sense of the variety. The versions range from flowery, ethereal translations, such as those of Feng and English (1972), to concrete, advice-based translations, such as that of Heider (1986). Our suggestion is to start with a translation that you find interesting in the bookstore, or possibly one that seems appealing to you from quotes in this chapter. Read a chapter and allow yourself time to contemplate its meaning in your life and your work. Ideally, read and discuss the Tao with a colleague. As time goes on, purchase a second translation and read the same chapter from each book, exploring the differences, similarities, and new images and concepts that the second translation generates. Over time, you'll find your understanding and experiencing of the Tao will grow and evolve. Therapists who embark on this journey will come closer to understanding their own Tao and its application to their role as a group leader. We encourage such individuals, when leading future groups, to remember to trust the process, to be present, and to trust their inner nature. If the process does not seem to be working, we suggest stopping to see where you may be interfering with the natural flow of things.

The flow of the river is always fine, except when we humans interfere with the nature of things. A river that floods its banks is a problem only if we have built homes, buildings, and bridges in the natural flood zone. When we need to slow down the flow of water or redirect its path, it is not because the river is a problem but because our construction has interfered with its flow.

REFERENCES

Dreher, D. (1990). *The Tao of inner peace.* New York: Harper Perennial.
Feng, G., & English, J. (1972). *Tao te Ching.* New York: Vintage Books.
Hartz, P. (1993). *Taoism: World religions.* New York: Facts on File.
Heider, J. (1986). *The Tao of leadership: Leadership strategies for a new age.* New York: Bantam Books.
Hoff, B. (1982). *The Tao of Pooh.* East Rutherford, NJ: Penguin Books.

Holt, G. R., & Steingard, D. (1990). The merely known mediator: Taoism and the metaphoric analysis of mediator behavior in divorce and custody mediation. *Mediation Quarterly, 7*(3), 251–284.

Knoblauch, D. L. (1985). Applying Taoist thought to counseling and psychotherapy. *American Mental Health Counselors Association Journal, 7*(2), 52–63.

Mitchell, S. (1988). *Tao te Ching.* New York: Harper Perennial.

O'Hanlon, W. H. (1987). *Taproots.* New York: Norton.

Rogers, C. R. (1970). *Carl Rogers on Encounter Groups.* New York: Harper & Row.

Wing, R. L. (1986). *The Tao of power: A translation of the Tao te Ching by Lao Tse.* Garden City, NY: Doubleday.

7

A Model for Leading

Task Groups

Robert K. Conyne, Lynn S. Rapin, and Jennifer M. Rand

*M*uch work in all areas of contemporary Western society is conducted through group efforts. Examples of these groups include teams, task forces, planning groups, committees, community organizations, discussion groups, study circles, and learning groups. The focus of task groups, the topic of this chapter, is on the application of group dynamics principles and processes to improve the practice and accomplishment of identified work goals (Association for Specialists in Group Work, ASGW, 1990).

Task groups however, share much in common with personal change groups, such as counseling and therapy groups (Conyne, 1989). For instance, core competencies for group work leaders, such as encouraging member participation and clarifying group member statements (ASGW, 1990), apply equally well to committees (a task group) and to counseling groups (a personal change group). Likewise, both types of groups generally can be expected to develop similarly over time, and many group developmental models exist to help predict their developmental evolution (e.g., Jones, 1973). This convergence of like factors for task and personal change groups represents a basic premise of group work.

Despite their substantial similarities with personal change groups, task groups can be demarcated by their attention to context and their emphasis on meeting performance goals that are directly connected to the external environment. Although task groups are concerned with personal and interpersonal growth, they are principally focused on accomplishing tangible goals that are responsive to some connected outside environment, such as the organization to which the task group members belong. As with all group work, the quality of task group functioning can range across a wide continuum. Task groups can be productive teams, but they also can be founts of conflict, they can wallow in confusion, or they can be just plain boring. The possibilities are numerous. We contend, however, that the quality of task group functioning can be influenced significantly by the type of interventions selected and implemented by the group leader.

Unfortunately, even though group leader interventions are intimately related to the quality of the group's functioning, no task group leader intervention model exists in the counseling literature to guide leader training and practice. In this chapter, we seek to address this deficit by describing a model we have found useful for task group leader intervention. This model is grounded in the struggles and challenges we have experienced in leading and participating in task groups and by our efforts to improve our practice in this area. We bring three different experience bases to our shared work.

Bob teaches group work courses, writes extensively about group work, serves as a task group leader in his academic department and in a national group work organization (the Association for Specialists in Group Work, ASGW), and has chaired ASGW's professional training standards committee. Lynn has worked with a wide variety of task groups in her consulting practice, serves as a leader in volunteer task groups and professional groups, and teaches a counseling program development and evaluation course designed to increase leader and member competencies. Jen, a recent counseling graduate, is providing new group services through existing private practice and agency settings and has been a leader in a local counselor association. As a person who wants to increase her competency in working with organizations and other task groups, Jen identifies with advanced counseling students who desire more knowledge and training in this important but somewhat neglected area.

Despite the differences in our types of work, we have experienced many of the same struggles. Each of us, for instance, has struggled with the need to balance the urgency in getting tasks completed with trust in the power of the group process in accomplishing goals. Lynn provides a recent example:

> *I have been working as a consultant with a self-directed work group made up of members of a department that was in serious trouble. The department had grown from a fairly effective group of 6 employees to a very ineffective and fractionated group of about 40. Morale was low. The department was divided into opposing camps. The manager was perceived by all as weak. Employees and organization leaders regarded the situation as being very serious even though the department was successful in meeting its performance outcome goals. Additionally, the department members faced an implied deadline for improvement,*

made by the organization's vice president, with a potential threat of firing key opposing department leaders. As the consultant, one of my responsibilities was serving as task group leader with the membership and management of the department. We had the shared task of identifying what was going wrong and what strategies could be implemented to effectively improve group functioning.

*The situation presented several familiar challenges. Because I was not the permanent leader of the department, I had to facilitate member involvement while not tying the members' progress to my leadership. I had the responsibility of helping the group learn about the relationship between content (delivering the service and identifying the barriers) and process (working effectively as a team). At the same time, I had to maintain my **own** trust that attention to both process and content would lead the group to more effective functioning.*

As in many of my consultations, I was faced with a multitude of considerations and options. Thinking about the elements of organization, group development, member and leader behaviors, and the outcome of developing a more effective self-directed group aided me in my leader role with the group. I recognized that my key struggle paralleled one that was affecting the group: I was challenged to work with the process issues present in the group and not succumb to the organizational pressure to generate a product or solution.

Lynn's example highlights some of the multiple dimensions in task groups that confront leaders as they seek to intervene. As the following questions, directed to task group and other group leaders show, the situations leaders face are often complex and ambiguous.

- Have there been times when you have left a meeting wondering what happened in those two hours?
- Have you been puzzled by confusing messages, conflicted relationships, and wandering agendas?
- Are you perplexed by how to handle feelings of members as you all work on task accomplishment?
- Do you wonder how to involve all members and reduce the domination by one or two?
- Do you wish you had a framework to use in leading task groups?
- Have you found that your counseling group skills do not frequently translate well into leading task groups?
- Are you, as a leader, adequately prepared to assist with these, and other, task group challenges?

These and other questions are addressed in our task group leadership model, which we discuss following a review of the literature.

RELATED LITERATURE

THE IMPORTANCE OF CONTEXT

The *team,* a highly visible form of task group, has become more or less a fixed goal for members of the current work environment (Muriel, 1993). Teams are centered around reaching performance goals, but in addition they are based on principles of mutual commitment and responsibility, a common vision, and an interdependent action orientation (Carr, 1992; Hood, Logsdon, Thompson, & Kenner, 1993; Katzenbach & Smith, 1993; Leftwich, 1994; Phillips & Phillips, 1993; Robbins, 1993). Team leaders or facilitators must effectively perform a wide range of task group competencies, including focusing on both personal and task issues, obtaining goal clarity in the group, implementing group decision-making methods, and using larger organizational issues in the group process (see e.g., ASGW, 1990; Bradford, 1976; McCorcle, 1982; Van Auken, 1992).

Task groups, including teams, usually do not function as stand-alone, independent entities in which the leader's and members' attention can be nearly exclusively devoted to the group members and other within-group phenomena. A task group is significantly influenced by its context, which is composed of environmental forces (or press), culture, performance demands, supports, and constraints. The group usually forms to meet the expectations and expressed goals of others within that setting (e.g., organizational managers) to produce a product, to modify agency procedures, or to design a strategic plan. The task group, then, functions in keeping with its particular context.

THE POWERFUL ROLE OF PERFORMANCE OUTCOMES

As we have stated, all task groups are expected to produce something that is tangible through meeting clear performance demands (Katzenbach & Smith, 1993; Walton & Nadler, 1994). Thus, the sharpest indicator of the success of a task group effort is to evaluate if the group met the performance outcomes specified, such as improvements in practice, procedures, product, or people. Illustrations include the following: Were cost-containment procedures developed, and how feasible are they for implementation? Did the group develop the workload standards specified, and do they seem endorsable? Did the personnel committee develop selection criteria for prospective candidates, and will those criteria be accepted by management? Was the staff training program created? Did the task force complete the organizational assessment project, and what are its results?

The task group exerts an indirect effect on its external press through its performance outcomes, as the following examples show. The workload standards that were produced are now being used within the larger organization to guide and evaluate employee functioning. The selection criteria that were developed are now being used to make decisions about which of five applicants will be offered a position. The staff training program is resulting in reduced stress and enhanced communication skills. Evaluations of these applications lead to ongoing feedback, which is used to refine, expand, or change the applications. Such a cyclical, dynamic interrelationship between the external environment and the task group is a characteristic associated with an "open system" (see e.g., Hrebiniak, 1978), an apt descriptor of task groups.

THE TASK GROUP PERFORMANCE MODEL

TASK GROUP INTERVENTION CHOICE

All task group leaders need to work with their groups within the open-system, performance-based framework we have described. This framework must inform their continuing group leadership functioning within the group.

We developed the task group performance model we are about to describe to guide leaders as they intervene in their groups (Conyne, Rapin, & Rand, 1995) and field-tested this model in two training settings: a group theory and process course and a national conference on group leadership. The insightful observations of participants in those field tests led to refinements in the model. Moreover, the seminal scholarly contributions of Cohen and Smith (1976) and of Lieberman, Yalom, and Miles (1973) to group leader interventions in personal growth and therapy groups importantly informed our thinking as we developed this task group intervention model. A discussion and presentation of this model can be found in Conyne, Wilson, and Ward (1997).

Our model is based on the premise that task group leaders must choose from a range of possible intervention options and that informed leader choice is a critical action. Three major components contribute to the choice of intervention (see Figure 7.1), and these components interact dynamically (as represented by the circles and arrows in Figure 7.1). The components are the following: (a) the *type* of leader intervention—problem-solving or group process emphasis; (b) the *level* of leader intervention—individual, interpersonal, group, or organizational; and (c) the *function* of leader intervention (modified from Lieberman, Yalom, & Miles, 1973)—caring, meaning, motivating, or managing emphasis. The leader intervention chosen for implementation produces an intervention effect (letter D, in the figure), which influences how the task group proceeds (see Appendix, which specifies and includes examples of these choices). The following sections describe the components of the intervention choice in more detail.

We see these task group intervention components as being intimately related to one another, with the leader having the capacity to choose various combinations, as appropriate. In a sense, the leader selects from revolving sets of

Intervention Choice

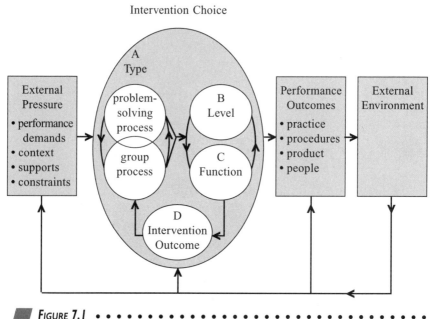

FIGURE 7.1 •

TASK GROUP PERFORMANCE MODEL

Note: Reprinted from *Comprehensive Group Work,* p. 133. Copyright American Counseling Association. Reprinted with permission. No further reproduction authorized without written permission of the American Counseling Association.

dynamic intervention options, arriving at an intersection that, according to his or her professional judgment, suggests the greatest possibility for success.

TYPE OF INTERVENTION

All task group interventions include both group process and group problem-solving components. For that reason, the group process and group problem-solving intervention types are shown as overlapping in Figure 7.1. The intervention type a leader chooses to focus on is a matter of emphasis.

No task group functions in either an all group process manner or an all problem-solving manner. Task group leaders need to monitor the ongoing balance between the two and select their intervention type emphases accordingly.

GROUP PROCESS. The task group leader can choose to emphasize group process interventions, which should be familiar to most counseling students. Group process interventions include giving attention to task functions, maintenance functions, norms, and the developmental stage of the group. Attention to group processes is often ignored in task groups, as well as other forms of group work, leading to negative consequences (Reddy, 1994).

PROBLEM-SOLVING. Alternatively, the task group leader can choose to emphasize group problem-solving, a frequent need in task groups. The problem-solving emphasis requires somewhat more discussion for two reasons: (a) counseling and therapy classes do not provide much detail about problem-solving process interventions in group work, and (b) as Schindler-Rainman (1981) observed, the major function of the task group leader is to help in the decision-making (problem-solving) process. The task group leader frequently needs to intervene to help group members to function as a team, to identify the situation they are facing, to assess that situation, and to determine what they need to do, how to do it, and if a strategy works when tried (Craig, 1978).

LEVEL OF INTERVENTION

According to Cohen and Smith (1976), leader interventions in personal change groups can range across three levels: individual, interpersonal, and group. Because performance outcomes often are based on an entire group effort, task group leaders need to place a high priority on group-level and interpersonal-level interventions. That is, the leader of a task group must continually attempt to connect people and tasks and to promote their interdependence. Less frequently, task group leaders may need to gear their interventions to the intrapersonal concerns of a single group member.

Task group interventions can also be accomplished at yet another level, one that is beyond the scope of personal change groups: the organizational level. This level of intervention connects internal task group functioning with the broader context of the group in the organization. At times, the leader, the group members, or both, will need to take action outside the group per se and within the organization (or community) of which the task group is a part. For instance, the leader may need to discuss portions of a strategic plan being developed by the task group with the director of the agency, or group members may request a meeting with all staff to discuss the findings of a survey with which they have been working. Such organizational interventions would then serve to shape future task group activity.

FUNCTION OF INTERVENTION

Task group leaders must pay explicit attention to motivating members and managing their activities and progress toward identified goals. These central functions, however, must be complemented by the functions of caring and meaning. Members need to feel supported and encouraged, which the caring function can provide, and they need to be able to make sense of their work together, which the meaning function can afford. Lieberman et al. (1973) described the motivating function as "emotional stimulation," the managing function as "executive functioning," and the meaning function as "meaning attribution." In practice, any leader function represents some blending of caring, meaning, motivating, and managing. At issue is how the leader emphasizes any or all of the four options.

STRUGGLING WITH TWO CRITICAL INCIDENTS IN TASK GROUP LEADERSHIP

The two critical incidents that are presented in this section illustrate the kind of struggles and challenges that may be faced by task group leaders. We use the same format of presentation, suggested by Cohen and Smith (1976) for personal growth groups, for each. A context for the incident is described, followed by dialogue specifying an event that preceded the intervention choice point faced by the leader. The choice point is then discussed from differing perspectives. Next, the reader is invited to develop three possible leader interventions that might fit the critical incident, drawing from the model. Finally, we provide a suggested intervention, realizing that no one choice is perfect. The principal goal in this exercise is to increase awareness of the range of possible intervention choices from which leaders of task groups can select while developing serviceable rationales for each one.

CRITICAL INCIDENT I: "I THINK WE'VE LOST IT!"

CONTEXT OF THE INCIDENT: The setting for this critical incident is a university graduate class on program development and evaluation. The incident occurs at the midpoint of the 16-week course, about two-thirds of the way through a class session. The course instructional format is that students are organized into a task group of eight members, with the instructor serving two roles: (a) that of a trainer, providing selected cognitive inputs and supplying general process management, and (b) that of a task group leader, attempting to help the students function as a task group in accomplishing the course goals. The task group is responsible for applying the six-step program development and evaluation model being learned (they are on step 4, planning for implementation, a particularly complex step) to a case example presented by the instructor. This application is intended to result in the task group's production of a comprehensive and specific plan of action. The group seems stuck, unable or unwilling to identify what is needed for continued progress. A growing sense of frustration is building among the members, and the leader appears to be uncertain about what steps to advise.

EVENT PRECEDING CHOICE POINT: Betty, a member, said to the group: "I think we've lost it. How are we ever going to get this thing done?" George, another member, responded: "And I am beginning to think all this is a waste of time. We're not going anywhere, and our plan needs to be done in, what, three weeks!" Jim, a third member, looked at Professor Sims, the instructor, and asked, "What can we do to get on with this?"

All eyes quickly turn to Professor Sims.

CHOICE POINT: The task group leader, Professor Sims, is feeling great responsibility. The organizational press on her is strong. Her group leading abilities and her instructional expertise are being questioned by her students. Moreover, this is a required academic course for all students, in which they are expected to master competencies in program development procedures and the evaluation of programs. Successful completion of the task group experience is fundamental to meeting the course objectives. Time in the semester is running out, and much remains to be done.

Professor Sims feels that she must come up with something—anything legitimate, almost—to move this task group forward. What would help the members to complete this step in planning for implementation?

She wonders if there is some better way she could present the information. Could the planning technique be clarified? Should she adjust the task group instructional method in favor of didactically presenting the program development and evaluation model? Should she give some concrete examples of how the members could complete the planning step? These possibilities relate to performance, centered around helping to make the instructional content clearer.

Alternatively, Professor Sims realizes she could focus on group process issues. Perhaps it would be worthwhile to legitimize the affect the members were feeling and help them to express it more directly. Perhaps she could enlist the members to devise a strategy together about possible next steps.

The critical issue in this situation seems to be how to get the group unstuck and able to move ahead in accomplishing its goal in a timely and an effective way.

INSTRUCTION TO THE READER: Suggest three possible group leader interventions that might be implemented at this point, drawing from the task group leader intervention model. Give a rationale for each.

SUGGESTED INTERVENTION: The suggested type of intervention is to focus on process, to work to validate the importance of the task group members to appropriately identify and express their affect in a caring environment. Professor Sims might say, looking at Betty, George, and Jim, "I hear your frustration about how we are doing. I, too, am feeling some concern. I wonder how the rest of you are feeling about our work." Here, the emphasis is on group process, the intervention level is the group level, and the intervention function is caring.

Professor Sims's intervention would serve to remove, for the moment, the intense emphasis on the task and to elevate for consideration attention to how members were feeling about the task and their work so far. After acknowledging the feelings Jim, George, and Betty had expressed, Professor Sims, making the comments suggested above, would seek information from the other five members (without naming each specifically) to discover and share how everybody was feeling. Turning to the group would also diminish the pressure on the three members who took an initial risk by questioning what was occurring so far. Task group leaders often need to remind themselves of the importance of the group process to effective functioning. In task groups, the immediate and continuing press is to perform and produce. When the group languishes for whatever reason, many members and too many leaders nearly automatically assume that the problem is a lack of pertinent information, technology, or resources. Although these factors may be present, two often overlooked contributors to ineffectiveness in task groups (as in personal groups) are poor process and a lack of validation and incorporation of member affect.

INTERVENTION OUTCOME: The group leader intervention suggested here may allow for the presentation and consideration of material previously unacknowledged by this task group: member and leader affect. Sharing feelings directly but appropriately will assist the group as a whole to more fully understand its situation while acknowledging the useful role that member feelings play in task accomplishment. Once affect is expressed, discussed, and incorporated, the whole group may be better able to focus on moving ahead with the task.

CRITICAL INCIDENT 2: "I DON'T KNOW WHAT OUR PROBLEM IS!"

CONTEXT OF THE INCIDENT: The setting for this critical incident is a meeting of the strategic planning committee of a non-denominational church that was established about a year before in a suburb of a city. The church has been rapidly attracting new members, including many single baby boomers and married couples with young children. Nearly all the members are professionals, many of whom seem interested in a church that emphasizes a sense of community while minimizing church traditionalism. The strategic planning committee was established by the minister at the request of the vestry to "determine a 5-year plan for the church, incorporating input from the congregation as a whole" in recognition that fast growth had outstripped the planning that had been done. The 12 members of the committee were selected by the minister to represent various important demographic categories, including race, gender, home location, sexual orientation, socioeconomic condition, age, occupation, and family status. The committee is cofacilitated by the minister and another church member, Sam, who is a human relations manager in a local company. All members of the committee have very busy lives. Finding time to meet is an ongoing issue, although a pattern of meeting twice a month has been generally kept. The committee has had six meetings to date, each one with differing membership due to individual scheduling conflicts. Two original members have withdrawn from the committee, apparently due to pressing work loads. The co-facilitators are also very busy. The time taken up by their professional and family lives has cut into the time they had hoped to spend planning and debriefing their work together. As a consequence, the functioning of the strategic planning committee appears to be floundering and fragmented, marked by unclear and inconsistent leadership and the absence of a framework on which to proceed.

EVENT PRECEDING CHOICE POINT: Sam, the co-facilitator, said to the other committee members toward the end of the seventh meeting: "I have been sitting here for a while feeling kind of bad about how our committee is doing. And I am not clear what is getting in our way. I wonder what's going on. What is our problem?"

Sheila, a committee member, responded, "I'm glad you mentioned that, Sam, 'cause I've been feeling the same way...I don't know, but it might be that we have never gotten 'on track.' We seem to have been drifting."

Others nod their heads in agreement.

Then Sam said, "I see lots of agreement on that, and it makes sense to me, too. I am beginning to think it might be good if we had a clearer plan of how we wanted to move ahead here. Maybe that's what we should develop."

The minister then enthusiastically responded: "Yes, that would help us to stay more on track as a committee! How about if we all think about this before our next meeting and see what we can bring back? Or, Sam, is that something you could do?"

Sam replied, tentatively, "Maybe it would be better if you and I met before the next meeting to develop a plan that we could present to everyone for reaction at the meeting. I think that might work better."

Charles, another committee member, then addressed the co-facilitators: "Forgive me, but I want to underscore what Sheila said. I think some sort of plan is what we have needed all along. We could really use some general direction about how to move ahead. This stuff is complicated, and we are all very busy. I think you [he was looking at Sam and the minister] could really help us to move ahead."

CHOICE POINT: Not only the minister but also the vestry had requested the 5-year plan. Therefore, there was an organizational expectation for the committee to deliver a product that would be useful for charting future direction for the expanding church. However, this committee is not working effectively. That is, it does not appear to have accomplished much after seven meetings. The co-facilitators and at least one member have noted the absence of an action framework to guide their activity. Even more pressing for this committee seems to be the inability or unwillingness of the co-facilitators to work well together, a point illustrated by their rare meetings outside the committee time for processing and planning. The co-facilitators differ on how the plan should be developed and, more particularly, on who would be responsible for producing its initial framework. Should it be the group members, Sam, or the co-facilitators?

The critical issue in this situation seems to be centered around direction and appears to have four components: (a) no action plan or framework exists to guide the committee members; (b) the co-facilitators are unsure of their mutual roles in relation to producing the framework; (c) the co-facilitators seem to be generally unclear of their respective and mutual roles and responsibilities in regard to this committee; and (d) the co-facilitators have not been able or willing to work together in attempting to resolve these issues.

How might the co-facilitators respond to the comments made by Sheila, Charles, and the other members, and to each other? Is the production of an action plan for the committee desirable? If so, who will have responsibility for creating that plan? Who should make that determination? Is there a general need for the co-facilitators to shore up their communication and planning function in relation to the committee?

INSTRUCTION TO THE READER: What three possible group leader interventions would you suggest at this point, drawing from the model? Give a rationale for each.

SUGGESTED INTERVENTION: The suggested type of intervention is for the co-facilitators to design a plan for working together that will more effectively aid the functioning of the committee. The minister might say to Sam (and, indirectly, to the committee): "Hmm, we seem to have different ways that we could go on this issue, but it seems important to come up with some direction. [Heads once again nod affirmatively.] Sam, your suggestion makes a lot of sense to me. If it is okay with everyone else, how about if you and I get together before our next committee meeting to see if we can map out a way to move ahead and then bring our plan back to the committee for discussion and possible approval? As a matter of fact, maybe that could be the start of our meeting at regular times to mull over our work. How does that sound to you, Sam, and to all of you?" Here, the emphasis is on problem solving, the intervention level is the interpersonal level, and the intervention function is managing.

The minister's intervention would acknowledge the importance of the task group members and facilitators being clear about their mutual responsibilities and roles. More specifically, it would illustrate how unclear responsibilities between co-facilitators can be openly addressed. Underlying this intervention choice is the premise that a major reason the committee was experiencing difficulties—beyond the busy schedules of its members and its lack of an action plan—was the failure of the co-facilitators to assume their rightful roles and responsibilities. Their ineffective communication and lack of planning had led to unfortunate but probably predictable inefficiencies for the committee. By applying their management function to themselves, and thereby creating an action framework to guide regular planning meetings, they would most likely enhance the overall clarity and coherence of the committee's functioning.

INTERVENTION OUTCOME: Meeting on a regular basis to plan and process would assist the co-facilitators in providing a more thoughtful and coordinated approach to committee facilitation. Out of this improved system of co-facilitator communication might emerge a tentative framework for committee consideration that could help the group move forward in its task.

APPLICATIONS TO GROUP LEADERSHIP

With its focus on performance outcomes, task group leadership requires explicit attention to operating within a system. The group leader must be continually aware of how the task group fits within the larger organizational structure and culture as well as with how interventions can be made to harness group resources to produce meaningful actions. As Donigian and Hulse-Killacky (1995) observed, the effective leader must carefully balance process with content (in this case, with performance demands and outcome).

Task group leaders need to follow a conceptual map that is grounded in group theory and process but that also is uniquely adapted to deal with the complex issues surrounding task performance and working with groups in organizations. Group work training components of counselor education and psychology programs would more comprehensively prepare students for group work if their curricular offerings included this kind of task group training.

FUTURE IMPLICATIONS

Group work today has a robust variety of applications, including task group leadership, and the opportunities in this field can be fully expected to increase in the future as individuals and work groups search for ways to enhance interpersonal connections, engender healthier lifestyles, and find better ways to produce and guide change. As counseling and therapy students become more broadly trained in group work leadership, they will be prepared more completely for practicing in the 21st century.

It is likely that the demands for task group work will originate from an increasingly wide range of settings, including schools and all educational units, churches and synagogues, neighborhood associations, community organizations, health and mental health organizations, and business and industry—wherever people gather to problem solve and to accomplish goals. By becoming involved with these groups as capable members, leaders, consultants, and researchers, counselors and therapists will become more fully mainstreamed in the ongoing social fabric of life and in that setting will have an improved capacity to promote effective functioning. We hope that the task group performance model we have described in this chapter will contribute positively to that highly desirable goal.

REFERENCES

Association for Specialists in Group Work. (1990). *Professional standards for the training of group workers.* Alexandria, VA: ASGW.

Bradford, L. (1976). *Making meetings work: A guide for leaders and members.* San Diego: University Associates.

Carr, C. (1992). Planning priorities for empowered teams. *Journal of Business Strategy, 13,* 43–47.

Cohen, A., & Smith, R. D. (1976). *The critical incident in growth groups.* La Jolla, CA: University Associates.

Conyne, R. (1989). *How personal growth and task groups work.* Newbury Park, CA: Sage.

Conyne, R., Rapin, L., & Rand, J. (Presenters). (1995, January). *Critical incident training in task group leadership.* Workshop presented at the Third National Conference of the Association for Specialists in Group Work, University of Georgia, Athens.

Conyne, R., Wilson, F. R., & Ward, D. (1997). *Comprehensive group work: What it is and how to teach it.* Alexandria, VA: American Counseling Association.

Craig, D. (1978). *HIP POCKET GUIDE to planning and evaluation.* Austin, TX: Learning Concepts.

Donigian, J., & Hulse-Killacky, D. (Chairs). (1995, January). *Effective group leadership: Balancing process and content.* Workshop presented at the Third National Conference of the Association for Specialists in Group Work, University of Georgia, Athens.

Hood, J., Logsdon, J., Thompson, J., & Kenner, J. (1993). Collaboration for social problem-solving: A process model. *Business & Society, 32,* 1–17.

Hrebiniak, L. (1978). *Complex organizations.* St. Paul, MN: West.

Jones, J. (1973). A model of group development. In J. W. Pfeiffer, & J. Jones (Eds.), *The 1973 annual handbook for group facilitators* (pp. 127–129). San Diego: University Associates.

Katzenbach, J., & Smith, D. (1993). The discipline of teams. *Harvard Business Review, 71,* 111–120.

Leftwich, C. (1994, October). *Culture and communication: Unlocking group process.* Paper presented at the annual meeting of the North Central Association for Counselor Education and Supervision, Kansas City, MO.

Lieberman, M., Yalom, I., & Miles, M. (1973). *Encounter groups: First facts.* New York: Basic Books.

McCorcle, M. (1982). Critical issues in the functioning of interdisciplinary groups. *Small Group Behavior, 13,* 291–310.

Muriel, A. (1993). Facilitating effective work teams. *SAM Advanced Management Journal, 58,* 22–27.

Phillips, L., & Phillips, M. (1993). Facilitated work groups: Theory and practice. *Journal of Operational Research Society, 44,* 533–549.

Reddy, W. B. (1994). *Intervention skills: Process consultation for small groups and teams.* San Diego: Pfeiffer.

Robbins, D. (1993). The dark side of team building. *Training & Development, 47,* 17–21.

Schindler-Rainman, E. (1981). Training task-group leaders. *Journal for Specialists in Group Work, 6,* 171–174.

Van Auken, P. (1992). Harnessing group dynamics for greater productivity. *Supervisory Management, 37,* 6–7.

Walton, E., & Nadler, D. (1994). Diagnosis for organization design. In A. Howard (Ed.), *Diagnosis for organization change: Methods and models* (pp. 85–105). New York: Guilford.

APPENDIX

TASK GROUP INTERVENTION CHOICE: LEADER INTERVENTION OPTIONS FOR IMPROVING TASK GROUP PERFORMANCE

A. *Intervention Type Emphasis*
  1. Problem-Solving
    • Forming a working group
    • What is the problem?
    • What makes it a problem?
    • What can be done to correct the problem?
    • Who will do what?
    • How has the problem been solved?
  2. Group-Process
    • Task: time frames, idea generation methods, decision-making processes, data gathering/clarification, agenda
    • Maintenance: participation, influence, gatekeeper role, collaboration, membership/inclusion, humor, physical posture
    • Norms: communication style, expression of thoughts and feelings, competition/collaboration, rigidity/flexibility, stiffness/humor
    • Group Development: personal and task relations
B. *Intervention Level Emphasis (Cohen & Smith, 1976)*
  1. Individual: directed at one person
  2. Interpersonal: directed between people
  3. Group: directed to the whole group
  4. Organization: directed to the parent organization
C. *Intervention Function Emphasis (Lieberman, Yalom, & Miles, 1973)*
  1. Caring: supporting, empathizing
  2. Meaning: interpreting, attributing
  3. Motivating: stimulating, catalyzing
  4. Managing: directing, regulating
D. *Intervention Outcome*

8

FROM GROUP LEADER TO

PROCESS CONSULTANT

CHUCK KORMANSKI AND LEEANN ESCHBACH

THE JOURNEY

*T*he journey from group leader to process consultant can have many forms. We begin this chapter with our own stories and then move on to discuss possible pathways for others. Our own professional development has taken each of us along a pathway to becoming a competent group leader and an instructor of training experiences that teach group process in a variety of settings. Chuck has followed two tracks that have periodically overlapped. His formal track and the degrees he has received have emphasized career development, student counseling, and teaching. His informal track, resulting from his passionate interest in group and organizational development, has led to consultation work in business, industry, community groups, and professional associations. In addition, his work with the National Training Labs (NTL), University Associates (now Pfeiffer & Co.), and related programs has provided a foundation for his continued personal growth and professional development. For LeeAnn, too, group process has been a key interest area and has been a major focus in her work preparing counselors and in actual counseling. She has also focused on extending her group work interest into creating presentations for teaching and training workshops, into building a framework for her research endeavors, and into laying a foundation for her involvement in professional organizations.

We have both found that our colleagues provide a valuable and stimulating resource for our continued professional and personal development.

Our paths have most recently turned beyond group leadership to involvement in a developing area called process consultation. In this chapter we highlight portions of the journey, examining and exploring the roles of process observer, process facilitator, and process consultant. We hope these stories will inspire others to explore their group work knowledge base, leader skills, and group experiences and to see the link and applicability between their work and the group process roles we describe.

We begin by describing some experiences related by Leslie, an enthusiastic young professional eager to take a journey similar to ours. The experiences Leslie describes have helped to heighten her awareness of her own professional development.

As the president of a professional organization, Leslie was about to lead a business meeting scheduled for a 2-hour period prior to the opening sessions of a state counseling conference. Leslie believed she could complete the formal agenda she had set for the meeting in the first hour and planned to devote the second hour to a discussion of future goals related to organizational growth.

The meeting, however, was a disaster. It started 20 minutes late and was interrupted twice by latecomers. The simplest of the agenda items created a 45-minute discussion, much of which was unrelated to the topic and which concluded with one member of the group issuing an angry outburst regarding unprofessional behavior and another member choosing to sulk quietly for the remainder of the meeting. The philosophical discussion of theoretical leadership styles that filled the second hour was dominated by three individuals who seemed to be competing to have the last word and repeated the same points time and time again. Additional, but critical, agenda items received less time and little attention as the group worked in a mad rush to complete its agenda. When the motion was finally made to adjourn, Leslie discovered that a quorum was no longer present as a result of members having left because of other commitments.

The surprising revelation, and the reason we describe this incident, is that the meeting was one of a professional counseling organization whose officers and members consisted of experts trained in group leadership. Their training, however, was completed within the context of group guidance, group counseling, and group therapy, and not organizational dynamics.

What follows is an account of a discovery made by two friends, Leslie and a colleague, Pat, and by ourselves concerning the relationship between group leadership and process consultation. Both Leslie and Pat teach group counseling courses to graduate students; we serve as their mentors. The learning journey is filled with awareness and insight brought about by the use of observation and reflection skills. Both Leslie and Pat have always found a variety of ways to apply the knowledge and skills taught in their classes to their own real-life experiences. Both have also modeled this type of learning for their students. Needless to say, they are not real people but represent a number of young professionals who have sought us out as mentors.

The conceptual journey begins with an exploration of how group dynamics and group leadership concepts are central to the roles of process observer and process facilitator. The journey concludes with an examination of the more complex role of process consultant. These three roles represent levels of a hierarchy that move from simple to complex, with each role becoming a part of the subsequent role as one moves upward on the hierarchy. Thus, the process observer role is a part of the process facilitator role and the role of the process consultant encompasses both process observation and process facilitation.

PROCESS OBSERVER ROLE

A few weeks after the meeting just described, Leslie attended a meeting of professional counselors interested in group work. She had just been elected a representative to the group. When introductions were made, one member was introduced as the process observer. In an effort to practice what it preaches, the organization had been experimenting with the process observer role as a means of increasing member involvement and task efficiency. The role of this person was to provide periodic feedback concerning group process, which would allow the president more time to focus on the agenda. The first portion of the meeting was devoted to members getting acquainted through a brief, structured exercise followed by a discussion and prioritization of major issues facing the organization. The process observer concluded this part of the meeting by describing the president's leadership style, the types of responses made by participants, and the developmental stage of the group. He also shared his observation of the president's anxiety concerning timing and keeping on task. He spent some time describing a conflict that had occurred during the prioritizing segment and then invited group members to share their feedback. As he provided descriptive feedback prior to involving the entire group, he modeled both a logical objectivity and a concern for feelings.

The remainder of the meeting flowed smoothly, for the earlier and more informal discussion and prioritization provided a vision for the group. The members worked cooperatively in building a pathway for the organization to follow. An additional self-initiated intervention by the process observer and a requested one by the president helped keep the group on task while providing for relationship building among participants. Each intervention provided more data concerning the developmental progress and growth of the group. Members rather quickly took on some of the leadership role by keeping on task and monitoring time usage. Just before the adjournment of the meeting, the process observer summarized the progress that had been made toward the goals of the group and identified the member behaviors that supported organizational values, including the use of healthy conflict and cooperative innovations.

Back at home after the meeting, Leslie became aware that the process observer used many of the skills that she taught in her group counseling course, such as goal setting, active listening, assertiveness, conflict management, affirmation, and feedback. Even more important, he gave priority attention to process, something Leslie constantly stressed with her students.

For Leslie, group counseling courses had traditionally been about group leadership. Group counseling theories and group development models were presented to provide leaders with guidelines to focus attention on both the task (content) and the relationship (process) dimension in their counseling groups. Thus, an effective leader accomplishes tasks and builds relationships. In addition, a caring leader provides opportunities for group members to fulfill their individual needs. Leslie frequently viewed the counseling setting as the primary forum for applying this group leadership knowledge and skill.

The experience with the process observer was eye-opening for Leslie. During a later discussion with us, she realized she had an entire class of group counseling students developing the needed skills for the process observer role. Together, we began to envision how to integrate process observation in settings other than counseling. Leslie left the discussion eager to tell her friend and colleague Pat about her new insight.

PROCESS FACILITATOR ROLE

Pat, like Leslie, teaches group counseling courses at a nearby university. He was recently invited to participate on a continuous quality improvement (CQI) team as part of the total quality management (TQM) initiative at his university. The team was made up of the team leader, a process facilitator, and the other team members. At the training workshop, Pat was introduced to the basic concepts and procedures of the TQM model. As part of the discussion, the process facilitator described her role as the owner of the TQM problem-solving model. She indicated that she would teach this model and appropriate techniques to the team, help the team members communicate with one another, share information about the experiences of other teams, and facilitate the group process.

During the first few meetings, the team members got acquainted, collected and shared information, and began to select an issue on which to focus their attention. Before long, the team was setting a goal and devising ways to measure progress concerning behavioral change.

At this point, Pat had the insight that all of the team tasks and relationships that were occurring mirrored what he was teaching in his group counseling courses. This team concerned with quality improvement was in the forming stage of group development. Based upon his knowledge of groups, Pat expected that as this initial stage of the CQI team achieved resolution, the conflict normally found in the storming stage would appear.

By the next meeting, Pat's expectation became a reality. A few members were reacting negatively to a small change that had been made in the meeting time, for it had necessitated rescheduling appointments. The absence of one team member who was to have brought some essential data caused additional tension. Then, as a few team members began generating solutions to the problem on which the team was focusing, others expressed concern that the problem had not been completely defined and said that it needed additional clarification. The team spent the remainder of the meeting discussing various viewpoints related to this issue. The team leader appeared somewhat anxious and uncertain as members expressed various feelings. The process facilitator, however, joined in the interaction without taking sides and began to instill some structure in the process. She encouraged and modeled active listening and assertiveness. She descriptively summarized her observations of the group's behavior, often revisiting the problem-solving model to clarify specific tasks and direction. She sought small points of agreement and used a larger, more visionary context to bring diverse points together, thus moving the team to consensus. By the end of the meeting, the immediate conflict had been resolved. In the team minutes, the group noted the possible problem solutions that had been generated as tentative and agreed to postpone further discussion of solutions until the issue was explored more thoroughly. A review of the TQM problem-solving sequence supported this decision.

Pat was convinced that he was teaching most of these skills in his group counseling course, and, so far, the team development process paralleled what he knew about the group development process. He reached the conclusion that all teams are groups but not all groups are teams.

Pat shared his insight with Leslie and us during a joint meeting. Leslie and Pat began to investigate their newly discovered insights, finding in them a wealth of information about organizational dynamics and the more complex role of process consultant. All of us collaborated on an article for a local counseling newsletter about process consultation, which included discussion of the process observer role and the process facilitator role. The newsletter article follows.

• • • • • PROCESS CONSULTATION NEWSLETTER ARTICLE • • • • •

Process consultation is guidance provided to some group by an individual trained in group dynamics and organizational development. Blocher defined process consultation as professional assistance to a group leader or organization that is intended to increase the effectiveness of the group (Blocher, 1987; Dustin & Blocher, 1984). Thus, it consists of intervention strategies to influence change. As Wheatley (1992) showed, a stream provides an excellent analogy of effective change in an organization. She observed that streams, like effective organizations, are very diverse and adaptable and take many forms that are constantly changing to meet the needs of the environment through which they pass. She suggested that leaders need to spend less time describing tasks and increase their efforts in facilitating process.

Process consultants help organizational leaders to accurately perceive, understand, and act on process events that occur during group interactions (Schein, 1969). Process consultants may be internal to the organization, such as a human resource professional specializing in group work or an external, contracted consultant. The job of the process consultant is to make the processes of the group more public and consciously rational so that group members are more aware of goals and procedures as well as their progress toward those goals (Schmuck & Schmuck, 1974). Process consultation encompasses distinct activities, and associated skills, best described as an action-research cycle. The activities include gathering data about process events, sharing the data with group members, planning actions designed to improve the process, and evaluating efforts at implementing those actions (Lewin, 1951; Weisbord, 1978).

The term "process events" refers to the relationship dimension of group interaction, or the manner in which things get done (Hellreigal, Slocum, & Woodman, 1986). Contrasted with content events, or the material that was discussed, process events focus on *how* the material was discussed. Examples of process events include individuals' behaviors and attitudes during meetings, formal and informal interactions, and, in general, the way the group addresses the content agenda.

Typical consulting skills needed in today's workplace include using a variety of group interview and consensus seeking techniques, analyzing organizational work processes, evaluating products and procedures, and delivering performance interventions, such as training. Typical consulting duties that require these skills are involvement in the organization's strategic planning, total quality management, employee assessment, training, needs analysis, team building, and other intervention processes.

An area that parallels process consulting is performance consulting. Whereas the former encourages emphasis on the relationship dimension of groups and teams, the latter stresses the task. Robinson and Robinson (1995) stressed the latter, suggesting that the focus and the measurements of outcomes be shifted from training to performance. Throughout their model, however, process is viewed as a critical contributor to the success of the performance. They encourage the development of collaborative working relationships with key individuals; a clear understanding of vision and achievement-oriented goals; performance standards for all; modifications of the work environment to enhance performance; and working with everyone to ensure successful interventions that will create high performance achievement.

Process consultation involves making an organizational diagnosis by examining the functions of purposes, structures, relationships, rewards, leadership, and helpful mechanisms as well as forces impacting on the organization from the external environment (Weisbord, 1978). Historically, the focus of organizational consultation has changed as the field of organizational behavior has evolved. In the early part of the 20th century, consultants were used as experts to solve problems for organizations. Around 1950, consultants began teaching others in the organization to solve problems. In the 1960s, the focus shifted to concern for process, and consultants were expected to improve the system. Currently, process consultants teach everybody in the organization how to improve the whole system (Weisbord, 1987). The current situation provides an empowerment role to employees, that is, the realization of a personally satisfying blending of individual achievement and relationship issues (Lewis, Hayes, & Bradley, 1992). Questions a process consultant might explore with employees and group members to accentuate empowerment include the following: How do you see your strengths being used in the organization? How do you envision yourself making key contributions to the organization? How do you see the organization assisting your future growth or enhancing your continued professional development? How do you see the organization meeting changing societal needs? Thus, the process consultant asks process questions about the future environment, whereas his or her predecessors answered content questions about the past environment.

Conyne (1989) described an excellent case study of process consultation with a task group. The committee chairperson regularly consulted with a social worker, who provided assistance in accomplishing the goals of the group by encouraging the chairperson to give attention to the process as well as the tasks. The social worker, functioning as a process consultant, and the chairperson established a time for discussion after each group meeting. During these discussions, the chairperson would describe a situation that had occurred at the meeting. Using active listening skills, the consultant would ask questions for clarification and to get needed information. After sharing observations and occasionally offering suggestions, the consultant would check with the chairperson to assure accuracy of perceptions. Sometimes the consultant would encourage the chairperson to reflect and answer his own questions. By learning about a group development model, the chairperson gained an understanding of the processes of getting oriented, becoming organized, generating data flow, solving problems, and bringing closure.

As U.S. society moves from the electronics era to the information age, the emphasis on understanding human process as a means of increasing productivity becomes more critical (Carkhuff, 1986). The work setting is becoming more complex and is involving increased numbers of interpersonal processes. As a result, attention must be paid to both maintaining effective processes that keep the organization viable in the present and planning strategically for the future in an environment that continues to change.

Process Observation

The use of process observation as a strategy to enhance leadership effectiveness can be traced to the research of Kurt Lewin (1951) and his students. Their systematic study of group dynamics in the late 1940s culminated in the establishment of the National Training Labs (NTL) and the creation of the T-group, or training group. Initially, an anecdotal observer recorded behavioral interactions that took place during small group meetings and made observational data available for discussion and analysis by groups involved in leadership training programs (Benne, 1964). The success of this strategy for understanding group dynamics and for contributing to the group's development led to the evolvement of the role of the process observer and the recognition of the important function of feedback. The T-group methodology gradually encouraged all group members to accept and take the role of process observer; thus, they experience what it is like to be a participant observer during group interactions.

At first, feedback about process was provided at the end of a group session. However, as group members began to accept the emerging role of participant observer, their feedback and related process interventions became legitimate at any time in the life of the group (Benne, 1964). The interventions call attention to any concerns the observers have about group process that is impeding the progress of the group. For example, the group may not be getting as much accomplished as was planned because members are spending too much time on insignificant items; because of misunderstandings, unmanaged conflict, or apathy; or because members are becoming too emotional.

Process observation has become an important component of experiential learning, which relies heavily on direct experience and the use of constant feedback to change behavior in an effort to create an action theory for growth and development (Corey & Corey, 1994; Johnson & Johnson, 1991). In groups, emphasis is given to descriptive data and perceptions concerning group functioning with a goal of increasing understanding and developing continuing action strategies.

Process Facilitation

Process facilitation includes performing the tasks of process observation but taking a more active role than the process observer in facilitating change. The purpose of the process facilitator, like the process observer, is to increase the effectiveness of group interactions and improve the process. One means by which process facilitators attempt to reach this goal is by monitoring the dynamics of the group interactions (Reagan-Cirincione, 1994). Casey, Roberts, and Salaman (1992) identified three steps for fostering process facilitation. These steps involve the facilitator (a) taking in what is going on (i.e., collecting data and information); (b) making sense of what he or she takes in without interpreting (i.e., summarizing and noting themes); and (c) intervening to help the group (i.e., sharing perceptions and "checking out" what members are thinking and feeling). After collecting process data, process facilitators typically share that information with group members and ask them process questions. One outcome of process facilitation could be ensuring that all group members have the opportunity to participate fully and that the group session is not dominated by a minority of group members (Keltner, 1989).

Process facilitators frequently choose a systems theory approach to change. Fuqua and Kurpius (1993) identified five characteristics of the use of systems theory with organizations: (a) Interdependence is a critical component of teamwork and refers to viewing each interaction as being connected in a dynamic, complex manner to an integrated whole. (b) Structural models are necessary to describe the relationships between the framework, methods, people, and goals of a system. (c) Open systems describe the functioning of human organizations as they undergo environmental change. (d) Equifinality suggests that many solutions exist for any given problem. (e) Effective strategies involve interventions in both the structural and human behavioral dimensions of a system to create a balanced process. The systems theory approach establishes a link between task and process (Senge, 1990), with the process facilitator providing feedback about group functioning to the group as they work on the task. These process interventions that feed data back into the system provide the basis for continued growth and change.

OPPORTUNITIES ABOUND

Group work has come a long way and expanded dramatically beyond the narrow scope of the counseling or therapy group. Today, it is increasingly used to meet personal, social, and business needs (Reddy, 1985). Gladding (1991) expressed confidence that group work will, in the future, permeate almost all segments of a changing society. Luft (1984) would agree. According to Luft, the rapidity of societal change is marked by one constant: the need for and importance of quality human interaction (Luft, 1984). Thus, as society approaches the 21st century, opportunities for increased process consultation and the need for professional process consultants will almost certainly increase. Naisbitt and Aburdene (1990) and Aplin (1985) identified a number of trends that are creating these opportunities:

1. Quality is becoming paramount.
2. Organizations are shifting from hierarchies to networking and are downsizing as well.
3. The leadership role is more frequently that of teacher, coach, or mentor with a team as group members.
4. The most valuable commodity in the marketplace is information.

5. Increases in technology are creating more interpersonal needs as more work is being done away from a central location.
6. The most valuable employees want involvement and ownership; the best organizations provide it.
7. Diversity of the workforce and feminization of the workplace are increasing.
8. Organizations are more frequently turning to third parties for consultation expertise.
9. Planning is changing from a short-term operational focus to a long-term strategic focus.
10. There are fewer and fewer simple solutions as society becomes increasingly one of multiple options.

As work groups, business teams, professional groups, and other gatherings of individuals search for greater effectiveness and deal with the impact of the changes occurring in society, quality communication and interaction will become critical. Groups will turn to professional process consultants to monitor and facilitate the quality of the interpersonal involvements among their diverse members. Professional process consultants will also be expected to provide direction to groups seeking a strategic focus for identifying the best possible solutions in the workplace. One of the biggest challenges for process consultants is to utilize the "power of the group" so groups can harness the resources within themselves constructively (Glassman & Wright, 1983).

Knowledge, skills, and experience are the keys for successful process consultation. Programs that prepare group practitioners provide the core training process consultants need. However, direct experience in business and organizational settings is essential. Individuals interested in this particular specialty will need to seek out practicums, internships, and related experiences that will round out their preparation. Specific experiences in observing, facilitating, and leading are needed to acquire the competencies necessary for effective process consultation.

• •

PROCESS CONSULTATION GUIDELINES

As Leslie and Pat continued their research on process consultation, we began to meet with them regularly. Together, we constructed specific guidelines we could use to incorporate process consultation into our advanced group counseling courses. In our discussions, we identified five areas in which we needed to conduct further investigation: entering the system, contracting for change, choosing a focus, providing feedback, and measuring progress. Guidelines for dealing with these areas follow.

ENTERING THE SYSTEM

Process consultation involves a somewhat different set of processes and issues than are typically encountered in other group leadership roles. Traditional group counseling takes place within a temporary and, to some extent, artificial system. Group leaders usually work on their own turf and their own terms. The process consultation situation is quite different, with some dynamics of the system less pronounced and roles articulated and assigned by others (Blocher, 1987).

The process consultant serves a system that is familiar to all but the process consultant as he or she attends to group climate from a systems perspective. He or she must develop an awareness of both the organizational and social contexts of the system (Umansky & Holloway, 1984). Initially, however, the process consultant, whether an internal or external consultant, enters an unknown system. The system could be the group that is the target of a specific process consultation or the larger organization of which that group is a "subsystem."

Relationship building with the consultee (or consultee system) is the first step for the process consultant (Russ, 1978). He or she must gain credibility as an accepted and trusted, even if temporary, part of the system (Blocher, 1987). A valued and respected relationship is built gradually and draws on the same relationship and leadership skills that are involved in group work. Blocher (1987) emphasized that such a relationship will support an open and thorough discussion of the consulting situation and process and of the cognitive and affective components of the group. When building relationships, attention should be given to the group leader, to people in supervisory capacities, and to the individuals in the system who hold the gatekeeper role. Johnson and Johnson (1991) defined the gatekeeper as the individual who translates and interprets information and developments to other group members. The gatekeeper plays a critical role in ensuring the group members' acceptance of the process consultant's role and is an essential individual with whom the process consultant must build a relationship prior to the beginning of group meetings.

Thus, the process consultant, by definition, is an outsider and an intruder into a system. As such, he or she needs to be sensitive to all members of the group as well as to the larger system.

CONTRACTING FOR CHANGE

People, and organizations, typically resist imposed change (Burke & Church, 1992). Thus, process consultants need to develop a contract for change with the consultee (or consultee system) and reach consensus among all parties involved. Doing so will increase the likelihood that all individuals will feel some ownership toward the planned changes.

The contract between the organization and the process consultant should not only define the roles of each entity but should also invite both to be a part of the change process. Statements about realistic expectations concerning the kind of data to be collected, who will collect that data, how the information will be presented to the group, when presentations will occur, and who will initiate the presentations constitute the heart of the contract. This contract may be a formal document that specifies a time frame, information about financial payment, and additional details, or it may be an informal, verbal agreement that highlights the tasks and relationships between the two parties.

CHOOSING A FOCUS

Experienced process consultants work at both a macro and a micro level. At the macro level, the focus is on the unit as a group with emphasis upon group development and the functions of task accomplishment and maintenance of relationships. At the micro level, the focus is on individual needs, interpersonal behavior, and leader-group interactions.

Leslie's experiences in leading the business meeting of a professional organization, described at the beginning of this chapter, illuminate the difference between a macro- and a micro-level focus. Leslie's emphasis on the formal agenda and goal-setting illustrate the macro-level dimension. The discussions unrelated to agenda items, the angry outburst between group members, and the other ineffective group member behaviors sparked by perceptions of not being heard by Leslie and other group members illustrate the micro-level dimension.

How does the process consultant decide whether and when to shift focus between the macro and micro dimensions? Organizational structure and situational variables guide the shift of focus. The organizational structure establishes an overall setting in terms of purpose and specific tasks assigned to the group. Situational variables include the management style of the leader, the readiness level of the group members, the amount of time the group will be together, and the contract between the organization and the process consultant.

Typically, the focus is initially on group formation. After group and organizational awareness levels have been heightened, interventions are directed at obvious events that are apparent to all. The process consultant models effective process observation and facilitates intervention behavior. Gradually, as the group members increase their interactions with one another, the focus moves to a shifting pattern between the more complex macro-level functioning of the group and the interpersonal (or micro-level) functioning among group members. Individual needs are addressed only after the group has gained some experience and willingness in giving and receiving feedback and a supportive climate has been established.

PROVIDING FEEDBACK

Feedback is an intervention strategy that offers possibilities for change and is a behavioral mechanism for creating and shaping the future. Feedback acts in a corrective manner, assisting individuals, groups, and organizations in reducing discrepancies between assumptions, perceptions, and reality.

Feedback is one of the most critical performance skills necessary for effective process consulting. In this light, Blanchard (Blanchard & Johnson, 1982; Blanchard, Zigarmi, & Zigarmi, 1985) called feedback "the breakfast of champions." Achievement-motivated individuals thrive on performance feedback. In fact, feedback is most effective when the person receiving it is motivated to improve. Process consultants constantly direct data back into the system through feedback (Senge, 1990). Delivering effective feedback may be viewed as a developmental process with situational components. Some helpful criteria include the following.

• **Feedback can be both descriptive and evaluative.** Process observation feedback and process facilitation feedback are most helpful and empowering when the comments are descriptive. The use of descriptive feedback places the decision making regarding change with the receivers. Developmentally, increases in descriptive feedback encourage a group to engage in increased shared decision making. Evaluative comments are best reserved for supervision and formal instruction. The most effective evaluative feedback consists of an adequate, but not excessive, amount of information.

• **Feedback can be both specific and general.** Specific feedback can be used effectively in groups to target behaviors that are preventing the group from making progress toward its goals. The narrow focus of this type of feedback can be helpful as a leverage point from which to initiate larger organizational changes. General feedback is less frequently used in group work but may be used when providing summaries of group progress.

• **Feedback can be monitored by all members and checked for clarity and accuracy.** Shepard (1964) called soliciting and discussing differing perceptions a triangulation procedure, which draws from the idea that views from at least two positions are needed to locate a point in space. Such monitoring of feedback is critical to building effective change strategies as well as to making sure all group members agree on the description of the issue around which change will occur.

• **Feedback should never be imposed.** Rather than being imposed, feedback should be given in a timely manner that takes into consideration the readiness level of the individual or group. The counselor can assess readiness level by asking if the group is willing to use the feedback just given and if they will be able to use it constructively. Feedback given to a group with low readiness level can contribute additional conflict, which may not be useful to a developing group. Interventions that build readiness may be more helpful at this point.

• **Feedback can provide direction for motivational energy.** To be effective, feedback should be directed toward behavior that has potential for change and that will fulfill group and individual needs. Often, it is used to assist in the identification of alternatives. The role of the process consultant, like the role of leadership, is to give individuals and groups opportunities to fulfill needs. As group members satisfy the lower level needs of security and belonging, they will increase their desire to focus upon the needs of esteem and achievement (Kormanski & Mozenter, 1987). Feedback can help direct their energy toward satisfying these needs.

The description of the continuous quality improvement team meeting presented earlier in this chapter illustrates the effective use of feedback. When the team leader was anxious and uncertain, the process facilitator encouraged and modeled active listening, provided specific behavioral descriptions, revisited the problem-solving model, asked members and the team leader for the opportunity to intervene, and clarified areas of consensus. The facilitator's visionary comments about the future directed the group's energy.

MEASURING PROGRESS

Goals are desired outcomes, and goal setting is an essential part of organizational change. Effective organizations begin with a value set and a mission (Goodstein, Nolan, & Pfeiffer, 1992) and move toward a vision. Process consultants facilitate that movement by helping to guide group behavior toward realizing group goals. Goals break the vision into manageable units. The process of operationalizing a goal makes it measurable. When describing goals, Blanchard (Blanchard & Johnson, 1982; Blanchard et al., 1985) used the acronym SMART as an operational criterion. Thus, goals should be specific, measurable, attainable, relevant, and trackable.

By assisting groups in identifying processes for which change interventions would be useful and in identifying a direction for each process to move, process consultants help the group form goals. Appropriate goals are jointly determined by both group members and leader (Gladding, 1991). Typical goals might be to improve communication, increase membership services, decrease budget overruns, or reduce meeting distractions.

Often, measurement techniques are employed to obtain a base rate (that is, to evaluate the process before a change is made) and to subsequently assess the effectiveness of strategies in moving the behavior in the direction of the goal. Examples include use of a Likert-type rating scale of communication effectiveness, determination of the number of membership services offered, calculation of the cost per budget overrun, and tallies of the number of distractions per meeting. The subsequent measurements produce change rates, which provide a means of measuring the gap between the present and the future. This evaluative feedback combined with descriptive feedback (about feelings, attitudes, and values) provides group members with an ongoing source of data. The group can use the data to shape the next set of strategies it will use to move toward the organization's vision.

PROCESS CONSULTATION INSIGHTS

As a new year began, we, as mentors, continued to help Leslie and Pat integrate process consultation concepts into their advanced group counseling courses. We became a learning group, sharing insights and outcomes with one another.

During our first meeting with this purpose, Pat described how he had introduced process observation into his course through a series of assignments that were to be completed over the duration of the course. As a first step, he instructed students to observe the dynamics of two groups each week and to share their observations in the first part of each class. After only a few classes, Pat had accumulated some excellent examples of real data, which came directly from student contributions, to use in his theory presentations.

Leslie had her students keep a process observation journal about their class. Following each meeting, the students wrote perceptions and thoughts to be used as feedback at the beginning of the next session. This initial feedback time provided an excellent review of the most recent class and, in addition, offered students another opportunity for skill development. Leslie read those journals that were voluntarily shared with her and gave additional feedback to interested students.

DEVELOPMENTAL STAGES OF GROUPS

During our second meeting devoted to sharing insights and outcomes, we discussed the developmental stages of groups. Pat noted that all of the models about group development were similar, frequently differing only in terminology. Chuck suggested that the number of group development stages specified by the models ranged from three to ten, with five being the most popular number (Kormanski, 1988). Typically, models with fewer than five units combined stages, and models with greater than five stages divided them into subparts.

Pat's favorite model was Tuckman's classic developmental model (see Figure 8.1), which consists of five stages: forming, storming, norming, performing, and adjourning (Tuckman, 1965; Tuckman & Jensen, 1977). LeeAnn noted that the use of student process observations in class made the model more realistic while providing a learning forum for understanding how real data fit a theory. As a result, lively discussions ensued in which reality and theory were brought together.

An early discovery made by Pat's students was that, like any process, group development flows, and one stage gradually evolves into another. Still, some critical, but subjective, measures can be used to assess task and relationship progress for each stage. Pat provided his students with an assessment instrument developed by Kormanski and Mozenter (1987) to measure the developmental stages of the groups they observed (see Figure 8.2). This Likert-type

Stage	Theme	Task Behavior	Relationship Behavior
One	Forming	Orientation (Orientation)	Testing and Dependence (Dependence)
Two	Storming	Emotional Response to Task Demands (Resistance)	Intragroup Hostility (Hostility)
Three	Norming	Expression of of Opinions (Communication)	Development of Group Cohesion (Cohesion)
Four	Performing	Emergence of Solution (Problem Solving)	Functional Role Relatedness (Interdependence)
Five	Adjourning	Separation	Disengagement

FIGURE 8.1 •

TUCKMAN MODEL OF GROUP DEVELOPMENT

Note: Adapted from the *Psychological Bulletin, 63,* "Developmental sequence in small groups," (pp. 384–399) by B. W. Tuckman, 1965; *Group & Organizational Studies, 2*(4), "Stages of small-group development revisited," (pp. 419–427) by B. W. Tuckman and M. A. C. Jensen, 1977.

rating scale measures team development, but it also effectively measures group development, because all teams are groups.

Another discovery made by the students concerned the specific task and relationship behaviors observed by the class members. Behavioral analysis revealed that even though groups in the forming stage exhibit mostly forming behaviors, behaviors related to all of the stages are represented during the groups' early interactions, including some references to adjourning (Lacoursiere, 1980). Likewise, in the adjourning stage, a few isolated forming behaviors are still seen. Thus, behaviors related to specific stages (e.g., goal setting during the forming stage) may appear at any time but are most likely to occur during their designated stage.

As we continued to discuss the process observations of groups at different developmental stages, it became evident that expecting groups to follow a se-

Instructions: Provide a rating from **one** *(low)* to **ten** *(high)* by circling the appropriate number that you think is most descriptive of your team.

1. **Commitment**
   Team members understand group goals and are committed to them.

10	9	8	7	6	5	4	3	2	1

2. **Acceptance**
   Team members are friendly, concerned, and interested in each other.

10	9	8	7	6	5	4	3	2	1

3. **Clarification**
   Team members acknowledge and confront conflict openly.

10	9	8	7	6	5	4	3	2	1

4. **Belonging**
   Team members listen with understanding to others.

10	9	8	7	6	5	4	3	2	1

5. **Involvement**
   Team members include others in the decision-making process.

10	9	8	7	6	5	4	3	2	1

6. **Support**
   Team members recognize and respect individual differences.

10	9	8	7	6	5	4	3	2	1

7. **Achievement**
   Team members contribute ideas and solutions to problems.

10	9	8	7	6	5	4	3	2	1

8. **Pride**
   Team members value the contributions and ideas of others.

10	9	8	7	6	5	4	3	2	1

9. **Recognition**
   Team members recognize and reward team performance.

10	9	8	7	6	5	4	3	2	1

10. **Satisfaction**
    Team members encourage and appreciate comments about team efforts.

10	9	8	7	6	5	4	3	2	1

FIGURE 8.2 •

KORMANSKI/MOZENTER TEAM DEVELOPMENT RATING SCALE

Source: Reproduced from *The 1987 Annual: Developing Human Resources* (p. 261), edited by J. W. Pfeiffer, 1987, San Diego, CA: University Associates. Copyright 1987 by University Associates, Inc. Reprinted by permission.

quential, step-by-step movement through the five stages was idealistic. Groups have both a developmental nature and a regressive nature. Unmanaged conflict, chaos, apathy, and individuals in crisis create regression, often causing the group to revisit earlier developmental stages. Groups working through the norming stage can revert to storming or progress toward performing. Groups at the forming stage can disband or move into storming. Some groups skip stages, particularly the storming one, but they usually enter the stages skipped at some later point during a regressive cycle. Bion (1961) presented one of the few models that is not sequential. His situational model provides a more realistic view of group movement. The model describes a beginning dependency (forming) stage followed by a move to a fight-flight (storming), pairing (norming), or work (performing) stage, based on the situational variables of the group.

Leslie spoke about her students' reactions to Schutz's (1958) FIRO (fundamental interpersonal relations orientation) theory. She had introduced the theory, with its focus on relationships, to the class after observing the students providing descriptive feedback to one another. The class was amazed at how their own interpersonal concerns about being in the class as a group were reflected by the theory. Leslie then offered the class the opportunity to take the FIRO-B (B for behavior), a self-assessment instrument that measures inclusion, control, and affection, the three behaviors that form the core of the theory.

When Schutz (1982) updated his theory, as he moved from working with encounter groups to organizational consultation, he changed one of the measures, affection, to openness, a more appropriate behavioral term. Leslie pointed out that even though the FIRO-B instrument measured only three concepts, the theory describes the interpersonal relationships of pairs or groups in five stages and involves two dimensions, an expressed behavior and a wanted behavior.

According to Schutz, when a relationship begins, individuals seek to gain inclusion (forming). This stage concludes when individuals are included (wanted behavior) and include others (expressed behavior). In the next stage (storming), individuals attempt to gain control and deal with the issues of leadership and influence. The stage ends when the members agree upon leadership and upon following specific roles. The third stage involves gaining openness (norming) and concludes when the group members take part in reciprocal communication, understanding, and involvement in a genuine manner. In the fourth stage, individuals in the relationship begin to give up control (performing), and the stage concludes when mutual trust is reached. This mutual trust is the heart of any group, including families, married couples, and friends. Giving up control is a critical prerequisite for empowerment. The final stage (adjournment) involves giving up inclusion and ends when the relationship or group disbands. In summary, Schutz (1982) presented his three concepts—inclusion, control, and openness—as a cyclic model that reverses itself when coming to an end.

FACILITATOR STYLE

The next time our group met, our agenda was to discuss facilitator style. As before, we all brought ideas that seemed relevant from our group counseling classes. LeeAnn noted that the literature on leadership style provides a useful framework for exploring facilitator styles. She also observed that leadership style is especially relevant if facilitating is viewed as encompassing opening up clear and direct communication within the group and helping members assume increasing responsibility for the direction of the group (Corey & Corey, 1994).

Leslie stated that she was unclear about which aspects of leadership were relevant to process facilitation. She asserted that even casual observation of facilitators in action reveals marked differences in their styles. Some facilitators seem to be autocratic, announcing policies and procedures without involving group members, and reluctant to give up control. Other facilitators could be described as democratic, allowing policies to evolve through group discussion and consensus decisions. For such facilitators, requesting the cooperation and involvement of group members appears to be a priority. Still other facilitators model what seems to be a laissez-faire style, not engaging or intervening in the group's decision making at all. Such differences, Leslie noted, should influence group productivity and the attitudes of group members, but Leslie was not sure that these three styles of leadership provided a comprehensive framework for process facilitator style. Johnson and Johnson (1991) mirrored her thoughts by suggesting that two shortcomings of this approach to assessing facilitator style are that different styles are effective under different conditions and an unlimited number of styles may be fairly similar.

Chuck brought other insights on facilitator and leadership style to the meeting. He observed that different leadership styles seem to be required in different situations, even with the same group. Chuck encouraged Leslie to examine a situational approach to leadership.

Situational leadership theory, which was developed by Hersey and Blanchard (1982), suggests that leadership style should move from a highly directive or autocratic orientation to a more democratic one as the task maturity level of the followers increases. Hersey and Blanchard defined task maturity as the ability and willingness to do a specific task. It is always task relevant. If the task is changed, the task maturity level changes. In subsequent adaptations of the theory Hersey (1984) referred to task maturity as readiness level.

Blanchard also related situational leadership theory to group development stages (Carew, Parisi-Carew, & Blanchard, 1984). Using the work of Lacoursiere (1980), he demonstrated how changing the nature of the group results in the need to change one's leadership style. Kormanski (1985) presented a similar theory using the Tuckman model (Tuckman & Jensen, 1977) and Maslow's (1954) hierarchy of needs.

In developing their theory, Hersey and Blanchard (1982) built on previous studies of leadership that determined that most leader actions could be categorized into one of two distinct behavioral dimensions: initiation of structure (task behaviors) and consideration of group members (relationship or maintenance behaviors). They clarified task behavior as being the extent to which a leader provides directions to group members, sets goals, and helps members define their roles. In essence, task behaviors communicate what group members are to do and when, where, and how they are to do it. Relationship behavior is defined as the extent to which a leader engages in "multiway" (or dynamic, interactive) communication, facilitates appropriate group member behaviors, and provides emotional support.

According to the situational leadership theory, task and relationship behaviors are two separate dimensions that are used in combination with each other to form a leadership style. Depending on the situation, group leaders and facilitators match their leadership style with the group's readiness level. A group development sequence following Tuckman's model would suggest that during the forming stage, group members are willing to understand the system but lack the ability to do so. A high task, low relationship style (directing or telling) would match this readiness level and address the issues of getting oriented and resolving dependencies as well as provide for security needs.

In the storming stage, unwillingness replaces willingness, which requires leadership style to change gradually to high task, high relationship (coaching or selling). This style combats the group members' hostility and resistance to task and aids in the fulfillment of belonging needs.

As the norming stage approaches and group members become more able, the leader must reduce task behavior but maintain a high relationship behavior to address the lack of confidence and unwillingness that often accompanies the start of open communication and cohesiveness. This low task, high relationship style (supporting or participating) also helps members to build esteem.

A reduction in relationship behavior and maintenance of low task behavior would match the readiness level of the able, willing group members in the performing stage. Such a low task, low relationship style (delegating) would contribute to group problem solving and interdependence as well as to the group members' fulfillment of Maslow's higher needs, particularly achievement.

A regressive crisis typically occurs during the adjourning stage of a group, manifested in a reluctance of able, willing members to leave the group (Kormanski, 1985). Moving backward on the leadership quadrant from a delegating to a supporting leadership style would increase the relationship behavior to address this change. This low task, high relationship style would assist members in terminating the task and disengaging from the group relationships. It would also revisit the group members' need for esteem and help bring closure to the life of the group.

Just as the group development stages move developmentally forward and regressively backward, the leader or facilitator must continuously change his or her style to match the needs of the group. In addition, because groups are composed of individuals, the leader's or facilitator's style must also change when he or she is interacting with any one member of the group concerning a specific task. The leader role is complex, with different demands made of the leader at a variety of levels. Figure 8.3 provides a summary of the relationship between group development stages, team development themes, leadership styles, member readiness, and individual motivational needs (Kormanski, 1985; 1988).

Group Development Stage	Team Development Theme	Leadership Style	Follower Readiness	Motivational Needs
1. Forming	Awareness	High task and low relationship	Inexperienced and willing	Physiological needs, security needs
2. Storming	Conflict	High task and high relationship	Inexperienced and unwilling	Belonging and social needs
3. Norming	Cooperation	Low task and high relationship	Experienced and unwilling or unconfident	Recognition and esteem needs
4. Performing	Productivity	Low task and low relationship	Experienced and willing	Achievement and higher needs
5. Adjourning	Separation	Low task and high relationship	Experienced and unwilling	Recognition and esteem needs

FIGURE 8.3 •

RELATIONSHIP BETWEEN STAGES OF GROUP AND TEAM DEVELOPMENT AND LEADERSHIP STYLE

Note: Adapted from *The 1995 Annual: Developing Human Resources* (pp. 217–255), by L. D. Goodstein and J. W. Pfeiffer, 1985, San Diego: University Associates; "Using Group Development Theory in Business and Industry," by C. L. Kormanski, 1988, *Journal for Specialists in Group Work, 13,* 30–41.

CRITICAL SKILLS

Our periodic meetings and discussions had been progressing well, and our interactions continued to be productive and meaningful. Leslie and Pat brought a few of their doctoral level graduate students to our next meeting, which became a lively seminar on identifying critical skills.

Leslie began the discussion by noting that the process consultant utilizes many skills throughout the life of the group. She identified eight skills that she felt were critical for the effectiveness of both group leaders and process consultants: active listening, reflecting, linking, summarizing, interpreting, blocking, disclosing oneself, and suggesting. These skills are defined and elaborated on in Figure 8.4.

Pat cited the work of Burns (1978), who described two major types of leadership with two different sets of skills. Transactional leadership is present-oriented with the leader's skills focused on getting the job done, whereas transformational leadership is future-oriented with the leader's skills aimed at providing inspiration and vision (Bennis & Nanus, 1985). Both types of leadership and skills are critical for process consultants. Kormanski and Mozenter (1987) suggested that transactional leadership and its related skills are emphasized early in the life of a group and that transformational leadership and its related skills are gradually increased until they predominate in the later life of the group. This integration of transactional and transformational skills is essential to effective group development. Figure 8.5 summarizes the transactional and transformational skills frequently used by process consultants at the different stages of group development.

PROCESS CONSULTATION APPLICATIONS

As Leslie and Pat continued to teach process consultation in their group counseling courses, they began to explore possible areas of application for their students. Initially, they looked for short-term activities that would be helpful in providing the students with hands-on process consultation experiences in non-counseling-group settings. We had suggested that they investigate professional and volunteer organizations, settings where we had found that group development knowledge and skills were directly applicable. Following this lead, Leslie had discovered that the human resources unit on her campus conducted a number of professional development programs that included skill training in a variety of areas. Specific programs offered currently included assertiveness, communication, supervision, and team building.

In our brainstorming sessions, a few other possibilities were suggested. A public forum on health care was being held on Pat's campus. LeeAnn had recently been part of a focus group that was collecting information and view-

Skill	What It Is	Why Do It	How to Do It
Active listening	Attending to the verbal and nonverbal aspects of what is being said	• Demonstrates care and concern for what is happening in the group • Assesses congruence between what a member is saying and his or her nonverbal communication	• Note both the content and underlying message of what a group member is saying and not saying • Use your eyes: scan the entire group and note nonverbal reactions to group members' comments
Reflecting	Conveying the essence of what is being said	• Helps eliminate ambiguity • Demonstrates that the group member was understood	• *Paraphrase* when focusing on content: repeat the substance of what was said without being mechanical • *Reflect* when focusing on feelings: state your best hypothesis of the group member's feelings; try to be accurate about both the specific feeling and the intensity of emotion
Linking	Relating what one person is saying or doing to another person	• Produces a sense of we-ness and cohesion • Identifies commonalities among group members	• Be alert to cues for common concern • Connect members in terms of similarities, similar phrases, ideas, thoughts, feelings, or experiences
Summarizing	Pulling together the important elements of a meeting or part of a meeting	• Promotes decision making about where to go next when the group process is bogged down or fragmented • Helps wrap up or end a group meeting	• Synthesize what has been communicated or highlight the major themes, both affective and cognitive; do not simply review the sequence of the discussion *(continued)*

FIGURE 8.4 •

CRITICAL SKILLS FOR GROUP PROCESS CONSULTANTS

Note: Adapted from Gladding (1991); Corey & Corey (1994); Jacobs, Harvill, & Masson (1994).

Figure 8.4 continued

Skill	What It Is	Why Do It	How to Do It
Interpreting	Offering possible explanations for certain group interactions	• Helps the group move beyond an impasse • Provides a new viewpoint for consideration	• Present your ideas tentatively as a hunch; allow the group to assess and consider their accuracy
Blocking	Intervening when group members engage in counterproductive interactions	• Protects group members • Enhances the flow of the group process	• Actually cut off a group member, stating reasons for your interruption • Alternatively, refocus on another group member by directly asking for input from others
Disclosing oneself	Sharing your reactions to the here-and-now events of the group	• Facilitates interaction • Models ways of sharing • Encourages members to reflect and react to the group process	• Use the individual counseling skill of immediacy—this is how I am feeling, this is what I am thinking, or this is my reaction to the events
Suggesting	Offering information, direction, or ideas for new behavior	• Helps group members develop alternatives	• Actually present information; least effective when it comes across as direct advice-giving

points about a specific topic. Pat contributed his own experiences from the continuous quality improvement team of which he was now an active member. Leslie noted that she had recently been appointed to a newly formed strategic planning committee on her campus. Finally, Chuck recommended reading a book about future search conferences, as he had recently participated in one. We were all certain we would discover other possibilities as our journey continued.

PUBLIC FORUMS

Pat accompanied a friend to a national issues forum sponsored by his university and the Kettering Foundation. Both sponsors were committed to increasing public awareness about the political process through a forum discussion of a preselected

Stage of Team Development	Transactional Skills (Management)	Transformational Skills (Leadership)
1. Awareness	Getting acquainted, goal setting, organizing	Value clarification, visioning, communicating through myth and metaphor
2. Conflict	Active listening, assertiveness, conflict management	Flexibility, creativity, kaleidoscopic thinking
3. Cooperation	Communicating, feedback, affirmation	Playfulness and humor, entrepreneuring, networking
4. Productivity	Decision making, problem solving, rewarding	Multicultural awareness, mentoring, futuring
5. Separation	Evaluating, reviewing	Celebrating, bringing closure

 FIGURE 8.5 •

TRANSACTIONAL AND TRANSFORMATIONAL SKILLS AND THEIR RELATIONSHIP TO STAGE OF GROUP DEVELOPMENT

critical issue (Mathews, 1988). This particular forum examined choices regarding the issue of health care. Pat observed that about 100 individuals representing all aspects of the community attended.

As the evening unfolded, the large gathering divided into small groups of 10 to 15 participants, each with 2 moderators who provided group leadership. Pat found himself giving more attention to the process than the topic under discussion even though health care was a controversial issue. He noted that the moderator role was really that of a group facilitator, not a group leader. The moderators did not lead the groups in any specific direction; instead, they facilitated movement toward understanding and making choices using group members' perceptions and contributions.

Initially, Pat's group looked at how the issue of health care affects people and identified key facts and emotions. Next, the group discussed the pros and

cons of three options discussed in an issue book. The group also had the opportunity to construct its own fourth option, and discussion on it ensued. Costs,
consequences, and values were important components. The moderators used the
skills of a group facilitator and involved the participants in a lively interaction.
Emphasis was given to hearing all points of view, working through conflicting
emotions, and discovering what makes choosing a difficult process. Individuals
noted what compromises they were willing to make, and the moderators facilitated the establishment of areas of common ground for further action. With the
aid of the moderators, the group acknowledged unresolved areas, which were
mostly related to values. The moderators summarized points of consensus and
provided feedback concerning the group work effort. Once again, Pat saw an
application of group process in action.

FOCUS GROUPS

LeeAnn responded to a memo from her university's Office of Assessment and
Institutional Research asking for volunteers to participate in one of several focus groups for faculty members. The director of the assessment office was interested in following up on the results of a survey on faculty perceptions, attitudes, and satisfactions that had been conducted by the Higher Educational Research Institute (HERI).

   As LeeAnn and six other faculty members arrived at their focus group meeting, they were greeted by two co-leaders. The co-leaders described the focus
group as a qualitative research technique. After securing permission from all
participants, the co-leaders began to audiotape the session. Although the topics
the group was to discuss were selected and focused by the co-leaders, the emphasis was clearly on exploring the perspectives of the group participants. LeeAnn
noticed that although the leaders asked a few key questions about faculty attitudes, perceptions, and experiences on campus, the interactions among the group
members provided spontaneous responses that were much more in-depth and
reflective than her initial response, or those of others, to the leaders' questions.
Also, one participant's comments seemed to provide new direction for the co-
leaders to pursue. After an hour of enthusiastic discussion, LeeAnn was amazed
at the amount of information she and the other group members had exchanged.
Group members' responses seemed to feed off one another and created insightful, synergistic data. LeeAnn observed the group leaders using the skills of active listening, linking, clarifying, summarizing, and reflecting. The skills they
exhibited mirrored those she taught in the skill development section of his class
on group leadership.

   LeeAnn talked to the co-leaders about focus groups after the session ended.
They stated that, for them, the key advantages of focus groups are that they
provide the opportunity to observe interactions among participants on the selected topics, to hear richer and more in-depth responses to questions than a

survey would allow, and to collect data from the group interactions that can later be reviewed in detail.

QUALITY IMPROVEMENT TEAMS

Pat continued his work with the continuous quality improvement team. The team had become heavily involved in a problem-solving model and was following a sequential set of steps designed to produce concrete results using statistical measurement tools. During the team meetings, the group developed process control charts; constructed a flow chart of the process they were working to improve; identified bottlenecks that they then analyzed using a cause-and-effect fishbone diagram; and built a decision matrix to use in selecting appropriate solutions.

Just as in counseling groups, the team dealt with the issues of inclusion, control, and openness (Schutz, 1982). While the team leader scheduled meeting times, supervised record keeping, and kept the group on task, the group facilitator monitored the group process and intervened when a situation involved relationship issues. The facilitator also provided a role model to the other team members and taught the various aspects of problem solving in a group setting. Most of the team members were good individual problem solvers but few had group problem-solving experience.

Pat was impressed with the facilitator's skill in bringing people and ideas together. By the time the group applied a new insight, it was hard to remember who had initiated it. Original suggestions were added to, modified, rearranged, and split into parts until they became the product of the team, not a contribution from an individual. The facilitator frequently combined ideas into team summaries. This integration was similar to the group counseling goal of building supportive relationships among group members. In this case, the process involved tasks as the primary focus although relationships were not ignored. Pat noticed that the facilitator used relationship support to solidify team effort and as a reward for team performance.

STRATEGIC PLANNING

Early in the semester, Leslie had been appointed to represent her department on the university's new strategic planning committee. The first meeting was a 2-day retreat held off campus and led by a process consultant. As Leslie participated in a sequence of experiences at the retreat, she specifically looked for similarities between what she was going through and the process of group development.

The retreat began with an exploration of the history and culture of the university, which included a values clarification exercise. By lunchtime on the first day, the committee was rewriting the university's mission statement to reflect its current purpose and the activities in which it was engaged. The afternoon and early evening were spent identifying and prioritizing critical issues. During the morning of the second day, a futuring exercise was conducted to examine key issue trends and desired positions of leverage. The exercise resulted in a statement of vision, which was completed around noon. During the second afternoon, small groups were formed to discuss goals and strategies; the groups would continue to meet when the committee returned to campus.

During the retreat, the process consultant demonstrated a comprehensive knowledge of strategic planning; however, Leslie was most impressed with her skill in working with, and her understanding of, the group process. She provided descriptive feedback concerning how the committee worked together throughout the retreat and facilitated the group through the developmental stages in a manner that built cohesiveness and helped the team to achieve its objectives. Overall, her process consultant role included being both a process observer and a process facilitator. Leslie noted how the process consultant's facilitator role smoothly followed her process observation summaries and how, when she was in the consultant role, she took the group beyond the immediate and operational issues into the future and strategic issues.

During one of the breaks, Leslie had a chance to ask the process consultant about her education and training for this role. To Leslie's surprise, most of her preparation was through specific skills training in weeklong and summer workshops plus a lot of direct experience. The process consultant stated that working with competent individuals in the field was most helpful. Although formal degree programs exist, there are, she said, many pathways to gaining expertise. Her final piece of advice was to constantly stay on the cutting edge by reading the current literature in a variety of related business, education, and counseling fields.

FUTURE SEARCH CONFERENCES

Following Chuck's suggestion, Pat and Leslie attended a book discussion of Weisbord's *Discovering Common Ground* (1992) held at Chuck's university. The discussion was sponsored by a group of organizational psychologists. In the book, Weisbord presented a variety of ideas with case studies about how to facilitate large organizational change. He suggested a format for change that brings 50 to 60 stakeholders of an organization or community together for a 2- to 3-day conference with the major aim being a search for the future. The conference agenda would include examining the past, looking at current trends, conducting an internal analysis, creating future ideal scenarios, and action planning.

Some participants of the discussion had been trained in the future search process, and others had been involved in actual search conferences. The latter described the conferences as dynamic, fun, and learning-oriented. One individual observed that action planning is easier when people work backward from an ideal future they have envisioned than when they work forward from specifics for which there often is disagreement. Another noted that the most important factor related to successful change is getting the key people involved. Leslie and Pat were struck by the fact that the discussion group involved very little teaching and instruction. The most frequent activity was learning in small groups.

Future search conferences, Pat and Leslie learned, are conducted by facilitators who might best be described as task facilitators rather than process facilitators. Their role is to keep the participants working at their task and facilitating their own processes. As Pat and Leslie completed some additional reading and talked with Chuck, they discovered that search conferences are quite different from the other process consultation applications they had investigated. Their focus on content and their de-emphasis of the leadership role, in particular, set them apart. The future search model provided a limited, but solid structure and empowered members of small groups to work with one another to manage change. There was no striving for consensus. Leaders did not intervene to facilitate process. There was no process consultant guiding the procedure. There was, however, a reliance on group dynamics and a constant search for common ground among participants. The focus was always upon creating an ideal future that everyone could live with.

PROCESS CONSULTATION IMPLICATIONS

As we continued our search for practical process consultation applications and reflected on what we had discovered, we realized that we had only scratched the surface. We had discovered some new roles in diverse settings for group leaders, but we had also begun to more fully appreciate the changing nature of complex roles in a changing society.

During the end-of-year semester break, we met to discuss the possibility of writing a chapter for a textbook on group work. Chuck presented the idea, which had come from two of his colleagues. The experiential journey we had taken during the past few months, which had led to a deeper understanding of the role of process consultant, was an appropriate content. Everyone was eager to begin.

LeeAnn suggested that we might also want to examine the process of our own group. In many ways, our group had mirrored the subject area we were studying. All of us had shared in the leadership role, and at different times each had become the process observer, the process facilitator, and the process consultant. Our periodic meetings had become more regular and more structured. Feedback had become the essential tool for shaping creative insights and setting direction. We were using all of the skills we taught to our students. Could this be the reason we each perceived our group as a stimulating and productive success? Were we actually practicing what we preached? Was each of us able to trust the process?

The fact that you are reading this book suggests that you have an interest in group process. You could create an experience similar to the one in which our group is engaged. As you read this book, think about whether any chapters strike you as possibilities for further exploration? Whom might you invite to form a group? What skills relevant to group process will be needed? Could the group benefit from the help of a process observer or a process facilitator? As you continue your own professional growth and development, might you aspire to the role of process consultant?

As the role of process consultant is evolving in our changing world, a major paradigm shift is occurring. The critical mission of influencing change is still paramount; the subroles of process observer and process facilitator are still intact. However, the goals and strategies that make the vision operational continue to change. Thus, contemporary process consultants tie the present to the future by focusing the attention of their clients on possibilities as well as on reality. As always, they continue to emphasize process over content, to ask questions instead of answering them, and to help everyone change the whole system.

REFERENCES

Aplin, J. C. (1985). Business realities and organizational consultation. *Counseling Psychologist, 13,* 396–402.

Benne, K. D. (1964). History of the T-group in the laboratory setting. In L. P. Bradford, J. R. Gibb, and K. D. Benne (Eds.), *T-group theory and laboratory method: Innovation in re-education* (pp. 80–135). New York: Wiley.

Bennis, W., & Nanus, B. (1985). *Leaders: The strategies for taking charge.* New York: Harper & Row.

Bion, W. R. (1961). *Experiences in groups.* New York: Basic Books.

Blanchard, K. H., & Johnson, S. (1982). *The one minute manager.* New York: Morrow.

Blanchard, K. H., Zigarmi, P., & Zigarmi, D. (1985). *Leadership and the one minute manager.* New York: Morrow.

Blocher, D. H. (1987). *The professional counselor.* New York: Macmillan.

Burke, W. W., & Church, A. H. (1992). *Managing change: Survey participant report.* Pelham, NY: W. Warner Burke.

Burns, J. M. (1978). *Leadership.* New York: Harper & Row.

Carew, D. K., Parisi-Carew, E., & Blanchard, K. H. (1984). *Group development and situational leadership: A model for changing groups.* Escondido, CA: Blanchard Training and Development.

Carkhuff, R. R. (1986). *Human processing and human productivity.* Amherst, MA: Human Resource Development.

Casey, D., Roberts, P., & Salaman, G. (1992). Facilitating learning in groups. *Leadership and Organization Development Journal, 13,* 8–13.

Conyne, R. K. (1989). *How personal growth and task groups work.* Newbury Park, CA: Sage.

Corey, M. S., & Corey, G. (1994). *Groups: Process and practice* (4th ed.). Pacific Grove, CA: Brooks/Cole.

Dustin, D., & Blocher, D. H. (1984). Theories and models of consultation. In S. D. Brown & R. W. Lent (Eds.), *Handbook of counseling psychology* (pp. 751–781). New York: Wiley.

Fuqua, D. R., & Kurpius, D. J. (1993). Conceptual models in organizational consultation. *Journal of Counseling and Development, 71,* 607–618.

Gladding, S. T. (1991). *Group work: A counseling specialty.* New York: Macmillan.

Glassman, S. M., & Wright, T. L. (1983). In, with, and of the group: A perspective on group psychotherapy. *Small Group Behavior, 14,* 96–106.

Goodstein, L. D., Nolan, T. M., & Pfeiffer, J. W. (1992). *Applied strategic planning: A comprehensive guide.* San Diego: Pfeiffer.

Goodstein, L. D., & Pfeiffer, J. W. (1985). *The 1985 annual: Developing human resources.* San Diego: University Associates.

Hellreigal, D., Slocum, J. W., & Woodman, R. W. (1986). *Organizational behavior.* St. Paul, MN: West.

Hersey, P. (1984). *The situational leader.* Escondido, CA: Center for Leadership Studies.

Hersey, P., & Blanchard, K. H. (1982). *Management of organizational behavior: Utilizing human resources* (4th ed.). Englewood Cliffs, NJ: Prentice-Hall.

Jacobs, E. E., Harvill, R. L., & Masson, R. L. (1994). *Group counseling: Strategies and skills* (2d ed.). Pacific Grove, CA: Brooks/Cole.

Johnson, D. W., & Johnson, F. P. (1991). *Joining together: Group theory and group skills* (4th ed.). Englewood Cliffs, NJ: Prentice-Hall.

Keltner, J. (1989). Facilitation: Catalyst for group problem solving. *Management Communication Quarterly, 3,* 8–32.

Kormanski, C. L. (1985). A situational leadership approach to groups using the Tuckman model of group development. In L. D. Goodstein & J. W. Pfeiffer (Eds.), *The 1985 annual: Developing human resources* (pp. 217–226). San Diego: University Associates.

Kormanski, C. (1988). Using group development theory in business and industry. *Journal for Specialists in Group Work, 13,* 30–41.

Kormanski, C. L., & Mozenter, A. (1987). A new model of team building: A technology for today and tomorrow. In J. W. Pfeiffer (Ed.), *The 1987 annual: Developing human resources* (pp. 255–268). San Diego: University Associates.

Lacoursiere, R. B. (1980). *The life cycle of groups: Group developmental stage theory.* New York: Human Sciences Press.

Lewin, K. (1951). *Field theory in social science.* New York: Harper.

Lewis, J. A., Hayes, B. A., & Bradley, L. J. (1992). *Counseling women over the lifespan.* Denver: Love.

Luft, J. (1984). *Group processes: An introduction to group dynamics* (3rd ed.). Palo Alto, CA: Mayfield.

Maslow, A. H. (1954). *Motivation and personality.* New York: Harper & Row.

Mathews, D. (1988). *The promise of democracy.* Dayton, OH: The Kettering Foundation.

Naisbitt, J., & Aburdene, J. (1990). *Megatrends: Ten new directions for the 1990's.* New York: Morrow.

Reagan-Cirincione, P. (1994). Improving the accuracy of group judgment: A process intervention combining group facilitation, social judgment analysis, and information technology. *Organizational Behavior and Human Decision Processes, 58,* 247–270.

Reddy, W. B. (1985). The role of the change agent in the future of group work. *Journal for Specialists in Group Work, 10,* 103–107.

Robinson, D. G., & Robinson, J. C. (1995). *Performance consulting: Moving beyond training.* San Francisco: Berrett-Koehler.

Russ, S. W. (1978). Group consultation: Key variables that effect change. *Professional Psychology, 9,* 145–152.

Schein, E. H. (1969). *Process consultation.* Reading, MA: Addison-Wesley.

Schmuck, R., & Schmuck, P. (1974). *A humanistic psychology of education.* Palo Alto, CA: National Press.

Schutz, W. D. (1958). *FIRO: A three-dimensional theory of interpersonal behavior.* New York: Holt, Rinehart, & Winston.

Schutz, W. D. (1982). *The Schutz measures: An integrated system for assessing elements of aware-ness.* San Diego: University Associates.

Senge, P. M. (1990). *The fifth discipline.* New York: Doubleday.

Shepard, H. A. (1964). Explorations in observant participation. In L. P. Bradford, J. R. Gibb, & K. D. Benne (Eds.), *T-Group theory and laboratory method: Innovation in re-education* (pp. 379–394). New York: Wiley.

Tuckman, B. W. (1965). Developmental sequence in small groups. *Psychological Bulletin, 63,* 384–399.

Tuckman, B. W., & Jensen, M. A. (1977). Stages of small-group development revisited. *Group and Organizational Studies, 2*(4), 419–427.

Umansky, D. L., & Holloway, E. L. (1984). The counselor as consultant: From model to practice. *The School Counselor, 31,* 329–338.

Weisbord, M. R. (1978). *Organizational diagnosis.* New York: Addison-Wesley.

Weisbord, M. R. (1987). *Productive workplaces.* San Francisco: Jossey-Bass.

Weisbord, M. R. (1992). *Discovering common ground.* San Francisco: Berrett-Koehler.

Wheatley, M. (1992). *Leadership and the new science.* San Francisco: Berrett-Koehler.

9

GROUP LEADERSHIP:

LEARNING FROM THE MACRO

TO IMPROVE THE MICRO

LORETTA J. BRADLEY AND ELAINE JARCHOW

As the president of a large professional organization and the dean of a college, we are both group leaders on the macro level. However, many similarities exist between our large group cultures and the culture of smaller groups. Indeed, lessons can be learned from the macro to improve the micro. Using our stories as catalysts, we stress the importance of the leadership ethic and the personal characteristics of leaders. Through four case studies, we connect with the leadership ethic and depict leadership in the college setting and the professional organization. To relate our large group culture to that of smaller groups and to speak directly to group counselors, we begin with our stories.

ELAINE'S STORY

My biographical paragraph tells the formal story—degrees and leadership positions that have resulted in my current role as dean of a large college of education. The informal rendering, though, is more interesting. I credit my mother with getting me started on the right path. When, in the ninth grade, I wanted to complete a "memorize a poem" assignment with a four-liner, she insisted on "The Highwayman." When I could not decide whether to run for student council or join the debate team, she suggested I give them both a try. Besides my mother's influence, I credit my all-girls Catholic high school with whetting my leadership appetite. All-girls schools provide plenty of food for jokes, but they also provide great opportunities for young women to lead. Because teachers and students are not distracted by "boys," expectations for young women differ from expectations in coed schools. Young women are expected to be the newspaper editors, debate team captains, and physics club presidents. I truly enjoyed my high school leadership roles and knowing that it was okay to be smart and to participate in a discussion of the Greek plays over a cafeteria lunch.

These foundations led me, when in college, to hold office in numerous organizations. I first was an officer in the Young Republicans and later in the Young Democrats. Dating the president of the Young Democrats probably had a little to do with the switch! I postponed my student teaching so that I could serve a full year as president of my dormitory. Later, as a young high school English teacher, I eagerly served on and chaired committees. Subsequently, as a full-time doctoral student, I joined the Graduate Student Organization.

I am now entering my 20th year of academic life and have taken advantage of numerous opportunities to lead. But why do I think that I have something to say to group counselors and other readers of this book? Deans actually spend considerable time in group settings. We meet with and chair faculty, student, and staff groups; we mediate disputes; we exhort our organization; we celebrate with our group; we facilitate growth and learning; we put out fires; we fight for resources; we create fertile environments for change; we nurture people; and we advocate for our college at all-university group settings. My experience as dean has led to insights that, I hope, will be useful to group practitioners and others.

LORETTA'S STORY

I grew up in Ashland, Kentucky, a small town with a population of about 50,000. Mine was a typical family of that era in that my father worked outside the home and my mother was a homemaker. I was always excited by my grandmother's visits. She often stayed a month with us and during that time would reminisce about her experiences as a young girl growing up in Kentucky. My grandmother was an independent woman who was always interested in events happening around her. My mother often described me as being like my grandmother, especially in terms of my independence.

I credit my mother and her eldest sister for encouraging me to have a career. My mother had planned to pursue a career as a teacher, but following her marriage, she did not pursue her college degree. My aunt taught for 5 years. But after she married, she did not continue teaching. Both my mother and her sister were kind, understanding women who always helped me to have a good feeling (self-confidence) about myself. Additionally, they encouraged me to be the best that I could be in whatever I chose to do. At this point, perhaps I should explain that our home was within walking distance of my aunt's home. Because my aunt and her husband did not have children, it was almost as if I had two sets of parents. Speaking of sets of parents, my father, although not always as vocal as my mother, nevertheless supported my ideas and encouraged my achievements. I never heard, or at least I do not remember hearing, the phrase, "Don't try this, for it may be too difficult." Instead, I was led to believe that with determination and hard work, I could do almost anything.

Throughout junior and senior high school, I was active in both academic and social activities. I received several awards and was elected to several leadership roles. I would characterize my years in junior and senior high as being pretty "normal." I remember that I enjoyed school and always seemed to have an insatiable curiosity about things. When I became interested in something, I would exert a lot of energy to satisfy my curiosity. In college, I served on several committees, and there, too, I held leadership roles. Following my freshman year in college, I married and directed my energies toward a dual career.

In graduate school, my major professor encouraged me to join professional organizations, and I joined three. On campus, I spent a lot of my time as an organizer. I remember that I and several other graduate women organized some activities focused on women's issues. While I was in graduate school, one of my friends nominated me for president of the West Indiana Personnel and Guidance Association. Running for a leadership position was the furthest thing from my mind, but I agreed to run. Even I was surprised when I won! This milestone marked the beginning of my leadership in professional organizations. The following year, I was elected treasurer of the Indiana Personnel and Guidance Association (IPGA), and the next year I was elected vice president of IPGA. I was later nominated for president of IPGA, but I had moved to another state and therefore withdrew my name from the ballot.

Readers of this chapter might question what we have to offer group counselors. Why would a textbook on group counseling have a chapter about leadership in a college and a professional organization? The answer is quite simple: Deans and presidents of organizations conduct a lot of their work through committees, task forces, and networks, which, in reality, are groups. In these groups, as in therapeutic groups, much attention is devoted to group dynamics and group processes (Beck, Eng, & Brusa, 1989; Hollander & Offermann, 1990). As president of a professional organization, my time, like that of any group leader, is spent facilitating positive interpersonal relationships and attempting to reduce problems. Similar dynamics occur within a counseling group. In our committees, the members work collaboratively to achieve a goal in much the same way as occurs in a counseling group. Leaders of both counseling groups and professional organizations must have a broad understanding of group dynamics and be capable of implementing this understanding in a variety of group settings. We hope this chapter will increase awareness of the similarities between leadership in counseling groups and leadership in professional organizations and colleges, for groups of all sorts are a natural way for individuals to communicate. We first discuss group leadership on the macro level, then explore what we call the leadership ethic through four case studies, and finally suggest implications of our work for group practitioners.

ELAINE'S WORLD

The culture of a college of education is similar to that of a business organization with the possible exceptions that, in the former, firings are rare and promotions and extrinsic financial rewards are few. Although profit does not drive them, faculty members in universities exhibit similar characteristics to their business counterparts. They enjoy exercising power, engaging in hallway politics, receiving rewards, and exhibiting such human characteristics as jealousy, regret, and nobility that make life interesting for the group leader.

So, a college of education can be thought of as a large organization with its own group norms. Sometimes, the dean meets with the faculty as a whole. I usually hold two to three of these meetings per year, having learned that conducting any more meetings than that only tends to alienate faculty and reduce attendance. During the first meeting, the one at the start of the academic year, I introduce new faculty, share my goals, and offer a progress report. Other members of the faculty also share information. Faculty members are welcome to raise important issues, but those issues are usually referred to committees for discussion. Wise deans do not allow these large group meetings to get out of hand. I devote the other full faculty meetings throughout the year to information sharing. In addition, they are a forum in which I establish my authority, acquire confidence in my own ability, use humor to "seduce" reluctant doers, set boundaries about what I will and will not accept, introduce values that I think are important, and present an agenda of business that can be efficiently accomplished.

Our college as a whole functions through its small group meetings. Each of the 65 faculty members belongs to a program, and the faculty in each program meet to make decisions about curriculum. Various other committees (e.g., Research, Graduate Studies, Promotion and Tenure) also conduct their work throughout the year. Finally, an elected Faculty Council composed of seven members engages in faculty governance.

The dean meets with these small groups periodically for a variety of reasons (e.g., to explain an issue, to request action). Perhaps the most difficult meeting is the one in which a dean must try to change the faculty's collective viewpoint. For example, a group of my faculty wanted me to take a strong stand about an issue with the faculty in another college, whereas I wanted our faculty to collaborate with them and to engage in a pilot test of a team taught course. I tried to convince our faculty but failed to do so; I will have to *ask* them to engage in the pilot test. Sometimes, the dean's dilemma is not easily resolved.

Our faculty is composed of two divisions, and the members sometimes perceive that the divisions are separated by a large chasm. For this reason, I often invite three members of each division to my office early in the morning for coffee, rolls, and focused discussion. I ask each person to share something noteworthy about his or her work and then to raise mutual concerns. These discussions help the faculty to appreciate one another's work, and they help me to better understand the faculty.

The college culture is exciting in the way it involves helping both large and small groups to embrace a common vision. The dean, like a group practitioner, must fully understand the group norms and settings, define the specific challenges, support the members of the group, and help everyone to realize the college's mission. The dean must articulate a clear vision, for college progress depends on the faculty buying into that vision.

LORETTA'S WORLD

Similarities between the climate of a professional organization and that of a counseling group are many, Both, for example, have a leader and members. Both are influenced by the style and skills of the leader and by member roles, group interactions, and group dynamics. Essentially, leading a professional organization is an exercise in group counseling, except the focus is usually on the organization and its goals rather than on individual members.

The leader's style in both the professional organization and the counseling group has a direct effect on the members. Some leaders are direct and keep the group focused. Other leaders are more person-oriented and offer support and care. Whether the leader is more direct or person-oriented often depends on what is happening in the group. In books and articles on group counseling, good leaders have been described as ones who facilitate and delegate and who model good communication skills (Richardson & Woverton, 1994; Sorenson & Savage, 1989). The same characteristics apply to good leaders in professional organizations. I view the leader of a professional organization as a person who, among other things, helps to open, and keep open, lines of communication between the leader and members and between different members of the organization. Recently, in my role as president of a professional organization, I appointed "new" persons to chair committees and networks because of terms expiring. I found myself implementing group counseling skills as I sought to facilitate these changes. In facilitating change, I would never want to dictate and require that a member relinquish his or her desire for a committee role. Instead, I would seek to encourage the member to find alternative ways in which he or she could be of equal or perhaps greater service to the professional organization. It would be my goal to work to help the member "own" the change and thus to understand and accept the change. In initiating this type of change it is also essential that I keep lines of communication open between "old" and "new" committee members.

In my role as president, I must, at times, resolve conflict. I have sometimes asked myself how this conflict can occur among counselors. One obvious answer is that counselors are attracted to power and control. Perhaps Kottler (1993, p. 90) aptly answered this question when he said that "restraining our [counselors'] egos is a challenge many of us will never meet." Despite my recognition of the narcissism of many counselors and its accompanying characteristics, as leader I must acknowledge that conflict occurs in all groups, including professional organizations, and that it is my role as president (leader) to manage conflict (Bennis, 1989). Although my approach varies depending on the situation, I generally work with conflicting ideas to reach a new solution or attempt to move the conflict into a compromise. I also, whenever possible, try to help members avoid win-lose situations. Additionally, I try to avoid using the power of my position. If power is needed, I prefer that it take the form of my being able to persuade the members that they can trust me and therefore support me in a particular course of action. In reality, professional organizations, such as the one to which I belong, function as several small groups commonly called committees and networks (Spangler & Braiotta, 1990). These committees (e.g., Awards, Budget and Finance, Membership, Strategic Planning) and networks (e.g., community counseling, multicultural, supervision, women's issues) meet throughout the year as individual groups to conduct their work. They also conduct their business at regional and national conferences. In both settings, group issues are clearly evident.

THE LEADERSHIP ETHIC

Everyone has known good leaders and bad leaders. But who among us can really define what good and bad mean in leadership, that is, what is ethical and what is not? The most salient component of good leadership is having a leadership ethic. The need for a good leader to be ethical is not only desirable, it is a necessity.

It is not easy to sort out all of the ingredients of a leadership ethic. We can, however, start by asserting that the leadership ethic operates on two distinct levels: (a) an internal level, which is the leader's personal values of right and wrong, and (b) an external level, which is the culture in which the leader's values are manifested. Both internal (personal) and external (climate or culture) ethics are crucial to the success of the leader. Evidence of the existence of a leadership ethic occurs when leaders walk their talk—that is, when their actions are congruent with their promises.

Another ingredient of the leadership ethic is related to the way in which a leader uses power. Power may take many forms. Sometimes it is visible, and at other times it is hidden. Sometimes it is sought, and at other times it is bestowed. It may be used fairly or unfairly. It may appear in a number of forms, including money, office, title, authority, and physical force. It is often exhibited differently by men and women (Jurma & Wright, 1990). Women in leadership roles, while exhibiting diverse leadership styles, are often more intuitive and adaptable and more concerned about relationships than are men in leadership roles (Conlon, 1991). Similarly, cultural differences influence leadership. For example, the United States, with its individualistic, achievement-oriented emphasis, is more likely to produce leaders with a more direct, individualistic style than is China or Japan, cultures in which relationships are more collateral. Although little or no research has been conducted linking cultures and leadership style to the leadership ethic, culture undoubtedly has a direct influence on the leader's approach to leadership, including his or her leadership ethic.

Leaders always have some power, if only a trace. Yet, holders of power are not always leaders. For example, an officer who stops a person and issues a traffic citation has power over that person at the moment, but he or she may not be a leader. An agent at an airport can force a person to either check one piece of luggage or forfeit his or her flight, but that agent is not necessarily a leader. In a college, a dean can force faculty to do what he or she wants them to do without being a true leader. Likewise, in a professional organization, decisions can be made that force actions on the membership. However, that action, too, is the use of power, not leadership.

Inevitably, leadership involves power, and power involves risk (Gardner, 1990). Although leadership and power are not often the same, their paths frequently cross. Leaders differ from one another in the way they exercise that power (Levit, 1992). In fact, Covey (1989) contended that it is the way power is used that differentiates a good leader from a bad leader. Some leaders use power to help their followers (e.g., Winston Churchill), whereas others use power to diminish their followers (e.g., David Koresh). Still other leaders exert their power by treating their followers well while simultaneously encouraging their followers to inflict pain on others (e.g., Idi Amin). Sadly, some leaders (e.g., Hitler and Mussolini) have used power to destroy the principles created by society. For the latter three examples, leadership can be characterized as a process reduced to the exertion of power to ensure a desired outcome. Although power is neutral and can therefore be either good or bad, it can, by virtue of its ability to dominate and take control, be exercised without regard to humanity. Essentially, power can be enforced without concern for right or wrong and therefore is not necessarily connected to a leadership ethic. However, leadership, void of the leadership ethic, is poor leadership. In contrast, good leadership is grounded in a leadership ethic derived from higher-order principles that ascribe to honesty and the worth and dignity of all people. Regardless of the situation, these higher-order principles do not change and are not compromised. Perhaps the hallmark of a good leader is that he or she serves as a catalyst for followers whereby the wants and the needs of both the leader and the followers are kept in alignment.

We believe good leadership derives from more than training or the accumulation of grades and credit hours. Although there is not a formula for being an effective leader, researchers, in study after study, have identified characteristics that seem to be prevalent in good leaders regardless of leadership setting. Consequently, the leadership ethic does not stand alone but is instead supported by viable leader characteristics.

LEADER CHARACTERISTICS

Researchers have described effective leaders as being charismatic (Carlton-Ford, 1992; Deutch, 1992), flexible (Zaccaro, Foti, & Kenny, 1991), honest (Stockton, Morgan, & Harris, 1991), humane (Deutch, 1992; Richardson & Woverton, 1994), open communicators (Blase & Roberts, 1994; Sorenson & Savage, 1989), and trustworthy (Gardner, 1990). Additionally, good leaders have been depicted as being accepting of individual differences (Bennis, 1989; Rose, 1987), being task-oriented (Ketrow, 1991), employing transformational rather than transactional or laissez-faire leadership (DeLuga, 1988; Hater & Bass, 1988; Yammarino & Bass, 1990), exercising good judgment (Rose, 1991), having intelligence and employing intellectual stimulation (Kirby, Paradise, & King, 1992), having good visionary skills (Carlton-Ford, 1992; Gardner, 1990), implementing conflict management skills (Abramson, 1989), using power positively (Gardner, 1990), and directing synergy wisely (Covey, 1989; Fiedler, 1967). This list of leader characteristics is, of course, exemplary and not comprehensive.

We focus the remainder of this chapter on four characteristics, drawn from or related to this list, that we believe a leader with a leadership ethic must possess and that have import for group counselors, who must themselves address the challenge of formulating a leadership ethic. As Figure 9.1 illustrates, the four characteristics are integrity, trust, vision, and synergy. We define a leader who possesses integrity as one who is honest. That is, he or she communicates openly and honestly, exercises power fairly, and resolves conflicts fairly. Essentially, we are saying that a good leader is truthful. With regard to trust, a good leader builds trust by demonstrating to followers that he or she can be trusted (Bennis, 1989). The leader demonstrates that trust both inside and outside the group. With regard to vision, we believe the test of a true leader revolves around whether the skills and behaviors he or she demonstrates today will have an impact on the future. Basically, a good leader must have the visionary skills to

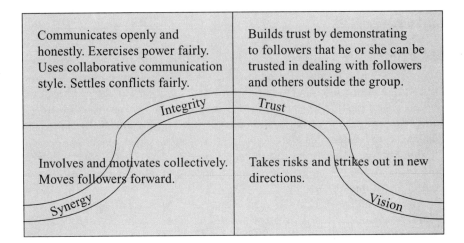

FIGURE 9.1 •

CHARACTERISTICS OF EFFECTIVE LEADERS

plan and implement decisions that will positively impact the future. To do so, the leader must take risks and strike out in new directions. Synergy, the fourth characteristic, is akin to vision, but synergy skills differ in important ways from visionary skills. With synergy, the leader is called upon to channel the group's collective thoughts and actions. Here, the leader is involved in motivating his or her followers to move forward. Covey (1989) described synergy as the highest activity of life. He stated that through synergy, one can unleash people's greatest powers by enabling them to leave the comfort zone of the base camp and confront an entirely new and unknown wilderness. With synergy, an atmosphere is created in which it is safe to talk. The leader unfreezes people, loosens them up, fosters new insights, and involves the group members in the problems. Covey concluded that the leader becomes a pathfinder and that synergy is embodied in one crucial ability: the ability to value and exploit the mental, emotional, and psychological differences among people.

To bring the leadership ethic to life, we now present four case examples drawn from our experiences with university faculty and professional organizations. In these examples, we illustrate the importance of integrity, trust, vision, and synergy in leadership roles. The cases of Sylvia and Richard depict leadership in a college setting; the cases of Sally and Bob depict leadership in a professional organization. The names of the subjects are fictitious.

Case Examples

Sylvia (Integrity)

Sylvia is the first African-American female dean of a college of education at a large midwestern university. She worked hard to reach her current position, and although she firmly believes that she has succeeded on her own merit, she also knows that affirmative action efforts had mandated the preferential treatment of minorities and women. As she began her first year as dean, she asked herself these questions: How do the faculty really view me? How can I convince them that I believe in collaborative decision making and that I view myself as an honest, fair woman of integrity?

The first task to which she needed to attend was the college's 5-year accreditation visit. The accrediting body had set a high standard for faculty diversity. Sylvia knew that the college's 70-member faculty, with 2 Hispanics, could hardly be termed diverse. She also knew that some of the faculty had applauded national efforts to strike down affirmative action laws. Sylvia, however, was a strong believer in faculty diversity because she knew that the college must mirror society and the school-age population, and must provide role models for students. What should she do, she wondered, about the nine faculty searches?

*Sylvia faced her dilemma by clarifying her position. She knew that in her role as a first-year dean, the faculty might not want her to take firm stands. She realized she could avoid the hiring issue for at least a year by suggesting **but not insisting** that the faculty become more diverse. Yet, she had been raised to stand firm on her principles, and she thought that some faculty might welcome a strong stand.*

Sylvia chose to project herself as a woman of integrity who stands for her principles. She asked the search committee chairs to form a pool of qualified candidates and from that pool to select the most qualified minority candidate as the first interviewee. She set the goal for the college of hiring at least four minority faculty members. Working collaboratively with the faculty, Sylvia convinced them that she was indeed fair and believed in faculty empowerment.

Sylvia was rewarded for her strong stand and modeling of leader integrity not only with a more diverse faculty but also with faculty support. Her faculty began to suggest ways to ensure that the new minority faculty would be successful. They offered to mentor, team teach, and co-author articles. Clearly, Sylvia's strong stand paid off.

Group leaders in any setting can model the characteristic of integrity. Certainly, they realize that "you can't please everyone" in the process of helping a group to come to a decision. Seeking win-win situations is certainly appropriate, but weighing alternatives may help the leader to exercise integrity and to bring a group to closure.

Richard (Trust)

Richard is an experienced dean of a college of education in a large metropolitan university. He knows that the faculty perceive him as both truthful and trustworthy, but the most recent crisis facing the university has provided a test to his attributes of leadership.

The provost had decided to eliminate two programs in the College of Education to cut costs. He shared his decision with Richard and ordered Richard to remain silent during the next 2 months as the central administration solidified its plans. At the end of the 2-month period, Richard would be asked to support the provost and to accomplish the program reduction swiftly.

Richard agonized over the provost's decision. He knew that his faculty saw him as a strong advocate of the college and of information sharing. He had always worked diligently to keep the faculty up to date and informed. He believes in faculty governance and has frequently empowered the faculty to make decisions. The programs slated for elimination strike Richard as viable programs. Could the provost's data be inaccurate? Could the provost's decision be altered?

Working closely with the program chairs but not betraying the provost's confidence, Richard worked to collect the data needed to build a strong case to save the two programs. As he analyzed the data, he realized that one of the programs had a strong case for survival.

*Richard presented that case to the provost, who agreed to eliminate only the other program. When the decision to eliminate that program was announced, Richard was able to provide a data-driven rationale for its elimination to the faculty and to reassign those working in that program to other programs. Richard's actions demonstrated that the trustworthy leader knows how to meet the needs of his superiors **and** his constituents.*

Although the hierarchical power structure of the university is not typical of therapeutic groups, the underlying concept of trust is certainly familiar to counselors. Whether in a therapeutic group or an organization, the importance of trust should never be underestimated; if trust is missing, the leader cannot function. Although trust is often described as if it were an internal part of leadership, in reality, trust is an outcome of good leadership. Basically, trust cannot be bestowed upon a leader; instead, trust must be earned by the leader.

Sally (Vision)

A hallmark of a good leader is vision. The effective leader must possess visionary skills not only for the present but also for the future and be able to communicate his or her vision. In essence, an effective leader must take risks to effect change that matters even after his or her leadership role ends. The following case of Sally illustrates the importance of visionary skills.

In Sally's role as president of a national professional organization, she had been entrusted with directing the organization for one year. A major portion of her role was to oversee and facilitate the day-to-day operation of the organization. Sally knew she could lead the organization while concentrating only on her year as president, but she also knew that for the organization to succeed, she would have to assert vision.

After assuming her role as president, one of the first things Sally heard as she tried to make change was, "We have always done it this way.... This has worked well for the past 20 years." She believed that committee reorganization, more centralized services, and budget reduction were needed in the organization. Yet, when she tried to effect changes along those lines, she met with resistance and politics. It immediately became clear that a consensus would be unattainable. The mere size of the organization presented a problem, and the politics of the organization added to the problem. Sally knew that she needed to reduce the size of the committee structure. However, to do so she would have to eliminate committees chaired by the very persons who had helped her to be elected. While Sally was quick to acknowledge that leadership usually involves politics, she was hesitant to take on the political power within the organization. Still, Sally understood that if this organization were to be solvent in 5 years, change must occur now. As Sally weighed her options, she knew she faced a dilemma. Namely, should she challenge the system and make changes knowing that she may never be elected to office again? Should she weigh the needs of the organization above her personal needs and make the changes she felt were necessary? Sally chose to do so.

Bob (Synergy)

Bob is a young assistant professor who is active in several professional organizations, including the American Counseling Association (ACA), the American School Counselor Association (ASCA), and the Association for Counselor Education and Supervision (ACES). Like many other bright, new professors, he knows the importance of networking with colleagues and being active in professional organizations.

Through networking at state and national meetings, Bob learned that another professional organization had been focusing on major licensure efforts that would omit counselors from a proposed licensure law. To make counselors aware of the impending problem, he contacted colleagues at other universities. Then, to reach an even larger audience, he presented a paper at a counseling conference alerting counselors to the growing licensure problem. His presentation was well attended and indeed alerted counselors to an imminent problem that could cripple the counseling profession, especially those engaged in private practice. Following the conference at which he spoke, a licensure committee was established to propose licensure standards for counselors. Bob had

effectively channeled collective thoughts and actions and by doing so had moti-
vated his followers to move forward with licensure standards for counselors.
Today, 41 states and the District of Columbia have counselor licensure laws.

From this example, one can see the impact of a leader through synergy in confronting a new, unknown path. Truly, Bob and his followers were pathfinders. Without their leadership, counselors might have been unable to practice their profession. Instead, because of the passage of counselor licensure bills, counselors today enjoy more secure careers.

DISCUSSION

Throughout this chapter, we have stressed the role and personal characteristics of the leader. We contend that the study of organizational leadership must be viewed from two major dimensions: a personal dimension and an ethical behavior dimension. In focusing on the leader's personal characteristics, we discussed how integrity, trust, vision, and synergy impact leadership. Likewise, we highlighted the leadership ethic. Basically, we believe that leadership is rooted in principles of good and right conduct and that these principles form a system of moral acts and values. Further, we believe that ethical behavior might be grounded inside (internalized) before it can be implemented externally with the followers. Consequently, we are asserting that the leadership ethic is a part of the leader's internal makeup and that it must function together with his or her competence to lead.

Imagine that a faculty member is asked to follow a dean whom she believes is competent but dishonest. Should the faculty member trust this person to be her leader? Most faculty would be unwilling to follow the dean because a very important characteristic, honesty, is missing. Now imagine that the leader of a professional organization is honest but incompetent. Although it is unlikely that members could "unseat" the president, most members would be reluctant to fully embrace this leader. The organization's progress could be impaired. Essentially, these examples illustrate that good leadership does not exist in isolation. Indeed, for a leader to be successful, his or her attributes must align in harmony.

In professional organizations, colleges of education, and counseling groups, followers may openly oppose leaders. What happens when the faculty oppose the dean or the members of an organization oppose the president? How does power influence the dean's or the president's behavior? How might the leader promote cooperation rather than competition?

Often, when faculty oppose a dean or the members of a professional organization oppose the president, the leaders are unprepared for this type of action and respond in an authoritarian manner. They use authoritative power or power based on their role as dean (or president) as a means of handling the dispute.

The dean might pull rank and say, "I am the head of this college, and in this role, I am responsible for decisions. In this situation, you will follow my directions." In response, the college faculty would likely unite and try to oppose the dean. At that point, the college will probably be in chaos, and if the problem is not settled quickly, the faculty could establish a vote of no confidence against the dean. A more advantageous approach would be for the dean to deal with the problem immediately in an open, nondefensive manner. To ignore the problem would only add to the frustration experienced by the faculty and would likely lead to the faculty launching an even greater attack against the dean. Although this example depicts leadership in a college, the principles also apply to group counseling. In group counseling as in the college setting, the leader must confront power conflicts between members and between members and the leader. As in a college, conflicts occurring in group counseling should be dealt with immediately and resolved in a manner that is as supportive as possible.

The extent to which power influences the behavior of the dean or president depends on how the leader views power. Power can be viewed as a given right, bestowed simply because one is the leader. When a leader views power in this way, it is likely that he or she views it as a means for winning. However, power does not have to be viewed from a win-lose perspective. Instead, it can be used positively to influence followers and help them to understand the reasoning leading to a particular decision. Influential power is almost always more effective than absolute power.

With regard to the question of how cooperation rather than competition may be promoted, we suggest that all leaders keep in mind the basic principles of group counseling. Decision traps between faculty and dean, members and presidents, and members and group leaders can usually be avoided if an atmosphere of cooperation is created among the members of the group. Instead of competing with one another, members should be encouraged to hold the belief that they can cooperate and collectively pool their resources to obtain the best outcome. In an organization or a counseling group, an atmosphere of cooperation should be fostered.

Throughout this chapter, we have focused on the similarities between leadership on a macro (college or professional organization) level and leadership on a micro (counseling group) level. In addition, we have highlighted some strategies for effective leadership. Further, we have asserted that even if a leader has good leadership training and skill development, the group is headed for a collision if the leader lacks leadership ethics. Although we recognize that leader characteristics are not as exact as a mathematical formula, we wish to remind the reader of the importance of leader characteristics and how they are embedded in a leadership ethic. The four leader characteristics that we highlighted are integrity, trust, vision, and synergy. We realize that we could have included other characteristics, many of which we listed earlier in the chapter. However, after carefully considering our own experiences and reviewing the literature on leadership characteristics, we concluded that the four leader characteristics we highlighted are basic to effective leadership. We believe that a leader must be ethical, and, accordingly, we discussed the importance of a leadership ethic. We know of no person from any era who can be called a leader if he or she lacks, or lacked, ethics. We do, however, know of some people (dictators) who lacked ethics and unwisely assumed themselves to be leaders. When we speak of integrity, we are simply saying that a leader must be honest and follow through on promises. With high integrity (or honesty), the leader will gain the trust of his or her followers. While we do not know of any formula for gaining trust, we do know that trust is a crucial ingredient in good leadership. Without trust, a leader will lack followers, and without followers, a person cannot be a leader. Good leaders are guided by a purpose or vision in which they believe and by which they are driven. Furthermore, good leaders can articulate this purpose to their followers. When a group of followers and their leader put their minds together to achieve a goal, the sum of their parts represents more than the simple addition of the part contributed by each member; this is synergy in action. In summary, the art of leadership is not a simple process. However, we believe that the basic tenets described in this chapter embrace the qualities necessary to enhance the work of leaders.

CONCLUSION

The four case studies presented in this chapter bring life and meaning to the leadership traits of integrity, trust, vision, and synergy and support their importance for all group practitioners. The strong, successful leader must exhibit what we have called a leadership ethic. Without a leadership ethic, leaders may misuse their power, cause their groups to lose their sense of purpose, and bring chaos to their groups' members. When strongly grounded in integrity, trust, vision, and synergy, the group practitioner will of necessity exhibit the leadership ethic. As Mohandas K. Gandhi said, "We must be the change we wish to see in the world."

REFERENCES

Abramson, J. C. (1989). Making teams work. (Special issue: Groups in health care settings). *Social Work with Groups, 17,* 45–63.

Beck, A. P., Eng, A. M., & Brusa, J. A. (1989). The evolution of leadership during group development. *Group, 13,* 155–164.

Bennis, W. (1989). *Why leaders can't lead: The unconscious conspiracy continues.* San Francisco: Jossey-Bass.

Blase, J., & Roberts, J. (1994). The micropolitics of teacher work involvement: Effective principals' impacts on teachers. *Alberta Journal of Educational Research, 40,* 67–94.

Carlton-Ford, S. L. (1992). Charisma, ritual, collective, effervescence, and self-esteem. *Sociological Quarterly, 33,* 365–387.

Conlon, I. (1991). The effect of gender on the role of the female group conductor. *Group Analysis, 24,* 187–200.

Covey, S. F. (1989). *The seven habits of highly effective people.* New York: Simon & Schuster.

DeLuga, R. J. (1988). Relationship of transformational and transactional leadership with influencing strategies. *Group and Organizational Studies, 13,* 456–467.

Deutch, M. (1992). The tough-minded and tender-hearted scientist. *Journal of Social Issues, 48,* 31–43.

Fiedler, F. E. (1967). *A theory of leadership effectiveness.* New York: McGraw-Hill.

Gardner, J. W. (1990). *On leadership.* New York: Free Press.

Hater, J. J., & Bass, B. (1988). Superiors' evaluation and subordinates' perceptions of transformational and transactional leadership. *Journal of Applied Psychology, 73,* 695–702.

Hollander, E. P., & Offermann, L. R. (1990). Power and leadership in organizations: Relationships in transition. *American Psychologist, 45,* 179–189.

Jurma, W. E., & Wright, B. C. (1990). Follower reactions to male and female leaders who maintain or lose reward power. *Small Group Research, 21,* 97–112.

Ketrow, S. M. (1991). Communication role specializations and perceptions of leadership. *Small Group Research, 22,* 492–514.

Kottler, J. (1993). *On being a therapist.* San Francisco: Jossey-Bass.

Kirby, P. C., Paradise, L. V., & King, M. I. (1992). Extraordinary leaders in education: Understanding transformational leadership. *Journal of Educational Research, 85,* 303–311.

Levit, R. A. (1992). Meaning, purpose, and leadership. *International Forum for Logotherapy, 15,* 71–75.

Richardson, R. C., & Woverton, M. (1994). Leadership strategies. In A. M. Cohen & F. B. Brawer (Eds.), *Managing community colleges: A handbook for effective practice* (pp. 40–59). San Francisco: Jossey-Bass.

Rose, J. C. (1991). *Leadership for the twenty-first century.* New York: Praeger.

Rose, S. R. (1987). The development of problem-solving skills in children's groups. *Social Work with Groups, 10,* 85–95.

Sorenson, R. L., & Savage, G. T. (1989). Signaling participation through relational communication: A test of the Leader Interpersonal Influence Model. *Group and Organizational Studies, 14,* 325–354.

Spangler, W. D., & Braiotta, L. (1990). Leadership and corporate committee effectiveness. *Group and Organizational Studies, 15,* 134–157.

Stockton, R., Morgan, D., & Harris, M. (1991). Factors influencing group member acceptance of corrective feedback. *Journal for Specialists in Group Work, 16,* 246–254.

Yammarino, F. J., & Bass, B. M. (1990). Transformational leadership and multiple levels of analysis. *Human Relations, 43,* 975–995.

Zaccaro, S. J., Foti, R. J., & Kenny, D. A. (1991). Self-monitoring and trait-based variance in leadership: An investigation of leader flexibility across multiple group situations. *Journal of Applied Psychology, 76,* 308–315.

Using Narrative Ideas

in Group Work:

A New Perspective

GERALD MONK, WENDY DREWERY, AND JOHN WINSLADE

*T*welve years ago, I (Gerald Monk) was a new recruit in a personal growth group that had been advertised as a workshop in active meditation and the development of the self. The male group leader, reported to be experienced and skillful, led the group of 20 people, most of whom were women although there was a sprinkling of men—a typical gender ratio for personal growth groups in our community. I remember little more of the content of the workshop than the group members shouting "no" at one another to practice being more assertive. What has stayed with me more, however, were the events that followed the exercises.

I had no particular difficulties with shouting no other than the fact that the exercise was becoming tiresome and not doing anything for me. But in the group round that followed, two people challenged me on the grounds that I was not saying no and wanted to know why. Did I have problems with saying no? Five or six other members of the group also noted that I had not participated fully in the exercise and wanted to know what I was avoiding.

I explained that I was avoiding getting a sore throat and had been finding the exercise a little tiring. Some of the group members wished to pursue their *line of concern. I said that I had said all that I wanted to say and that the group could get on to other business. We all sat in silence for what seemed like 20 minutes but may have been only one or two. The group was waiting for me to say more. I didn't say anything more. Clearly, the group was annoyed by my silence. My position of acceptance in the group deteriorated for the rest of that day and the beginning of the next. As I reflect on the incident now, I realize that both I and the group did not see that I had indeed passed with flying colors in my ability to say no. Instead, I experienced painful feelings of ostracism, isolation, and exclusion, the result of my defying the unstated assumptions of the group leader and group members about performing in a particular way. The group leader and the participants had clearly expected compliance in both the exercises that were arranged and the expected way of talking.*

Although group therapy may have moved on from these 1970s-type "personal growth rituals," most group leaders still have particular ideas about the kind of group environment they are trying to create. In groups, counselors typically encourage or permit certain kinds of talking and displays of emotion, value specific types of behavior, and consider certain activities appropriate or inappropriate, successful or unsuccessful.

Most group leaders work hard to create and manage a particular culture within their groups. People experienced in group leadership would agree that facilitators have an effect on helping to shape the cultural practices that form in the group. Yet what culture do they participate in creating? What expectations and practices emerge from that culture? And what is it that facilitators inadvertently participate in assembling in their groups that they deem unquestionably desirable?

In this chapter, we explore these questions using a social constructionist approach to understanding group leadership, group process, and outcomes. This paradigm, which originally emerged out of the discipline of sociology, has encouraged us to rework how we interact with therapeutic groups. The chapter introduces a range of new vocabulary to the group work literature. Where possible, we have used lay terminology to describe our orientation. However, in places, we have deliberately used such words as discourse, deconstruction, discursive, and positioning—words specific to the social constructionist model—for these terms convey a way of thinking that would take a less precise shape if recast in another form.

A New Look at Group Process and Practice

Social constructionism is an exciting and potentially highly significant theoretical shift in the way therapy in general and group therapy in particular can be understood and practiced. The theory is now widely discussed in relation to identity formation (see, e.g., Gergen, 1985b, 1991; Parker & Shotter, 1990; Shotter &

Gergen, 1989), developmental psychology more generally (Burman, 1994; Harre, 1986; Olssen, 1991), and individual and family therapy (McNamee & Gergen, 1992; White & Epston, 1989). However, we feel that the theory is still in its infancy in terms of exploring these implications, especially in terms of how group work can be understood and practiced. To that end, we introduce here a social constructionist model that we call narrative group work. Its purpose is to help bridge the infamous gap between events and experiences occurring at an individual level and events and issues occurring on the larger sociocultural stage. Applying narrative theory, therapists can help their clients identify how their past history and present culture mold their lives and at the same time can help them become aware of new ways of reshaping their lives that are more conducive to well-being.

TRYING TO GET IT RIGHT

In this section we outline our dissatisfaction with the models of group work that are dominant today. As counselors and counselor trainers in New Zealand through the 1980s, we were challenged deeply by the apparent powerlessness of the dominant therapeutic models to respond to the emerging voice of Maori people. As the indigenous people of New Zealand, Maori were, and still are, in the process of reviewing the consequences of colonization, including their overrepresentation in hospitals, benefit queues, and prisons and their underrepresentation in school achievement, boardrooms, and parliament. Voices of protest, both Pakeha and Maori, were more and more represented in our classes at the same time that we were recognizing the ineffectiveness of Western-style therapeutic models with many such clients.* Although this story of the emergence of the voice of the Maori people is important, it is not unique. Similar stories can be told with respect to minority populations in North America and elsewhere.

WE ARE NOT ALL MOVING TO THE BEAT OF THE SAME DRUM

Group members are often, though not always, aware of the expectations placed upon them, and they are sometimes startlingly docile in moving into their "group membership roles." An experience one of us had as a group participant is illustrative.

---

*Pakeha is the Maori name for the white people who came to colonize New Zealand. For reasons that may be apparent in this statement, the meaning of this term is always in contention.

On one occasion, I (Gerald) and the other group participants were asked to line up according to our "present stage of development" within the group. The group was relatively homogeneous—mostly Western, white, and middle class. What was most astonishing about this activity was how quickly we all complied and placed ourselves in a linear order with very little disagreement. On no occasion was the "present stage of development" defined, yet all of us appeared to know what to do. What knowledge had we drawn upon? How did we "know" what to do?

Recently, one of us conducted a group that included a Maori male, Mat, who was familiar with Western values and Western culture but was, understandably, more influenced by his own ethnic cultural practices. Mat would resist putting forward personal goals within the training group other than those goals his *hapu* (subtribe) had presented to him either directly or indirectly. When he was asked to make positive evaluative judgments about his performance, he would respond with an anecdote illustrating that it was inappropriate for him to evaluate himself. He typically replied with, "A *kumara* [a root vegetable] does not speak of its own sweetness." Never did he push himself forward in the group, and he tended to speak only when asked. When he was challenged to be more forthcoming and outspoken, he replied that it was not his place to challenge and direct others within this context given his "student status"; to do so, he felt, would be disrespectful.

In traditional Maori culture, to talk about one's ideas in the presence of people deemed to be more senior is to show *whakahihi* (arrogance and boastfulness) and is considered a breach of *mana tangata,* or the personal dignity of the person (Ritchie, 1992). No doubt the culture of the group just described, which was dominated by white, middle-class participants and facilitated by leaders from a Western culture, placed certain constraints on Mat's being understood or finding a voice in this setting. But from a Western cultural framework, his non-involvement and lack of participation could have been seen as an obstacle to healthy group behavior.

Working as group leaders with mixed ethnic groups, particularly groups including the indigenous people of New Zealand (Maori) and the Pacific Islands, we, as white, middle-class New Zealanders, have continually experienced difficulties. Indeed, nonwhite members of the groups have begun to articulate that they want something different from our usual offering.

Our experiences with these groups have led us to seriously question what it is that we value in group work and group leadership and how we come to value things in the way that we do. We have become skeptical and cautious about defining "healthy" functioning, "competent" group leadership, and "successful" group culture. In addition, we have become interested in how dominant cultural practices in our community influence what gets labeled as problems. As a result, we have become more aware of how cultural practices influence the way we go about resolving such problems in psychotherapy groups.

When we speak of cultural practices that influence the group, we are not referring to the ethnic or racial makeup of the group. We are referring to the wider, commonly shared beliefs and ideas that are held by the group members and leaders both prior to and within the life of the group. From our own experience, we have noted that many of these values, beliefs, desires, and behaviors are associated with our histories of membership; for example, our sexual orientation, our socioeconomic class, and our gender and ethnic background. Obviously, the cultural histories that are dominant in the group will have enormous bearing on what form the culture of the group takes. The challenge lies with the group leader to manage the culture of the group so that the group's evolution does not inadvertently replicate the dominant societal norms and in so doing diminish or restrict the validity of the contributions and learnings of some members while privileging others. The empirical research clearly demonstrates, for example, that men tend to take up more talking time in a group than women do and can dominate group interactions (Spender, 1985; Tannen, 1990). For a group leader to ensure that the dominant societal norms do not inadvertently become the group norms, the leader would need to monitor and attend to the amount of talking time used by the men in comparison to the women.

The values group members and leaders from the dominant culture hold may result in a requirement or expectation of specific forms of behavior and conduct from minority members. Indeed, the literature discusses the dropout rate of non-Anglo group members due to culture-bound values that produce conflict and diminish the degree of understanding between members of different ethnic groups (Mokuau, 1987; Pedersen, 1988; Sue, 1990). To attend to these issues, group leaders need to modify their own concepts and techniques.

We have found that the social constructionist paradigm has helped us guard against unquestioningly replicating mainstream societal norms in our groups and inadvertently foisting dominant majority values on our group members. We use the tools of discourse analysis, deconstruction, and positioning to help us identify and manage the dominant cultural practices that are expressed within the group. Doing so allows us to avoid replicating rigid or unjust practices in the group counseling setting. In addition, theorizing group process in this way has opened up a considerable range of new therapeutic tools that we have begun to use to facilitate attitudinal and behavior change in group members for whom conventional group work techniques have not been successful.

LOOKING THROUGH ANOTHER LENS

Social constructionism has emerged from a philosophical movement located in several key disciplines, including philosophy (where it is allied with language), anthropology (where it is allied with the development of cultural meanings), and sociology (where it originated with Berger and Luckmann's [1966] seminal volume, *The Social Construction of Reality*). It has more recently appeared in psychology (Gergen, 1985a).

Social constructionism emphasizes how language works and how meaning is created (Gergen, 1985b; Harre, 1986; Olssen, 1991). Put quite simply, words are not thought of as having meaning in themselves. Rather, words derive their meanings from the contexts in which they are produced or constructed. As stated by Harre (1992, p. 157), talk and conversation are the "intransigent background to all human action." Human interactions are more than what is expressed or performed between speaker and hearer. They illustrate the cultural practices to which the interacting parties subscribe. Shotter (1989) suggested that the central function of speech is to give shape to and coordinate social action. Similarly, Edwards (1991) suggested that communication is a "form of social action" (p. 517). On this basis, groups can be viewed as contexts in which meanings are produced and constructed. Thus the meanings, conversations, narratives, explanations, accounts, and anecdotes observed in groups not only describe but constitute what becomes accepted as real (Wetherell & Potter, 1992).

The process of making meaning from the constructions produced within a particular context has been described as discourse. Edwards (1991, p. 523) suggested that discourse is "not just a way of seeing, but a way of constructing seeing." Thus, discourses are sets of coherent social practices and statements about the nature of the world (Fairclough, 1992; Hollway, 1983). The identification of discourses provides a tool by which the discursive practices operating within a group can be observed. Use of this approach assists the group leader in understanding how personal identities are socially constructed and how people are located as actors in the discourse.

NARRATIVE CONSTRUCTION

One particular version of social constructionism that is attracting the attention of therapists working in individual, family, and group counseling is the narrative metaphor (O'Hanlon, 1994). Narrative therapy, as it is sometimes called, was developed in the mid-1980s by two family therapists, Michael White and David Epston (Monk, 1993; Zimmerman & Dickerson, 1994). White and Epston (1989) drew upon the ideas of the ethnographer Edward Bruner and integrated them into a narrative model of therapy. In keeping with the social constructionist orientation, Bruner (1986) noted that although people come to understand their lives through their lived experience, they construct their lives by storying that experience. He suggested that people make meaning about themselves using stories as a vehicle. In his view, people arrange their experiences of events in a sequence across time, weaving together events in the past with those in the present and those predicted for the future to produce a particular account of the self.

White and Epston (1989) identified in the work of Bruner and his colleague Clifford Geertz that self-narratives do not encompass all of a person's lived experiences. According to Geertz (1986), people construct dominant stories that tend to be immediately available for use in making sense of themselves, but the dominant narratives do not encapsulate their unstoried lived experiences that are dormant and unactivated.

The Constitutive Effects of Stories

White (1989) described how stories circumscribe the meanings that people give to their experiences as well as the aspects of those experiences that they select for expression. In this light, stories are not seen merely as passive descriptions of people's experiences, separated from their active engagement in day-to-day life. Rather, narratives have real effects in shaping lives and relationships; people live their lives according to their own private stories, which are constantly rehearsed.

Virginia had been sexually abused over a 3-year period in childhood. In group, she described her mother and father as highly restrained people who spoke very little about their private concerns. She explained that she spent much of her adolescence in virtual silence, sometimes being silent for months at a time. She felt her role as a young woman was to be silent and self-effacing. The dominant account she gave of herself was of a person who was damaged, did not belong, and did not deserve. Virginia lived her life according to this story of herself for about 28 years. During this period, she selected negative events that fit the description she had about herself.

The development of a narrative often involves the act of pruning experiences that do not fit the dominant story. Narrative therapists are interested in the potential for co-authoring the unstoried acts with their clients so that new, more preferred accounts of self can be constructed. Although many of Virginia's life experiences did fit with her dominant problem story, numerous experiences did not. A powerful example of an experience that stood apart from her story occurred in a recent group therapy session when Virginia volunteered to talk about aspects of her life in front of the group for a substantial period of time. This event stood in stark contrast to the descriptions that had followed her around for most of her life. During a subsequent group session, we interviewed Virginia about how she was able to develop her abilities to present herself so publicly within the group. The conversation illuminated numerous competencies and abilities of which Virginia had not previously been aware.

Because the social constructionist perspective emphasizes how individuals become constituted as persons through language, there is little interest paid to discovering an essential self, some stable inner core that can be unsheathed and polished through some form of self-actualizing process. According to this perspective, the self, or identity, is constantly in a state of change as it operates in the world in relation to the stories that the individual actively subscribes to at any given point in time.

POSITIONING WITHIN DISCOURSE

Individuals do not produce on their own many of the private stories that they hold. The stories are co-constructed with others in their families, school, and community.

The material available for constructing self-narratives comes from prevailing cultural practices, such as those referred to earlier. The themes of the stories derive from these dominant discourses, and the stories are produced according to the discursive frameworks from which they arise. Depending on the particular discourses operating on an individual at any particular time, he or she will be positioned in the story line either as an active agent who has a major part in his or her own production or as a passive character trapped or constrained by the edicts of the discourse.

Our present understanding is that if we, as group leaders, can assist group members to see that they are silenced or trapped by the dominant meanings that construct their way of understanding themselves, we can then assist them to reposition themselves in more active and preferred ways of functioning in relation to the issue at hand. Consider the story of Josh.

In a narrative training group, Josh was feeling trapped in a set of circumstances that were unfolding in his wife's family. His mother-in-law had been treating his wife badly, which left his partner feeling defeated and angry at her mother. It was painful for Josh to observe the damaging effects his mother-in-law's behavior was having on his wife. Josh was not unfamiliar with tense relationship issues. On occasions when they arose in his own family, he had been able to challenge the involved family members to stop the level of abuse that had been occurring. Now, however, he did not feel as if he had any options but to watch from the sideline. He had been taught that it was not his place to meddle in other people's affairs. This story about himself was stopping him from offering some help and making suggestions. During the group, Josh was given the opportunity to reflect on all of the abilities he had that he could use to manage this difficult situation. He began to see that he had numerous options for proceeding constructively to support his wife. He was able to recognize that to do nothing was only one option among many.

Group participants seeking to make some kind of transformative movement in their lives are typically affected by a problem-saturated story line. This type of story constrains them from being active agents in their lives. The group leader and the group participants can, however, co-construct the meanings by which problems are generated and solutions found. This process is discussed next.

NARRATIVE PRINCIPLES IN ACTION

In this section we present actual applications of the ideas we have outlined. The first task that faces us as group leaders is to identify the discourses operating within the group. After doing so, we can begin to take apart the assumptions present that relate to the topic at hand and work to create space for members to speak, not only in the voices they have been "given" (the voices of the dominant discourses) but in their own voices.

INTERNALIZING

People have a tendency to internalize societal discourses that carry the shared cultural understandings of the community in which they were raised. Consider the story of Maria.

Maria, who was in a counselor training program near the community in which she lived, wanted to look at her internal struggles and therefore put herself forward to be interviewed in a narrative therapy training group. She explained that she had been struggling in her counselor training program and often felt out of place. At times, she said, she found it difficult to be in the group. She had seriously considered finding other work. Maria had been raised in a traditional Hispanic family where familial and communal responsibilities took precedence over individual and private wants. Her family could not understand why Maria wanted to pursue a career, which would take away from her involvement with her family. They did not understand why she wanted to be concerned with other people's problems.

Maria described the enormous disjuncture between the dominant discourses in her culture, which privileged family responsibility over personal wants, and those in the counselor program, which privileged self-development and self-actualization. In the program, she would often feel selfish for being concerned with her own wants and could not block from her mind the voices of family members asking her to give up her private ambitions and consider the needs of her family. Maria was blaming herself and internalizing the problem as her fault. When she came to the group, she was unaware of the struggle that existed for her between the discourses that were being presented in her life. She did not understand that the problem related to a cultural clash of different ways of understanding the world and not to any particular personal inadequacies.

Maria came to see that the struggles were much bigger than she originally thought and lay in the field of conflicting discourses rather than internal intrapsychic forces. Upon seeing the bigger picture, her level of self-blame di-

*minished to the point that she was ready to make a more dispassionate decision
regarding her future, one that was less controlled by her own private guilt.*

People often fail to notice the source of the problem discourses they internalize and as a result feel alone and isolated from others while unknowingly
being subjected to the full force of those discourses. Because of the private manner
in which people internalize and come to own the problem discourses, some degree of self-blame and shame is inevitably attached to them. Many of the presenting issues for group members relate to these internalizing conversations.
People tend to judge others and themselves for being caught by the intercon-
necting web of discourses that position them in painful problem narratives. Maria's
story presents an excellent illustration of the problems that can emerge with the
clash of opposing discourses.

We have used narrative therapy in our work during the past few years with
groups of counselor trainees, many of whom have been in their 40s and 50s, in
which we have taken them through outdoor physical education activities including
rappelling down an 80-foot cliff and blackwater rafting, where group participants travel in rubber tubes down an underground stream. Not surprisingly, there
is a measured degree of physical risk in these activities. To prepare the participants, we place them in small groups in which they are encouraged to recount
their private stories about their abilities in participating in activities involving
physical challenges. Until this time, some of the group members' private stories
have spoken only about their limitations in engaging in the outdoor activities.

These private conversations describe them as fearful, personally inadequate,
and singled out as not being able, too old, claustrophobic, and so forth. However, when participants bring forward these private accounts of self and place
them in a public context, that is, in the group context, the conversations take on
a new form and meaning. Each person sees his or her own story alongside others that share a similar theme. When discourses concerning fear, middle or old
age, or claustrophobia are externalized, new openings emerge. No longer do the
participants feel isolated by their private accounts; instead, they feel the support
of the group in challenging the discourses of fear, age, or inadequacy.

The isolating and separating effects of internalization begin to crumble when
a group member's private narrative is brought into the history of the group. Not
only does bringing forward one's personal descriptions help the individual confront the challenges of separation and isolation, but these public accounts also
influence the life of the group in overcoming the restrictive nature of oppressive private stories.

The Problem of Certainty

For many counselors trained in empiricist theories, the importance of theoretically formed truths has been central in their initiation to group work practice.
Empiricist models of training tend to promote a pre-knowing stance; the coun-

selor looks for certain patterns and characteristics to emerge and then names them in an authoritative and expert manner (Anderson & Goolishian, 1992). In the West, the immersion of some psychotherapies in the positivistic sciences over the decades has prompted counselors to seek predictability, continuity, and certainty in their professional interactions.

Amundson, Stewart, and Valentine (1993) stated that "in therapy, certainty often emerges as expertise or privileged knowledge that claims to capture the 'essence' of things. In trying to be helpful there is the temptation to enact our privilege; to impose upon others normalizing standards or to be blinded to diversity by the professional certainties of our practice" (p. 111). Certainly, clients are susceptible to this position-taking by the therapist or counselor and, indeed, often encourage this behavior.

In our groups, we work to interrupt the discourses that place group facilitators in some superior role in the group and see them as being able to determine categories of adequacy. The facilitator works to undermine notions of "good enough" behavior and the "right" responses.

As facilitators, we characteristically model through personal disclosure our positioning within what we experience as problem discourses. For example, one of us worked recently with a small group of trainee counselors who were experiencing a high level of anxiety about performing in a counselor role and gave the group an account of their struggles with shame and inadequacy about their performance. For the group members, the facilitator's willingness to express their own private struggles gave them openings to reduce or give up the restrictive evaluative judgments they were placing on themselves while interrupting the authority of the "knowing" group leader. We have found considerable value in moving away from the notion of "self-actualized" and "knowing" group therapist on one end of the continuum and the naive group member on the other.

The discourses that accompany the ideas of knowing leader and naive participants tend to place participants on a continuum of adequacy that produces inherently oppositional categories of people who "have made it," "are making it," or "have not made it." Instead, we attempt to open spaces for all participants to take up full group membership even though they may not fit in with the dominant societal norms. Included here are, for example, people from minority ethnic groups, those with more communal than individual values, and those with homosexual rather than heterosexual orientations.

GENUINE CURIOSITY

The task of the group leader is to encourage and value the diversity of human expression, even when this expression may contradict some of the prescriptions of Western group norms, such as extreme individualism. It is easy for group leaders to impose dominant culturally prescriptive expectations on minority culture group members who do not adhere to some of the traditional Western group norms of self-disclosure and self-promotion. In response to these concerns we have began to promote a therapy of curiosity in our groups where the role of the "naive inquirer" is dominant (Clayton, 1989). Our focus is to move away from the taken-for-granted way in which we understand our meaning making. We have found the "not knowing position" described by Anderson and Goolishian (1992) to be an excellent standpoint from which to engage with another's world. As Anderson and Goolishian stated, the not-knowing position invites the therapist to not prejudge a situation and instead demonstrate "an abundant, genuine curiosity" (p. 29). A position of curiosity, naiveté, and not knowing is useful for deconstructing dominant problem narratives. This approach can be used as a way to guard against applying one's expertise to try to change a person in the direction one sees fit.

The group leader's use of curiosity creates leverage for both the group leader and the participant, for the approach encourages participants to bring forward their own private stories about their realization, orientation, and meaning-making with regard to their experience. The curiosity employed is a specific kind, one that has the group leader asking questions of the person about "how things might be otherwise, a curiosity which falls outside of the totalizing stories that person has about [his or her life], and outside of those dominant practices of self and relationship" (White, 1993, p. 59).

After a lifetime of experience, people can be regarded as experts on their own lives. From this perspective, the group leader may easily become curious about how group members understand things to be. The narrative group leader might, in this regard, begin a session on dealing with anger by asking the group, "What would you want from a discussion about anger?" (Silvester, 1994).

As group leaders we have asked group members how they were able to challenge or fight fear to the extent that they could rappel down a cliff. In other instances, we have asked group members to give an account of their private conversations that enabled them to complete the rappel. We have also asked participants how they made use of the public conversations of the other group members' stories and whether they might now be able to revise their own self-narratives. The experience of telling one's self-narrative to an audience, we have found, presents many people with the opportunity to revise that part of their identities in which they may have labeled themselves as claustrophobic, nonactive, old, or fearful.

DECONSTRUCTION

By using curiosity with the technique of deconstruction, we have been able to take apart the taken-for-granted assumptions that are present within a group. Deconstruction covers a range of different methods, though most "render strange these familiar and every day taken-for-granted realities and practices by objectifying them" (White, 1993, p. 34). Bourdieu (1988, cited by White, 1991) described deconstruction as "exoticizing the domestic." Here are two examples taken from the anthropology literature.

Lutz (1985, cited in Sampson, 1993) described an anthropological study in which it was reported that the child-rearing practices of the Japanese were "indulgent" and the parents were quick to "shame" their children. If one were to deconstruct this commentary it would be necessary to consider the notions of "indulgence" and "shame" as being implicitly assumed by some group's standard. In this case, it was likely the anthropologists' judgment, based on their own cultural standards. Of course "indulgence" is not an intrinsic property but rather a relational one.

Linnell and Cora (1993) described the use of deconstruction in a group for women who have been sexually abused. The facilitator may ask group members to identify how dominant cultural stories about gender and about the incidence and effects of child sexual abuse have exerted an influence on their lives. Later, in a session on self-blame, the women explored how common cultural myths polarize "woman" as, on the one hand, a source of evil and temptation and, on the other hand, the custodian of moral and family values.

In a group on dealing with anger, the narrative group leader may ask the participants, "What constrains women from expressing anger assertively?" This question would open up the investigation of the effects of gender discourse on the expression of emotion.

In a group influenced by traditionally gendered discourse, the group leader may ask the participants why more women than men in the group were emotionally expressive and why many of the men were emotionally constrained. Alternatively, the group members could be asked to consider why men tend to exhibit more linear thought processes than women and why women tend to be more multitasked in orientation. Other useful questions would be, "How is it that many more of the men than women in the group express and assert their ideas and claim group time for doing so while the women are more likely to hold back and provide space for others and be more tentative in presenting their ideas? How is it that some members in the group have been completely silenced, and how does discourse, rather than the individual members per se, maintain the silence?"

When dominant themes are identified by group members, the group can more clearly identify the strength of discourse and how it is operating on the group members in their interactions both within and outside the group. In fact, it is easier to identify the operation of discourse in a group setting than in one-to-one work. Interactions in a group setting are more easily attributed to the influence of discourse than to an individual's personal inadequacies or intrapsychic conflicts. The more voices there are in the group identifying the dominant discourses, the easier it becomes to locate the constraining influences of dominant discourse as opposed to individual pathology.

Further, when group members express views that are counter to the dominant cultural patterns, the group facilitators and other members can ask how these alternative positions were established. For example, how can this man or these men in the group exhibit sadness, hurt, shame, or fear when these responses are more typically expressed by women? Identifying alternative histories to the dominant, culturally prescribed ones opens up alternative discourses for other group members to consider.

Deconstruction is most successfully achieved when group leaders look at familiar habits and social practices as though they were observing an alien world. When deconstruction is applied successfully, the group leader questions his or her own preconceptions and preferred points of reference, beliefs, and judgments, which are often called common sense.

Deconstruction has, in our view, far-reaching implications for group counseling and therapy. We use deconstruction as a means to assist group members to identify how discourse or dominant cultural stories can produce their privately held accounts of themselves. These private accounts can, in turn, produce self-blame as a result of the person's sense of failure to conform to certain expectations or replicate certain specifications or norms. In our training groups, we often use deconstructive methods to review how dominant counseling discourses invite the participants to adhere to essentialist descriptions of the self. Such discourses suggest that there is an untainted and pure essential core within each person that is trapped by defense mechanisms and self-protective layers. For self-development to occur, people must peel away the protective layers to show their uniqueness and whole self. Social constructionists would deconstruct this dominant humanistic discourse by retracing its history and its emergence in present-day counseling and group therapy. In the process, they would call attention to the discourses shaping social constructionist theory that provide an alternative account of growth, change, and development. Social constructionists view the notion of development as occurring when individuals reposition themselves within discourse, from what they may have deemed culturally appropriate to what they would now regard as a more preferred discursive field. In doing so, they would draw on alternative discourses or on unstoried experience lying outside the discursive world and therefore often overlooked in the process of meaning construction.

When group participants begin to disassemble specific cultural norms, they experience an opening in the way they understand themselves and begin to objectify the specifications rather than themselves. Typically, when people deconstruct their previously unquestioned assumptions about themselves and others, they experience a greater degree of agency.

THE USE OF RELATIVE INFLUENCE QUESTIONS

Relative influence questions can be used to aid group participants in the process of deconstruction. In the early 1980s, White (1986) developed questioning techniques that enabled clients to explore the impact their problem concern or problem narrative was having on their lives and to explore the resistances they had developed so that they would not be completely dominated by the problem. With this technique, the group leader asks questions about the origin of the problem narrative and the group members historicize the problem stories' effects on their lives, with the result that everyone gains a fuller grasp of their concerns. Congruent with the telling of a story, clients are asked to give an account of the effect the story is currently having on their lives and to predict the most likely "ending" to the story given its present course.

In our experience, people can become accustomed to their problem story, and they initially tend to report a diminished account of themselves as active agents in the story line. When they have the opportunity to devote time to investigating the complete extent of the problem story, particularly when the theme of their problem-saturated account lies within the dominant cultural practices and societal norms, clients tend to become more actively willing to be repositioned in a more preferred account of themselves.

In a group we facilitated that was focused on physical challenges, we were interested in exploring the effects that fear, age, and sedentary lifestyles had on the way group members confronted physical challenges. We asked the participants to consider how fear had, in the past, dominated or controlled them and the effects fear had on influencing the choices they had made in their professional and personal lives. The group members discussed occasions when fear may have taken charge of them and placed constraints on the choices they made for themselves. Subsequently, they told stories of occasions when they had made fear less persuasive in their lives. When the group members presented these accounts of their own private struggles in the group context, the public nature of the storytelling contributed to significant shifts in how some of them described themselves following their engagement with the physical tasks.

One member, for example, felt that the title "claustrophobic" did not suit her new understanding of herself. Another member described a change from seeing herself as a person who is entertained by watching others engage in physical tasks to seeing herself as a full and active participant in creating new adventures. These accounts demonstrate the influence of the person over the identified problem or issue. The group members' responses were revealed through the use of relative influence questions.

The following are examples of relative influence questions taken from accounts of a range of narrative groups that explored the effects of a problem concern on the group members.

- "Do you think alcohol might set some traps for you to try to trip you in your success, or have you discovered enough about the lies of alcohol to not get caught out?" (Smith, 1994, p. 32)

- "How has chemical use affected your life?" (asked of members of a cocaine recovery group) (Campbell & Brasher, 1994, p. 67)
- "In terms of your childhood experience of sexual abuse, how do you think you got these ideas, feelings, and habits?" (Linnell & Cora, 1993, p. 63)
- "How has depression influenced your life story?" (Laube & Trefz, 1994, p. 32)
- "Can you tell me how stress affects the organization?" (Silvester, 1997, p. 244)

Questions such as these encourage group members to reflect on the impact of a problem's effects while inviting them to move away from blaming themselves for the problem. Such questioning and reflection tends to invite initiative and activate the group members to engage more purposefully in diminishing the problem's effects. To build on this new momentum, the group leader can ask additional relative questions that can help members explore the impact that they are having on the problem. This approach tends to remind the group members that they have already been taking some action against the problem, which encourages them to see themselves as active and resourceful with competencies that previously may have been only dimly recognizable. Examples of this type of question include the following:

- "How come you were able to be successful [combating the demands of alcohol] so quickly?" (Smith, 1994, p. 31)
- "What is your longest period of clean time?" (Campbell & Brasher, 1994, p. 67)
- "What positive thing does it [a picture] tell you about yourself that you were able to challenge this particular problem on this occasion?" (Linnell & Cora, 1993, p. 63)
- "How did you figure out how to be a person in the group whose thinking isn't controlled by depression?" (Laube & Trefz, 1994, p. 33)
- "What does it mean that everyone has spoken in the whole group? Does it mean that assertiveness is present?" (Silvester, 1997, p. 235)

EXTERNALIZATION

White (1991) discovered that if the counselor and client can title the problem discourses or problem story, such naming externalizes the problem discourses and the client experiences a shift in the objectifying and totalizing effects of the discourses. From such externalization, the client experiences an opening in language use concerning the problem.

Using this technique, Zimmerman and Shephard (1993) asked members of a narrative therapy group on bulimia to name the negative influences of the bulimia. The members made up descriptions for the bulimia, giving it titles such as "Ilsa," which stood for how ill the group member would feel after bingeing and throwing up. Michael White (1991) is known for naming problems in this way, using titles such as "sneaky poo" for children who are attempting to stop soiling.

Externalization has been used to separate the effects of the problem story from the person in order to help the person challenge unhelpful habits or address totalizing discourses about, for example, patriarchy, dominant gender attitudes, and racist attitudes and hatreds that might be in operation (Zimmerman & Dickerson, 1993). When a clear separation occurs between the problem and the person, any blaming response by the therapist toward the person tends to be averted and any self-blame tends to be undermined, opening space for that person to join the group leader in resisting and protesting against the problem discourses (Tomm, 1993). White's frequent phrase (1991) has been, "The person is not the problem; the problem is the problem."

As we have already described, in our narrative therapy groups we use externalization of a problem such as fear to relocate the problem. The subtle language change assists the group members in joining together against the problem and supporting one another. With this technique we can monitor the progress of the group to determine the extent to which the group has made inroads into the problem concern. We can thus determine how much the group is in charge of fear in comparison to how much fear is in charge of the group.

ALTERNATIVE STORIES, OR REPOSITIONING IN PREFERRED DISCOURSES

It becomes apparent to the group leader and participants, when "abundant and genuine curiosity" is used, that people are not completely and utterly dominated by the problem discourses. We do not espouse the notion that people are "blank slates" to be passively written on by problem discourses (Linnell & Cora, 1993). There are, as we suggested earlier, lived experiences that stand outside the dominant problem story line. It is these unstoried lived experiences that are of most interest to the narrative group therapist.

To identify lived experiences that are located outside the sphere of the problem, the narrative group leader encourages an atmosphere of curiosity in the group about occasions in which the problem did not dominate. Often, group members have lived with a sense of diminished potency in relation to the problem, and seldom are they able to easily identify an absence of the problem's influence or the presence of their own influence on the extent of the problem-saturated story. To help them do so, the group leader must be resourceful and persistent in his or her genuine curiosity about lived experiences with which the group members are only slightly acquainted.

The group leader needs to ask such questions as, "Has there been an occasion where [the problem] hasn't completely dominated your thoughts?" If the answer is no, the group leader might ask, "Has there been an occasion even for a few moments when you've noticed its temporary absence?" "Have there been moments in this group when you may have considered that the problem could be beginning to lose total hold on you?" "Have there been occasions when other group members' stories about their struggles with this issue have inspired or strengthened you in your own struggle?"

White and Epston (1989) described such moments that are not problem dominated as "unique outcomes." Using a story metaphor, the group leader can help the group member to link unique outcomes together to produce an alternative, more preferred account of self. Participants tend to view recent unique outcomes as more significant than earlier ones; hence, events that occur in the context of the group interactions have much potential. If the lived event is not considered a unique outcome for the person concerned, then it cannot be considered as useful in the construction of an alternative account.

The group leader's intention, using this approach, is to assist group members in producing more preferred accounts of the self within a non-problem-dominated story line or to assist group participants to be located in a more favored group of discourses. Knowledge of alternative discourses may enable the group member to produce stories that present them as being active agents in their lives and in the life of the group. In the same way that individuals develop a problem story, they can historicize the alternative story's source, note its present effects, and make predictions about the story's future and their place within it. They can also consider the impact of the alternative story on other group members and on the evolving ethos of the group.

Within the group, members can play the role of audience or assist one another in noticing the development of an alternative account of self in group interactions. The alternative story is thus co-constructed by participants and the group leader based on material provided by a particular group member that has already been performed, however minutely, in the life of the group or in the world. Just as naming the externalized problem story assists the individual in challenging it, naming the alternative story is a shorthand strategy for identifying the emergence of the new.

Not surprisingly, the group leader's role in helping the group member construct an alternative account of self requires a persistent and determined effort in the early stages. However, it is important for the leader not to have a stronger investment in the participant's alternative story than the group member has, as a story line can easily become the facilitator's story about the person and not the group member's own account. The group leader can assist the group members to position the emerging alternative accounts alongside their dominant stories, but it is the group members who must choose which story is a more preferable account of themselves.

A useful strategy is for the group leader to ask the group members whether they favor their dominant problem accounts over the emerging accounts. If they answer "no," then the subsequent dialogue can contribute to their being more fully acquainted with their abilities as an active agent in their lives. It is helpful for the group leader to be aware of how the dominant problem discourses may be reestablished. To acquire this knowledge, the leader should encourage the storying of unique outcomes in relation to the identified problem throughout the repositioning phase.

EXAMPLES OF GROUP WORK USING NARRATIVE IDEAS

Although narrative ideas have been widely applied in work with individuals and families (Laube & Trefz, 1994), only recently has this work been featured in the group work literature (Laube & Trefz, 1994; Linnell & Cora, 1993; Zimmerman & Shephard, 1993). Four of the most common problem-related themes that have been addressed in the literature are substance abuse, depression, eating disorders, and sexual abuse. Group members experiencing these problem-related concerns have benefited from working in a group format. Significant advantages to addressing these issues in a group context are that members work with peers who have similar difficulties and who can serve as an audience to the changes that an individual is making.

THE AUDIENCE

The value of the audience in witnessing a group member's submergence of a problem narrative and his or her active engagement with a more preferred account of self is seldom underestimated by group leaders. It is not surprising that the group context has become an important avenue for the exploration and development of narrative ideas in group work.

The group participants are the initial audience for the telling of stories in a safe setting in which there is validation, commonality, and affirmation about how the identified "problem" has become a dominant influence in a participant's life. The members help one another transform their tales by being an audience for discovering exceptions and noticing differences. In addition, members help one another identify audiences in their private lives who will help perpetuate their new stories. In the audience role, participants can ask others to identify family members or significant others who may have some interest in the private events going on in their life and to reflect on how a significant other might react to them after hearing an account of some new development taking place in their life.

In a recent group, one of us (Gerald) asked a participant about a loved but deceased maternal grandfather's possible reaction to the changes she was making in her life in relation to her ability to become less controlled by perfection-

ism. As she reflected on what her late grandfather's response might be, a whole new dimension was brought into play that enabled the participant to feel her grandfather as a intimate observer to her life-changing circumstances. She became aware of the acceptance and understanding this loved man had of her and his probable assurance that the time she was taking to make these changes in her life was totally acceptable. This interaction illustrates the potency of an audience even if that audience is not present in the room.

Acknowledgment of the value of the audience led to the development of what Anderson (1987) and White (1995) termed the reflecting team, a group of people, usually professionals and paraprofessionals, invited to become intimately involved in the therapeutic context while observing a therapist working with individuals and families. Members of the reflecting team, after observing a session, are asked to question one another about the impact a particular person's story had on them and the implications the favored lived experiences might have on the person's future directions. The team discusses how the group participant was able to make the changes he or she reported. The members also interview one another about their own private stories that may have become activated by listening to group participants presenting concerns. This awareness adds to the likelihood that some of the members of the team will have some point of connection with the participant's problem narrative. Presenting one's private story to an audience typically reduces feelings of isolation, alienation, and rejection, for the group member's concerns become normalized through the public hearing. In addition, through the reflecting team's discussion the group participants usually become aware of possible developments of their preferred narrative that had not surfaced in the earlier part of the session.

The value of the audience in witnessing change has been documented in many articles and books on group leadership (Kottler, 1994). The literature shows that spectator effects, a concept similar to the notion of group members as audience to changes being made by fellow group members, can be highly beneficial in group work.

Externalizing the Problem in the Group

When working with a group whose members have problems with, say, depression, the use of externalization is particularly helpful. With this technique, the group members can become aware of how depression has affected their lives and how it may immobilize the group. In addition, the group members can be encouraged to learn how depression can be influenced by the group and to develop a group story that parallels their individual private stories. This co-created group story would contain accounts of influencing depression and creating nondepressing experiences. The group does not merely focus on helping individuals express their pain in relation to what the depression has done to them, they construct the stories they live by in the group life. Further, they pay attention to the evolving story of the group, noting each stage in the unfolding group story.

Laube and Trefz (1994) explored the effects of depression on the individual lives of group members by observing how depression interferes with a group's life and how it can be undermined, moment-by-moment, by the interactions of the group members. They asked their groups such questions as, "How does it feel to all of you when depression comes into the group so strongly?" In line with the use of unique outcomes and more preferred redescriptions for people being affected by problem narratives, they asked, "How did you figure out how to be a person in the group whose thinking isn't controlled by depression?" (pp. 32–33).

It is often useful for members to identify the strategies they use to perform their more preferred accounts of themselves outside of the group and to consider how developments that occurred within a group session might affect the development of their continuing story between sessions. A comment to assist this process might be, "Think about what you revealed today and how, as a result, you are different during the week and think about how these differences will reveal themselves in the group in the future." At the beginning of subsequent sessions, the leader can ask group members to report unique outcomes that occurred between meetings so that the group story can be updated. Another comment that can assist this development might be, "Think about the kind of character you have been in your story and the character you anticipate being in the group." The group can record these developments so that absent members can become informed and the group's evolution can be fully documented.

PREPARING TO INTRODUCE NARRATIVE IDEAS INTO GROUPS

The narrative metaphor is generally appealing to group members. Most people warm to the effects that stories have on their lives and are fascinated or intrigued to contemplate the nature of the dominant stories they have constructed about themselves. To prepare individuals for a group that will employ narrative therapy, the leader can ask prospective members to consider how the unfolding of the group story will have an influence on their own private stories. The leader can also assist group members in preparing themselves to integrate their stories with those of others to discover exceptions to the problem discourses presently impacting their lives. The following are examples of questions, (Laube & Trefz, 1994, p. 34) that can be used in preparing new members who are about to participate in a group using narrative ideas:

- "How would you like to tell your story in this group?"
- "How has your story begun to change since you made the decision to join the group?"
- "As you continue to add to and contribute new stories about yourself, how will you be different?"

Because group members can work with narratives in a variety of ways, it is important for the group leader to give participants the message that these differences are acceptable. Some people want to give a full account of their story regarding the problem narrative, whereas others want to tell a snippet. Still others find it more beneficial to listen to stories than to relate them; from others' stories they glean ideas about how to deal with their own concerns.

CONCLUSION

The narrative approach to group work is more than a collection of new techniques. It is a way of thinking about how problems are made and solutions produced. It is a third-wave therapy that represents a fundamentally new direction in the therapeutic world, drawing attention to the wider systems that impact on group members such as family, schools, media, and peers.

As is evident from the discussion in this chapter, group leaders using narrative ideas are interested in naming the cultural practices that create what comes to be known as normal and natural and in deconstructing the oppressive practices that typically emerge in sexist, racist, classist, and ageist discourses.

This approach to group work endeavors to move away from the didactic and advice-giving interactions that are typically prevalent when the broader sociocultural world is introduced into the group work context. The group leaders instead draw upon narrative ideas to assist group members to reflect personally on the effects of unjust practices both on themselves and on other group members. Using narrative ideas in group therapy is not about seeking scapegoats in the form of white, male, middle-class capitalists. It is not about engaging in philosophical discussions about the social construction of reality. It is an approach that helps group members to identify the culturally oppressive practices and habits of action that affect everyone. Narrative ideas, when incorporated into group therapy, can help individuals put ideology into action, producing visible and practical changes in their lives.

REFERENCES

Amundson, J., Stewart, K. & Valentine, L. (1993). Temptations of power and certainty. *Journal of Marital and Family Therapy, 19*(2), 111–123.

Anderson, H., & Goolishian, H. (1992). The client is the expert: A not-knowing approach to therapy. In S. McNamee & K. Gergen (Eds.), *Therapy as social construction* (pp. 25–39). Newbury Park, CA: Sage.

Anderson, T. (1987). The reflecting team: Dialogue and meta-dialogue in clinical work. *Family Process, 26*, 415–428.

Berger, P., & Luckmann, T. (1966). *The social construction of reality.* Garden City, NY: Doubleday.

Bruner, E. (1986). Ethnography as narrative. In V. Turner & E. Bruner (Eds.), *The anthropology of experience* (pp. 139–155). Chicago: University of Illinois Press.

Burman, E. (1994). *Deconstructing developmental psychology.* London: Routledge.

Campbell, T., & Brasher, B. (1994). The pause that refreshes: Opportunities, interventions and predictions in group therapy with cocaine addicts. *Journal of Systemic Therapies, 13,* 65–73.

Clayton, G. M. (1989). *Group work training manual.* Victoria: The Australian College of Psychodrama.

Edwards, D. (1991). Categories are for talking: On the cognitive and discursive bases of categorization. *Theory and Society, 1,* 515–542.

Fairclough, N. (1992). *Discourse and social change.* Cambridge, MA: Polity Press.

Geertz, C. (1986). Making experiences. In V. Turner & E. Bruner (Eds.), *The anthropology of experience* (pp. 373–380). Chicago: University of Illinois Press.

Gergen, K. J. (1985a). Social constructionist inquiry: Context and implications. In K. J. Gergen & K. E. Davis (Eds.), *The social construction of the person* (pp. 3–18). New York: Springer-Verlag.

Gergen, K. J. (1985b). The social constructionist movement in modern psychology. *American Psychologist, 40*(3), 266–275.

Gergen, K. J. (1991). *The saturated self.* New York: Basic Books.

Harre, R. (1986). The step to social constructionism. In M. Richards & P. Light (Eds.), *Children of social worlds* (pp. 287–296). Cambridge, UK: Polity Press.

Harre, R. (1992). What is real in psychology: A plea for persons. *Theory & Psychology, 2,* 153–158.

Hollway, W. (1983). Heterosexual sex: power and desire for the other. In S. Cartledge & J. Ryan (Eds.), *Sex and love: New thoughts on old contradictions.* (pp. 124–140). London: Women's Press.

Kottler, J. A. (1994). *Advanced group leadership.* Pacific Grove, CA: Brooks/Cole.

Laube, J., & Trefz, S. (1994). Group work using a narrative theory framework: Application to treatment of depression. *Journal of Systemic Therapies, 13,* 29–37.

Linnell, S., & Cora, D. (1993). *Discoveries.* Australia: Dympna House.

McNamee, S., & Gergen, K. (Eds.). (1992) *Therapy as social construction.* London: Sage.

Mokuau, N. (1987). Social leaders' perceptions of counseling effectiveness for Asian-American clients. *Journal of the National Association of Social Leaders, 32*(4), 331–335.

Monk, G. (1993, October). *Narrative approaches to therapy: The fourth wave in family therapy.* Paper presented to the New Zealand Association for Research in Education, Hamilton, New Zealand.

O'Hanlon, B. (1994, November/December). The third wave. *Family Therapy Networker,* pp. 19–29.

Olssen, M. (1991). Producing the truth about people. In J. Morss & T. Linzey (Eds.), *Growing up: The politics of human learning* (pp. 188–209). Auckland: Longman Paul.

Parker, I., & Shotter, J. (Eds.). (1990). *Deconstructing social psychology.* London: Routledge.

Pedersen, P. (1988). *A handbook for developing multicultural awareness.* Alexandria, VA: American Association for Counseling and Development.

Ritchie, J. (1992). *Becoming bicultural.* Wellington, New Zealand: Huia Publishers.

Sampson, E. E. (1993). Identity politics. *American Psychologist, 49*(5), 412–416.

Shotter, J. (1989). Social accountability and the social construction of you. In J. Shotter & K. J. Gergen (Eds.) *Texts of identity* (pp. 133–151). London: Sage.

Shotter, J., & Gergen, K. (1989). *Texts of identity.* London: Sage.

Silvester, G. (1994). *Psycho-educational groups.* Unpublished manuscript, University of Waikato, Hamilton, New Zealand.

Silvester, G. (1997). Appreciating indigenous knowledge in groups. In G. Monk, J. Winslade, K. Crocket, & D. Epston (Eds.), *Narrative therapy in practice: The archeology of hope.* San Francisco: Jossey Bass.

Smith, L. (1994). *Working with people experiencing problems with alcohol.* Unpublished seminar booklet, Waikato University, Hamilton, New Zealand.

Spender, D. (1985). *Man made language*. London: Routledge & Kegan Paul.

Sue, D. W. (1990). Culture-specific strategies in counseling: A conceptual framework. *Professional Psychology: Research & Practice, 21*(6), 424–433.

Tannen, D. (1990). *You just don't understand: Women and men in conversation*. London: Virginia Press.

Tomm, K. (1993). The courage to protest: A commentary on Michael White's work. In S. Gilligan & R. Price (Eds.), *Therapeutic conversations* (pp. 62–80). New York: Norton.

Wetherell, M., & Potter, J. (1992). *Mapping the language of racism: Discourse and the legitimation of exploitation*. London: Harvester Wheatsheaf.

White, M. (1986). Negative explanation, restraint and double description: A template for family therapy. *Family Process, 25,* 169–184.

White, M. (1989). *Selected papers*. Adelaide, Australia: Dulwich Centre Publications.

White, M. (1991, No. 3). Deconstruction and therapy. *Dulwich Centre Newsletter,* pp. 21–67.

White, M. (1993). Deconstruction and therapy. In S. Gilligan & R. Price (Eds.), *Therapeutic conversations* (pp. 22–61). New York: Norton.

White, M. (1995). *Reauthoring lives*. Adelaide: Dulwich Centre Publications.

White, M., & Epston, D. (1989). *Literate means to therapeutic ends*. Adelaide: Dulwich Centre Publications.

Zimmerman, J. L., & Dickerson, V. C. (1993). Bringing forth the restraining influence of patterns in couples therapy. In S. Gilligan & R. Price (Eds.), *Therapeutic conversations* (pp. 197–214). New York: Norton.

Zimmerman, J. L., & Dickerson, V. C. (1994). Using a narrative metaphor: Implications for theory and clinical practice. *Family Process, 33,* 233–245.

Zimmerman, T. S., & Shephard, S. D. (1993, Spring). Externalizing the problem of bulimia: Conversation, drawing and letter writing in group therapy. *Journal of Systemic Therapies, 12,* 22–31.

SUGGESTED READINGS

Awatere, D. (1981). Maori counselling. In F. Donnelly (Ed.), *Time to talk* (pp. 198–202). Auckland: Allen & Unwin.

Braidotti, R. (1991). *Patterns of dissonance: A study of women in contemporary philosophy*. New York: Routledge.

Bruner, J. (1987). Life as narrative. *Social Research, 54,* 11–32.

Bruner, J. (1990). *Acts of meaning*. Cambridge, MA: Harvard University Press.

Calvert, S. (1994, March). Psychology and a feminist practice: Opponents or complements? *Bulletin of the New Zealand Psychological Society,* No. 80.

Corey, M., & Corey, G. (1992). Groups, process and practice. Pacific Grove, CA: Brooks/Cole.

Davies, B. (1991). The concept of agency: A feminist poststructuralist analysis. *Postmodern Critical Theorizing, 30,* 42–53.

Davies, B. (1993). *Shards of glass*. Sydney: Allen & Unwin.

Davies, B., & Harre, R. (1990). Positioning: The discursive production of selves. *Journal for the Theory of Social Behavior, 20*(1), 43–63.

Drewery, W. (1990). Listening, hearing and power relations. *New Zealand Association of Counsellors Journal, 12*(1), 27–38.

Flax, J. (1990). *Thinking fragments: Psychoanalysis, feminism, and postmodernism in the contemporary West*. Berkeley: University of California Press.

Fox-Genovese, E. (1991). *Feminism without illusions: A critique of individualism*. Chapel Hill: University of North Carolina Press.

Gannon, L., Luchetta, T., Rhodes, K., Pardie, L., & Segrist, D. (1992). Sex bias in psychological research: Progress or complacency? *American Psychologist, 47,* 389–396.

Garnets, L., Hancock, K. A., Cochran, S. D., Goodchilds, J., & Peplau, L. A. (1991). Issues in psychotherapy with lesbians and gay men: A survey of psychologists. *American Psychologist, 46,* 964–972.

Gergen, K. J. (1989). Warranting voice and the elaboration of self. In J. Shotter & K. J. Gergen (Eds.), *Texts of identity* (pp. 70–81). London: Sage.

Gergen, K. J. (1994). Exploring the postmodern. *American Psychologist, 49*(5), 412–416.

Gilligan, C. (1982). *In a different voice: Psychological theory and women's development.* Cambridge, MA: Harvard University Press.

Graham, S. (1991). "Most of the subjects were white and middle class." Trends in published research on African Americans in selected APA journals, 1970–1989. *American Psychologist, 47,* 629–639.

Harre, R. (1984). *Personal being: A theory for individual psychology.* Cambridge, MA: Harvard University Press.

Herek, G. M., Kimmel, D. C., Amaro, H., & Melton, G. B. (1991). Avoiding heterosexual bias in psychological research. *American Psychologist, 46,* 957–963.

Ho, M. K. (1984). Social group work with Asian/Pacific Americans. In L. E. Davis (Ed.), *Ethnicity in social group work practice* (pp. 49–61). New York: Haworth Press.

Lee, P. C., Juan, G., & Hom, A. B. (1984). Groupwork practice with Asian clients: A sociocultural approach. In L. E. Davis (Ed.), *Ethnicity in social work practice* (pp. 37–47). New York: Haworth Press.

MacKinnon, C. A. (1989). *Toward a feminist theory of state.* Cambridge, MA: Harvard University Press.

Oakley, A. (1981). Interviewing women: A contradiction in terms. In H. Roberts (Ed.), *Doing feminist research* (pp. 30–61). London: Routledge & Kegan Paul.

Riger, S. (1992). *Epistemological debates, feminist voices: Science, social values, and the study of women.* Washington, DC: American Psychological Association.

Semp, D. (1994). *Nurturing sense-able men: Resisting and revisioning masculinity.* Unpublished master's thesis, University of Auckland, Auckland.

Waldegrave, C. (1990, No. 1). Just therapy. *Dulwich Centre Newsletter,* pp. 6–45.

Young, I. M. (1990). *Justice and the politics of difference.* Princeton, NJ: Princeton University Press.

11

MENTORING

GROUP LEADERS

RICHARD J. HAZLER, REBECCA POWELL STANARD,
VALERIE CONKEY, AND PAUL GRANELLO

*A*ll group therapists can name those special individuals who had the greatest influence on their professional development. They were perhaps mentors who helped lead them to a great career choice or possibly away from a specialty that looked good at one time but could later be recognized as a bad idea. Likewise, most group therapists can recall people who led them to nothing more than wasted time, disastrous choices, and worthless ideas that they never used as group leaders. Then there were the people who wanted to tell them how to do therapy but whose help they resisted at all costs, often for reasons they could not fully identify. One's history of mentoring relationships and potential mentoring relationships is commonly a mixed bag of positive and negative experiences.

How are the mentoring relationships that proved to be wonderful gifts different from those sought unsuccessfully, those that were not sought but should have been, those found but later regretted, and that majority that seemed to be good ideas but were never completely successful? If one discusses these questions with experienced group workers, the answers that typically surface are related to isolated personality characteristics of the mentor or protégé or to some other factor of fate. We have found that it is hard to hold the attention of experienced group counselors on a discussion of this topic as their need for a mentor is primarily in their past and their need to practice successfully is their immediate concern. However, most experienced group leaders also recognize the opportunities available to help mold new group leaders through mentoring roles, and although their time and energy are in short supply, their motivation to help is persistent.

In this chapter we identify the complex issues involved in mentoring group leaders and discuss the critical factors that mitigate successful mentoring. Mentoring group leaders is a qualitative and highly personal experience that must be viewed in that context if its theoretical concepts and practice are to be meaningful. For that reason, we begin the chapter with accounts of our personal experiences as protégés and mentors; indeed, such accounts surface throughout the chapter, helping to provide a context that matches the personal nature of mentoring. Following our opening accounts, we provide a review of the literature, highlighting the overlapping issues of mentoring and co-leadership in advanced group work and providing a foundation for comparing the research that has been conducted to the lessons we have learned from experience. Next, we convert the concepts, experiences, and information provided in the first portion of the chapter to applications for group practitioners who wish to mentor or be mentored. Important themes are identified that practitioners can use to initiate and maintain productive mentoring relationships. In the final section, we provide conclusions developed from the points of emphasis in the discussion that can be used to guide the application of these ideas.

PERSONAL INTRODUCTION

EVEN PROFESSIONALS NEED SUPPORT

I (Richard Hazler) am a 50-year-old professor with a Ph.D. and a great deal of counseling experience, yet I still wake up with nightmares about my experiences, more than 20 years ago, in leading my first counseling group of middle school boys. I am embarrassed that I cannot let this memory rest after so many years and so many successful group experiences. At the time, I felt like I lacked all knowledge and experience in group work, although that was far from the truth. I had received a solid education and had already gained substantial group experience as both a leader and a supervisor with military substance abusers and prison inmates. Before working as a counselor, I had been a sixth-grade teacher. I had no reason to feel incompetent or inadequate; but that was exactly how I felt before, during, and after this group.

The boys group met several times, and when the group disbanded I felt greatly relieved but also disappointed with myself. It seemed as if the group had gone on for 100 years. Every time a boy made a comment, I would reinforce it and followup, no matter how trivial the statement was. In retrospect, I am sure that the boys could see that I felt desperate to promote any kind of conversation and that they toyed with my insecurity. We talked about more irrelevant junk in that group than in any group I have facilitated either before or since. I knew the group had not run the way it should have, and I knew its failings were my fault!

I knew I needed help, but help was not readily available as I was the only counselor within a 50-mile radius. Even more relevant than the distance, however, was the fact that I was new to the area and embarrassed that my previous training and experience had not adequately prepared me to do a good job with a relatively normal group of seventh-grade boys. I did not lead any groups for the rest of my first year as a school counselor even though I recognized my hesitation to do so as a simple act of avoidance.

Even today, whenever I see students entering their first group or experienced counselors trying something different, the memories of that nightmare group return. The memories serve a positive purpose, though, by reminding me of how important it is to have a fellow professional providing a solid base of support, particularly in the complex format of group work. I did not need someone to teach me or even to run the boys group for me. I needed someone to work with me; someone who would be there in the tough times, someone who would help me recognize and recover from mistakes, someone with whom I could bounce ideas. Best would have been a professional who had worked with groups of kids similar to those in my group. Colleagues have told me that the needs associated with my nightmare are not mine alone. I believe all experienced and novice professionals can benefit from similar support from a viable mentor. However, being a viable mentor is easier said than done.

PROVIDING SUPPORT TO PROFESSIONALS IS EASIER SAID THAN DONE

When Richard told me (Val Conkey) of his experience with his first group, I nearly lost my breath. Surely the experience could not be that of the self-confident professor I have leaned on for his knowledge, skills, and stability. Then I thought about my own development from student to respected professional to mentor and back to student. I recalled the fear and anxiety I felt in facilitating my first group and in later groups in which I was the less experienced co-leader. At those times I, too, felt frustrated and, like Richard, vowed to become helpful to others in similar situations. However, the first time I found myself in the mentor role for a less experienced group leader, the experience provided a rude awakening. Mentoring was not the simple task I had thought it would be. Simply being motivated and able did not get the job done.

Before my first mentoring role, I had successfully run many groups. As an experienced counselor, my confidence was high, as was the confidence of others in me. Thus, when I was asked to co-lead an adolescent group with a new counselor, I was pleased and excited to have the opportunity to share my skills and experience in the ways that I felt they were needed—something not provided to me when I was new at group work.

What a frustrating first attempt at mentoring that was. I couldn't find the time to discuss things. My co-leader couldn't find the time to see me. I didn't know how to best involve her in the group. To my surprise, she responded to my efforts in that regard in much the same fashion I responded to a more experienced counselor's efforts when I was a beginning counselor. She would rarely talk or participate in the group. She looked no more pleased, comfortable, or satisfied than I had felt with my first potential mentor. I tried to do those things I had wanted done for me, but my efforts did not change her behavior, which just about drove me crazy. There was clearly some aspect of performing mentoring that was not yet a part of me—something I still needed to learn.

COMBINING KNOWLEDGE AND EXPERIENCES FROM DIFFERENT VIEWPOINTS

The four of us (Richard, Becky, Val, and Paul) have seen good mentoring, bad mentoring, no mentoring, mentoring when it was needed, and mentoring when it was not wanted, and we have all tried to act as mentors for those whom we thought wanted or needed mentoring. In co-leading groups we have sometimes been a mentor, sometimes a protégé, sometimes a colleague, and sometimes a mixture of all three. Perhaps the most consistent piece of knowledge we have gained is that having a helpful working relationship as a mentor, protégé, or co-leader is never the easy task it may appear to be. Sometimes the relationship works well, and sometimes, try as we might, it is a disaster.

We know that we cannot control every interpersonal or group situation in just the way we want and we have no pretenses that anyone else reading this chapter will approach perfection either. What we offer here are ideas that we believe mentors can use to help make their support of emerging group leaders as valuable and consistent as possible. The ideas presented should offer a base from which mentors can operate that is supportable by both theory and practice even if it does not approach perfection.

WHAT THE LITERATURE REPORTS

Mentoring has been a topic of discussion for years in many professional areas, including education, business, and scientific disciplines such as nursing. Mentoring relationships may begin as informal or even chance encounters and grow into strong relationships that benefit the mentor, protégé, and the organization (Wright & Werther, 1991). Or they can be formally established staff development mod-

els designed to promote continuity and maximum accomplishments in an organization. Mentoring does not relate to one isolated role. Teachers, advisers, supervisors, employers, and friends have all been recognized as having potential
mentoring responsibilities.

The concept of mentor, long established in some disciplines, is just beginning to be addressed directly in the counselor education literature (Brinson &
Kottler, 1993; Robinson, 1994). Counselor educators have been identified as
the most appropriate professionals in the field to take on the responsibility of
mentoring practitioners on how best to integrate field research into their practice. Working together in a mentoring relationship should, in theory, help both
mentors and protégés improve their client services and should advance the profession as a whole (Robinson, 1994). However, research on the methods and
outcomes of mentoring and of student-faculty relationships in general is limited (Hazler & Carney, 1993). The concept of an other-than-instructor relationship seems to be well accepted, but reliable information on how, when, and where
such relationships should be put into practice is often missing.

Brinson and Kottler (1993) acknowledged the complexity of these issues in
their look at the personal challenges and professional responsibilities inherent
in cross-cultural mentoring of minority counselor education faculty. The potential benefits, problems, and techniques of mentoring emerging group leaders
have not yet been directly studied. Ideas similar to mentoring have, however,
been indirectly addressed in discussions of group co-leadership, and similarities can be seen between the two functions (Corey, 1995; Jacobs, Harvill, &
Masson, 1994).

Group co-leadership has been touted by several authors as a preferred model
for leading groups and for training group leaders (Corey, 1995; Jacobs et al.,
1994). It has been seen as a means of offering new group leaders a degree of
safety that will allow them to explore more than they might without the support
of a more experienced co-leader as backup. The inexperienced professional, whose
early responses to group behaviors are likely to be a patchwork of guesses, is
provided a safety net by the co-leadership of an experienced and mentoring professional, making co-leadership a viable part of any group therapy training program (Fenster, 1991). Experienced professionals can also find a degree of safety
in co-leadership, for it allows them to give up some control in the group setting
to a less experienced leader while still being available to intervene as necessary.

Co-leadership offers additional advantages as well, including benefits to
group members (Corey, 1995). Having two leaders offering their experiences,
insight, and perhaps different perspectives can add depth and variety to group
sessions. Plus, because both leaders bring their unique strengths and abilities to
the group, every potentially helpful skill and bit of knowledge does not need to
be encompassed in one individual. Yet another advantage of co-leadership is
that it presents many opportunities for relationship modeling, which can aid
both group members and the less experienced leaders. The co-leaders, for ex-

ample, can re-create dynamics that two group members may have had with each other or that members may have had with a parent or outside individual.

The skill improvement and learning that result from a co-leadership model may derive from either a formal or an informal mentoring relationship. Jacobs et al. (1994) discussed three models of co-leading, one of which has a great deal in common with mentoring. In the first model they discussed, the co-leaders alternate in taking the primary leading role. The second model, shared leading, requires more flexibility on the part of the leaders. Their interactions must flow together as the co-leaders jointly lead. The model closest to a formal mentoring concept is an apprentice model in which the group is primarily led by the more experienced leader. The inexperienced leader mainly watches, listens, processes, and provides limited but increasing input as his or her understanding and confidence increase.

In many settings, the advantages of a mentoring relationship for both the protégé and the mentor are numerous. Protégés in higher education settings have reported gaining insight into their preferred methods of learning and working through the help of mentors. Research has shown that protégés in this setting became increasingly confident in their own abilities (Graham, 1994) and were more likely to pursue available educational opportunities (Johnson, Simpson, Williams, & Kotarba, 1993). These benefits in the higher education arena appear to be reinforced by findings that the early career promotion histories, general work satisfaction, and career satisfaction of early career managers and professionals were increased by mentoring (Whitely & Coetsier, 1993). A developmental theory of mentoring presented by Haensly and Parsons (1993) suggests that mentoring facilitates the task accomplishment characteristic of early life stages in addition to enhancing the general process of creative and intellectual growth.

For group work, co-leadership can provide valuable feedback that can benefit the more experienced professional as well as the protégé. Both leaders benefit from observing, learning, and working together, because experienced therapists recognize and react to more complex factors than do novice group therapists (Kivlighan & Quigley, 1991). Another set of benefits is more directly related to the mentor, who, through the process of mentoring, is reminded that his or her experience has value not only for the clients and the protégé but also for him- or herself. This recognition of one's value is easily lost or discounted when inadequate opportunities exist for receiving positive feedback from less experienced professionals. Mentoring gives experienced professionals the opportunity to review their own professional practices as they convey those experiences and their meanings to others (Graham, 1994). An increased sense of personal satisfaction and an increased enthusiasm for one's own work appear to result from helping a protégé (Atkinson, Neville, & Casas, 1991). Additional rewards for the mentor include expanded competence and increased feelings of confidence in one's own abilities, which can lead to further enjoyment of mentoring (Newby & Heide, 1992).

The element that seems to be essential to the development of both effective mentoring and effective group co-leadership is a quality relationship. The personal growth and professional vitality of the individuals involved, bolstered by the development of an effective mentoring relationship, appear to influence the development and maintenance of a productive relationship (Rogers & Holloway, 1993) as well as effective group co-leadership. Closeness, affection, trust, commitment, acceptance, encouragement, and respect appear necessary to allow and promote the openness, risk taking, and self-disclosure that are necessary for both of these concepts.

LESSONS FROM THREE MENTORING RELATIONSHIPS

The idea that the quality of a mentoring relationship is the core of its success is an easy one for professional therapists to embrace. In one form or another, it emerges as a central ingredient in all theories of therapeutic group practice. However, how and when one can successfully implement those quality relationship skills as a mentor to group leaders is much less clear.

The three experiential accounts of mentoring relationships that follow illustrate the complexity of issues that arise when an individual's development from novice to expert group counselor interacts with mentor and protégé personalities and situational conditions. The first example of Richard and Jim explores the fear and anxiety levels of the novice group counselor, how those feelings impact the counselor's thinking and behavior, and how the mentor must provide opportunities for the protégé to experience both safety and additional challenges that force the confrontation of anxieties. The protégé may recognize these competing needs, but it is the mentor who must ensure that they are met.

RICHARD AND JIM AS PROTÉGÉ AND MENTOR

The guard locked the door behind me (Richard Hazler), as I was the last to enter the room. Eight men waited for my mentor and I to begin our first co-led counseling session. The men, I sensed, saw me as the new white-boy counselor, and through just their looks they conveyed their disdain for my life, my lack of knowledge about their lives, and my skills. They were bigger, meaner, harder, more angry, and, at that point, much more confident than I was. If the guard had not locked the door, I might have run and given up my counseling career right there and then. I found it hard to imagine that I could ever face these men alone, without my experienced mentor, Jim.

Fear, self-doubt, and threat caused a throbbing in my head, a pounding in my heart, and near hyperventilation in my chest that first day. Jim and I would work with this group of inmates for the next 3 months, and I eventually felt bet-

ter, but that first day I could hardly speak. Jim handled everything, and I was very grateful.

Jim had taken time before the first session to tell me what to expect of the inmates, their problems, racial issues, control issues, and what it felt like being locked in a cell alone with them. He had reassured me that it was safer than some other places but that it certainly was no country club atmosphere. He also assured me that I would initially feel anxious but that I would later get over much of that anxiety, and he told me that it would be the skills and knowledge I had developed that would get me through the rough spots. He encouraged me to do as much as I wanted but asked me to do nothing on that first day other than introduce myself, which was about all I could handle.

Things went smoothly as Jim handled everything for the first few weeks. During that time I began to find places to provide input even though my part did not seem to be very therapeutic. After each group session, we talked about what Jim had done and how it had affected the inmates. He knew what he was talking about, and I listened closely hoping that I would eventually be able to emulate his skills and knowledge. The more difficult time for Jim and I came several weeks after the group started, when Jim told me it was past time that I got more involved. I went home feeling like I had failed by not doing enough and scared that I might not be able to do the job Jim did. I knew there was no turning back. I would just try to do the best "Jim" I could next time.

I have never been much good at being anyone but myself, and that next session was no different. My attempt at doing what I thought Jim would do only brought on a loud reaction from the most aggressive inmate in the group, who said, "Hey, Jack, what you do'in man? You got som'in to say, then say it. Don't be talk'in 'bout some shit you don't know. You just a person like the rest of us."

I looked to Jim for support, but all he had to say was, "You are different today. What's the story?"

Jim was throwing me to the wolves. Where was the Jim that had always been there for me? Why was he not protecting me? What was I supposed to do now? Because I could not think of any other options, I answered the question honestly. I told the group members about my fears, my desire to help, and how I felt so much less experienced and skilled than Jim. No one in this group made any attempt to soothe my pain and help me get out of this hard spot. Instead, the group members demanded that I get on with being me or get out. I opted for the former because I could not face Jim, my peers, my family, or myself if I quit. I knew that getting on with being me was the right thing to do, but someone else had to make me see that.

During the time we co-led the group, Jim taught me much about himself as a person, the people in the group, group work, leadership, co-leadership, and mentoring. The difficulties involved in learning and implementing group leadership and mentoring skills are not entirely explained in the literature but are at least given attention. Mentoring relationships force counselors to look at diffi-

cult issues within and outside themselves and to consider change as a form of growth (Wright & Werther, 1991). Mentors and groups offer security to the less experienced counselor only to later replace that security with the challenge to demonstrate one's development as relationships and situations change (Hillerbrand, 1989). Mentors offer models to observe (Gladding, 1991) and then demand that their protégés create their own personal models as they grow in expertise.

Jim's mentoring helped me to build my life and helped make me better as a person and a professional. The things he did and the ways he did them were probably not always right, but they helped me tremendously.

Richard and Jim shared a traditional mentoring relationship that produced clearly positive outcomes. The power differential they experienced was one they had informally agreed upon, where Jim was the definitive leader and Richard chose to follow to an extent that eventually needed to be challenged. Many potential mentoring and co-leading relationships, however, begin with much less agreement on the extent and implications of this power differential. The experiences of Becky and Val illustrate some of the challenges that such differences in perception can foster in mentoring and co-leadership relationships.

Becky and Val as Co-leaders

In my first experience as a group leader I (Becky) found an absence of support that is unfortunately typical in many community mental health agencies. I had been working in the agency for a very short time and did not yet really have a caseload. One day, a co-therapist was needed in an adolescent therapy group, and I was asked to fill in. I had no idea of what the group was about. I had only worked with adults, and I did not know the other leader; in fact, we were not even introduced before the group session began. All I knew was that my co-leader was an experienced therapist, someone who might become my supervisor. I was not prepared, and I was scared. This situation was not one I would have chosen, and a great deal of trepidation followed me into the group.

The group got started, and I sat for the entire hour and a half without so much as saying more than my name. I was completely intimidated by the co-leader and the group. I had thoughts and observations that seemed appropriate, but I was not sure about them or my role, so in no way was I going to open my mouth. I was no help. Fortunately, if the truth is to be known, my co-leader probably had no need for me to be there.

Subsequently, I have had positive experiences as a co-leader of groups. One that comes to mind was a group I ran with a co-therapist (Val), whose experience was at a similar level to mine. The group was made up of sexual abuse survivors, a population I had a fair degree of experience in working with in individual counseling. My supervisor suggested that I write up a proposal for forming the group, and I agreed.

After the proposal was accepted, I began to talk with potential co-leaders. One was rude, condescending, and argumentative about the format of the group, focusing on how it was different from her mentor's model. It was clear that she did not respect my knowledge or ability in this area and that working together would be a disaster. We decided not to work together for the sake of everyone.

Val and I wound up running this group together. It was the first time either of us had facilitated such a group and the first time either of us had worked with an equal as a co-leader. Our greatest fear was whether we could get the group members to talk about their abuse. What a shock we experienced when they talked eagerly, and indiscriminately, in the first session. We had hoped for appropriate disclosure, not indiscriminate revelation! We did not know if we would ever be able to get them to disclose appropriately!

We needed to find someone who believed in our ability level and our desire to grow who could offer some much needed advice. The mentor we chose listened, reassured us of our abilities and plan, and encouraged us to continue, offering key bits of advice. She suggested that we utilize our own skills to our best advantage and pointed out ways in which our styles could mix well. I was more spontaneous, interactive, and willing to try different things than Val was. Val, in turn, was process oriented and better able to work through the happenings of the group, the members' actions, and their reactions. It proved to be a very effective combination, in part because we used our skills in a complementary fashion rather than butting heads with our differences.

Good communication between Val and me and our discussions with our trusted mentor were two keys to the rapid development of our group leadership abilities. In addition, working with an equal rather than with someone more experienced freed us to discuss our own ideas and try new approaches. We found that we were more confident in our approach to our mentor after first reasoning out our ideas together. Placed with a more experienced co-leader, I probably would have deferred to experience and played a more supportive role than the productive one forced upon me.

The journey from novice to expert includes the acquisition of information and skills and finding an effective context in which to use them. One's mental ability to lead a group involves more than a numerical count of experience, for experience does not, by itself, assure expertise (Hillerbrand & Clairborn, 1990). One's preparation and ability to lead a group must be judged more on how the person conceptualizes the group process than on how long he or she has been in the profession. New group leaders do not all begin as equals, and mentors must recognize the differences. Where the beginning group leader falls on the continuum should have a primary influence on the nature of the mentoring relationship and the amount of time given to it, as is illustrated by the experiences of Paul and Gil.

PAUL AND GIL IN THE MIDDLE STAGES OF A GROUP

The purpose of the mentoring relationship is often perceived as moving a novice from the beginning point in a process to a logical expert ending. The experiences of Becky and Val provide examples of how differing perceptions regarding the nature of the mentoring relationship can interfere with the initiation and implementation of the relationship and also its outcomes. The experiences of Paul and Gil illustrate another model, one in which the protégé is presumed to be an inexperienced co-leader and follower but the mentor demonstrates confidence in his ability to quickly take over a more independent leadership role.

In his early work with groups, Paul was fortunate to be given the immediate information and responsibilities needed for his rapid development toward greater expertise. He was presented with verbal and written background on the group he was to co-lead, on its individual members, and on the theory and practical approach of his experienced co-leader. Here, Paul describes an unplanned occurrence in the group for which he was cognitively but not experientially prepared and which provided the type of immediate natural learning tool that has great meaning for both emerging leaders and group members.

Psychodrama groups were new to me (Paul), and I knew relatively little about what to do as a group leader or how such groups work. Gil was serving as my mentor, showing me the techniques and how to use them. Although I had the title of co-leader, it was clear to me that Gil was the one who really knew what he was doing. His experience, knowledge, and reputation were outstanding. However, my cognitive-behavioral orientation would offer plenty of opportunities for providing input, and I felt that I would be able to ease my way into this new set of techniques.

This experience, I felt, was going to be just the mentoring and learning model I had been looking for. I would have the opportunity to learn from someone with experience, to make positive use of my own skills, and to try to make concepts that were new to me work the way they were designed without having to take responsibility for doing so successfully in an environment in which I would have an expert as a safety net. Gil and I related well, and Gil expressed that he would be happy to process with me both before and after group. I was going to be able to relax, learn, and do my own thing.

The group had been in session for several weeks prior to my involvement. Gil briefed me by providing a solid background on the group. He let me read his group notes and explained where the group had been, what they were doing now, and where they were headed. He informed me that early conflicts and anxieties had been resolved, and the group was working very effectively at this point. He gave me an overview of the individual members, their reasons for being in this particular group, and how they tended to react. Gil even told me of his own past history of seizures but said that none had occurred recently and that if one did occur, he needed only to be left alone for a short while because the seizures were not dangerous. All this seemed to be more information than I would ever want or need. I just wanted to get on with the group.

The background Gil provided became more important than I ever expected in just my second session with the group. Gil was casting roles for a drama shortly after the beginning of the session when it became clear to everyone that Gil had stopped directing, was standing quietly, had a blank look on his face, and had begun to gently shake. He was having a seizure, and the group members were looking to me to act. Without thinking, I stood up, sat Gil down, and reassured the group members that he would be all right. They were not convinced, and neither was I, but they had enough experience with the group process, their interactions, and the role of the leader to go along with me. We continued the process of casting roles, something they had done many times before.

To everyone's relief, Gil came out of his disorientation after only a few minutes. I explained to him where the group was, and he said, "Continue." In a short while, he smoothly reentered the leader's role and I gladly became the follower again. I found it remarkable how well the group members adjusted to Gil's situation, to my role change, and to continuing group work at such a difficult time.

It is impossible to imagine how one will react to events that are as unexpected as Gil's seizure. Yet, it is just this type of unplanned and natural experiential problem that is vital to testing and advancing the training of a group leader. Gil's briefings about the stage of the group, the nature of the clients, and his own background made a world of difference in how I was able to react.

By showing confidence in me without forcing me to do things I was not ready to do, Gil treated me as a professional who wanted to learn rather than as a learner who wanted to be a professional. He recognized that I was in the middle of the novice-to-expert developmental process rather than assuming I had to be either a novice or an expert (Etringer, Hillerbrand, & Clairborn, 1995). He recognized much better than I ever could have that I needed information and observation opportunities, and at the same time I was thrust into situations that forced me to employ and expand my abilities. The group itself provided an additional safety net, as the members already knew their roles and responsibilities.

APPLICATIONS TO GROUP PRACTITIONERS

Most group counselors could readily relate personal experiences to match the themes of our samples. Nearly all counselors have experienced the struggles of developing or even avoiding supportive professional relationships with a mentor or co-leader. Whether they wished to enter such a relationship and tried to do so or avoided the possibility of such a relationship because of their particular needs and fears, they gave consideration to the possible benefits and problems involved as well as the actions that might be needed to follow through successfully in an actual group situation.

The literature reviewed previously provides some clues that can help direct the impact of mentoring relationships on group leadership. For the remainder of this chapter, we describe those themes from the literature and from our experiences that we believe are most critical for assisting the development of group leaders through mentoring and co-leadership.

Select the Relationship Based on Novice-to-Expert Development

Richard was pleased to have a more experienced mentor, whereas Becky benefited from a co-leader of a similar experiential level. How can a potential mentor or protégé know which model is best? Certainly, as in all other relationships, individual needs and situational variables play critical roles. However, recognition of these unlimited variables only increases the complexity of conceptualizing the problem rather than helping to make the path to selecting the most appropriate relationship more clear. A better way to select the best model for a relationship is to recognize the extent of the protégé's cognitive development on a novice to expert scale.

One emerging leader may need to follow for a time in order to prepare for leadership. Another may want to follow but, as in Richard's case, need to be pushed into leading in order to overcome fears and utilize his or her true potential. Still another person, like Becky, may have reached a stage at which her knowledge, skill, and confidence have made her ready to jump in and do things on her own. Mentors can most accurately decide how to deal with the endless variety of potential protégé situations and personalities only after they and their protégés have developed an honest and understanding relationship that highlights the conceptualizing abilities of the protégé (Etringer et al., 1995).

Richard found that he had little insight about what was happening in the group or why such insights seemed so natural to his mentor. Becky, however, was able to make many connections between past experiences and the new group she was going to run. Richard and Becky both had information about the people and process, but Becky had additional awareness, drawn from her past experiences, of the insights that group members would be having. This conception of how people develop insights seems to occur more frequently in experienced counselors and has a positive effect on counseling (Cummings, Slemon, & Hallberg, 1993).

An effective mentoring relationship is one in which the mentor recognizes the protégé's level of insight as a measure of his or her viable expertise. The protégé's position on the novice-to-expert continuum is one of the factors that can help mentors determine how much freedom of operation the protégé should have as a group leader. The further along this dimension a counselor is, the more a mentor can and should provide opportunities for independent direction seeking.

RECOGNIZE ABILITIES AND EMBRACE IMPERFECTIONS

An appropriate early relationship between mentor and protégé is typically one that is supportive, does not require perfection, and provides continual opportunities for progressive steps. Paul's co-leader, Gil, recognized that Paul needed to be a follower in the practice of psychodrama, which was new to him. At the same time, he knew of Paul's counseling skills and could therefore express confidence in his ability to take over if necessary. The confidence he placed in Paul was not blind but based on Paul's proven skills. Gil's recognition of Paul's ability conveyed that he believed Paul would be able to provide modeling to the group members (Gladding, 1991), bring new material to their therapeutic work, and provide group management in his absence (Simon, 1992).

Gil was supportive of Paul but did not try to protect him from potential problems. Likewise, the counselor who supervised Becky and Val's group experience did not panic when things did not go as planned. She provided advice and support but, recognizing Becky and Val's commitment and ability to make things work, allowed them to make correctable mistakes, to learn from those mistakes, and provide a quality experience for the group members. Mentors and protégés who require that both people in the relationship make no errors, or never admit to making errors, will produce a false sense of security that can prove damaging for clients and lead to future problems in the development of their relationship as professionals. An open-to-error approach is critical to the development of novice counselors, who almost always exhibit a perfectionistic thinking style (Miller, 1986) that needs to be challenged.

Differences in styles, beliefs, theories, and background do not eliminate the possibility of a mentor and protégé working effectively together. Instead, such differences can be embraced and their exploration can become a growth factor for both protégé and mentor. One of Paul's more frustrating experiences was with a co-leader whose approach was much more affective than Paul's cognitive-behavioral approach. "When I would be trying to focus the group on the idea that their thinking was driving their affect," Paul said, "the co-leader would say, 'Yes, that's true, but go ahead and express yourself. Just let yourself cry.' We were fighting each other *to see who was right* rather than being supportive." Paul and his co-leader's contrasting styles, beliefs, and theories were a problem only because the two leaders were seeking to find who was "correct" rather than how to interpret and best use their two sets of ideas. They needed instead to reflect on the situation, gain a broader perspective, and find a win-win outcome (Ellis & Douce, 1994). They finally realized they had to either stop working together or communicate better and thereby make adjustments. They chose to find out more about each other's positions and about themselves as persons and began to realize the potential value of this newfound information in their group work. They succeeded in developing complementary instead of contradictory strategies, something they could not have done had they not given the necessary attention to their theoretical positions, practical techniques, and the interpersonal dimensions of their relationship.

ADDRESS POWER AND CONTROL ISSUES

For mentoring relationships to progress, both parties must recognize and address issues of power and control. Who is in charge? Who will make the final decisions? Whose words carry more influence? When will the balance of power in the relationship change? What are the consequences of challenging the other person or the system? These concerns are integral to relationships of unequal power but are rarely discussed openly and honestly. As a result of these nondiscussions, the mentor and protégé make assumptions based on past experiences and personal anxieties rather than reasoned decisions based on the terms they set for their professional relationship.

Early in a relationship power and control issues differ based on the people involved, their self-selected roles, and their organizational roles. Both parties need to recognize the fact that people differ in the extent of their need to control themselves and others. How much control the mentor and protégé need and how those needs blend together will affect the specific ways they handle their roles. Novice professionals will most often be eager to accept information relayed by mentors about content and techniques, typically taking almost no directive role themselves. More advanced leaders, however, are more like the typical teenager who fluctuates between wanting autonomy and control at one time and desiring support and direction at others (Ronnestad & Skovholt, 1993).

The mentor must recognize the protégé's increasing need to assume control in the mentoring relationship as a natural step in becoming a professional. By providing increasing opportunities for the protégé to assume more control in ways that will confirm both areas of growth and areas in which growth is still needed, the mentor can promote productive changes in the relationship. Defensive or inflexible actions designed to maintain the current status of power and control issues will lead to a lesser quality of relationship and, ultimately, the cessation of the relationship.

The discussion thus far has concerned informal mentor-protégé roles, but organizational roles also have an effect on relationships, particularly with regard to power and control issues. For example, the relationship between a faculty member who needs to make major professional judgments about a student and that student will be affected by many different perceived and real power issues. Less formal power issues are also present between a new counselor and an experienced colleague. Getting off to a good start requires that those involved in a relationship give recognition to these dual relationship issues rather than discount them or presume they can ignore them.

Attend to the Relationship's Development Stages

Our experiences as protégés and mentors have brought us to the recognition that there at least three broadly conceived stages that mentors and protégés must negotiate if they are to continue working together productively over time. The stages reflect both the changing nature of the protégé as he or she develops from novice to expert (Etringer et al., 1995) and the mentor's continuing need to find personal or professional value in the relationship.

Initial Stage

The beginning stage of the relationship is marked by identifying and responding to official factors affecting the relationship. Organizational roles, such as supervisor-supervisee, teacher-student, and higher-lower official rank, are often the first criteria used to identify a relationship. The obvious and formal nature of these roles make them stand out as potential first choices, particularly in organizations in which formal professional interaction is more acceptable behavior than personal interaction. These roles may sometimes form the basis for assigning or accepting mentorships, but they probably do not make the best mechanisms for doing so. It appears from the literature that "true mentors" cannot simply be assigned (Cesa & Fraser, 1989). Nevertheless, these more formal roles often seem to be used as starting places by people who want to define a mentoring relationship and have experience with such roles. People tend to do first what they already know how to do.

The examples of Richard, Becky, Val, and Paul demonstrate varied starting places for them and their mentors. However, regardless of the widely varied knowledge, competence, and confidence with which they entered these relationships, their initial reactions conformed to the traditional roles of supervisee and student or follower. Richard sought the follower relationship; Paul saw himself as a student; Becky and Val, although more aggressive than the others in getting their needs met, first looked to find someone who would take the traditional mentor role to assist them as well as confirm their strength and independence. Such formal relationships are the type most people have been offered all their lives, and it would not be one's first thought to exchange such a relationship for a more nebulous mentor-protégé relationship. Roles and interactions that have familiarity provide people, including novice group leaders, with the security and confidence they need (Ronnestad & Skovholt, 1993).

The power differential between mentor and protégé is great at this beginning stage, and the tasks of the mentor are likely to be directive. One person in the relationship appears to know more of the answers and one appears to know fewer. The confusion inherent in the beginning of a relationship often leads the mentor-protégé pair to attempt to find order by attending to the areas of inequality in their relationship rather than negotiating those areas in which they operate on a more equal footing. For this reason, too, they are likely to start out adhering to traditional, clearly defined leader and follower roles.

MIDDLE STAGES

The growth of the mentor, the protégé, and their relationship, as well as the progress of their group work, all serve to diminish the continued effectiveness of their initially adopted roles. The second general stage of the relationship emphasizes the need for accommodating these changes. As protégés begin to gain more confidence and conceptualizing ability, they move from desiring short-range, learning-specific challenges toward seeking to address long-term and more global concerns (Lowe, 1994). To support this growth, a decrease in the power and control differential with their mentor is needed.

In the examples in this chapter, the change in Richard's relationship was forced by his mentor, whereas the change in Paul's relationship was promoted by circumstances. Their mentors recognized the need for their increasing independence and, in their own ways, helped create situations in which they could encourage the risk-taking needed for their protégés' further development. Both relationships were being pressured to expand toward more equality, more mutually responsible interactions, and broader conceptualizations of the mentor-protégé roles. Both Richard and Paul initially viewed their mentors as being mostly nonflawed group leaders and professionals. That status, however, began to erode as a more realistic picture emerged that incorporated more mentor fallibilities and protégé competencies.

Roles that were useful in the beginning stage lose their effectiveness as similarities and equality begin to overshadow the dissimilarities and inequality emphasized earlier. Discussions of these changes, their potential benefits and problems, and the new relationships that might evolve become necessary. Conflict often occurs, and the parties will choose either to face the conflicts and changing needs and find solutions or to avoid the issues and try to hold on to the past. The latter option holds little more likelihood for success in the mentor-protégé relationship than it does in any other relationship in which people have moved beyond the characteristics and needs on which their relationship was built.

LATER STAGE

The third relationship stage is marked by continuing recognition of ongoing real and perceived changes that support greater equality between mentor and protégé. Moving from degrees of inequality to equality accompanied by the common selection of directions is a difficult step in any relationship. A common alternative is for either or both parties to allow the relationship to become stagnant, to deteriorate, or to end. Feeling sufficient satisfaction with earlier stages of the relationship and having insufficient commitment to the hard work of seeking new levels of involvement can put strong pressures on the parties to end the development of a relationship. The mentor or protégé may decide that the relationship was good the way it was and there is no need for anything new.

However, one cannot achieve long-term success in a relationship by maintaining it in its initial form. In the mentor-protégé relationship in the field of group therapy, protégés need to be given fewer "things to do" with groups and more information about ways to initiate and maintain interactions within the group as their experience increases (Wiggins & Carroll, 1993). Developing mentor-protégé relationships should model such a shift in focus from information and skill distribution to an emphasis on the interaction of equals. Val and Becky expanded their relationship in this way so that it continued to be productive and promoting of future growth. Paul and Richard, although grateful for the supportive mentoring provided to them, had no continuing contact with their mentors because more equal and interactional relationships did not evolve.

Growth and change force the need for new, more equal, and different styles of relationships. One cannot expect the bliss of an early relationship to continue by simply doing the same thing repeatedly. Openness, honesty, objectivity, and hard work are required to maintain the feelings of productivity and pleasure in an environment of personal and professional change.

Make Time and Place Available

Learning and relationship building take time. Group counselor mentoring relationships that do not incorporate sufficient processing time outside of the group experiences will provide correspondingly less value to everyone. Val's description of the frustration she felt in her first protégé-mentor relationship is not unusual. Her mentor had other groups to run, individuals to see, consultations waiting, and paper work piling high. There was not enough time for her to develop the necessary relationship with Val, to process what was happening, to explore Val's anxieties, and to create new alternatives. Without the necessary time being made available, Val could not determine what factors or actions might have made her first mentoring situation more productive.

Arrangements must be made for places, ways, and times to meet; they cannot just be expected to occur. Richard was unsure of himself in leading his initial group of junior high boys even though he had a good deal of quality group experience. He needed reassurance from someone, but such feedback was not available because of distances between schools and counselors. His eventual involvement in the regional counseling association helped him to recognize that people were available and very willing to provide that kind of support. Unfortunately, they were still 50 miles away. Only when the organization began planning for cooperative ways for members to support one another did availability begin to match the degree of willingness.

People sought as mentors are generally very busy individuals with many important professional responsibilities. Both mentor and protégé must realize that time and energy are limited and plan within those limits. Starting a mentoring relationship when the time, place, and energy needed to make the relationship a success are not available will doom the relationship to mediocrity at best and significant dissatisfaction or failure at worst. A better alternative may be to not even begin the relationship.

MENTORS NEED TO STRETCH THEMSELVES

Successfully working with a co-leader is never a one-sided growth process no matter how great the differential between the co-leaders' experience and knowledge. Although it may seem that flexibility and growth will occur only for the less experienced person in relationships in which one person is clearly the mentor and one clearly the protégé, such is not the case in many instances, in which mentors report getting the most from relationships. Consider these comments made by a dedicated mentor:

> Mentoring is much more than case sharing for me. It stretches me. It makes me question the things that I do automatically. I have to be able to communicate the "how" of getting those things done that I normally do almost by reflex. It is hard to do and even challenges my views. It makes me articulate my views, which often brings a realization that they are not as clear as I thought they were. The whole process also makes me feel good about the protégé, the field of counseling, and myself. It is not easy growth, but it sure feels good when I can see the growth.

Meeting the needs of beginning counselors and expanding oneself in an evolving relationship are challenging but rewarding feats. One cannot experience the full rewards without taking on the challenges. Mentors who lead by example can demonstrate the value of stretching themselves and the ability to learn from each situation and example.

CONCLUSIONS

A recent disturbance in our organization caused a noncounselor to question, "How can you guys be like this among yourselves? You're all counselors. You should be able to deal with these things better."

Giving and taking support and assistance through mentoring and co-leading with beginning group leaders at first appears to be such a natural and positive process for therapists. Perhaps these presumptions are the reason relatively little research has been done on this topic in the field of group counseling. Therapists expect mentoring to be easy even though a realistic look at a variety of experiences shows the opposite.

Therapists are human beings first and professionals second when it comes to needs, weaknesses, and fallibility. Training and personal development may serve to offset these traits but they are never eliminated. Therapists must continuously explore themselves, their professional behaviors, and their relationships if they hope to keep pace with the changes that go on around them. The same type of continuous growth and development is required for one to be an effective mentor, protégé, or group co-leader or to be in a relationship that involves these roles.

The experiences, literature review, and discussion of applications of mentoring to group practitioners provided herein serve as a general model for mentoring emerging group leaders. The model is based on relationship building and the realization that change in the mentor-protégé relationship must occur as an outcome of the growth that is expected in the participants. Exact ways to behave in every relationship cannot be identified because only the generalities and not the specifics of the mentoring situation are consistent. A strong relationship is the key to promoting positive growth, and those involved must give maximum attention to the relationship.

Certain personal behaviors do seem appropriate for individuals in mentoring relationships, however, based on the information available. They begin with acceptance of the protégé's and mentor's styles, levels of knowledge and skills, and needs. This acceptance, when combined with an identification of the strengths and weaknesses of the protégé, the mentor, and the situation, creates the opportunity for progress for these qualities help to establish a realistic foundation. This foundation, in turn, can support planned activities designed to affirm recognized strengths and facilitate improvement on weaknesses within a co-leadership experience.

A relationship that begins with these qualities does not automatically result in continuing growth and progress. Both mentor and protégé must exhibit flexibility to deal with the recognition of and reaction to changes that occur in the relationship. Little can remain static in an evolving relationship, and both participants need to continually reevaluate where they are and how supportive their position is of where they need to go. The changes they identify should direct their next set of actions.

Mentors who seek the most basic things they can do to support the development of their protégés can look to three primary elements. One is to exhibit patience, a virtue continually needed in a professional world that is becoming increasingly more hurried and goal oriented. Because mentoring of group leaders should occur only after potential protégés have had, at the least, substantial training and some directed experience, protégés are typically more trained than untrained and more knowledgeable than ignorant. In this situation, protégés should be given leeway in how fast they are forced to progress. Mentors must recognize the professional status of their protégés and exhibit sufficient patience for them to find their own way as professionals.

Another thing mentors can do is to seek complementary roles for co-leaders in groups. Co-leaders with the same skills and roles sometimes wind up simply sharing time at running their group. Such a structure, however, makes sense only when one co-leader is helping to develop the skills of another. Co-leaders with different strengths and with complementary roles can better serve their group.

Finally, mentors must be role models. Successful mentors have the pleasure of seeing people develop. If all else were forgotten, mentors who "practice what they preach" would provide their protégés with a great deal of success. The mentor will be viewed as some degree of a role model regardless of what anyone wants. Being successful thus demands that mentors model those behaviors they would have their protégés adopt. The more consistently that modeling is done both inside and outside of groups, the greater the potential that the protégé will recognize, accept, practice, and internalize new and better ways of behaving as a professional.

REFERENCES

Atkinson, D. R., Neville, H., & Casas, A. (1991). The mentorship of ethnic minorities in professional psychology. *Professional Psychology Research and Practice, 22,* 336–338.

Brinson, J., & Kottler, J. (1993). Cross-cultural mentoring in counselor education: A strategy for retaining minority faculty. *Counselor Education and Supervision, 32,* 241–253.

Cesa, I. L., & Fraser, S. C. (1989). A method for encouraging the development of good mentor-protégé relationships. *Teaching of Psychology, 16*(3), 125–128.

Corey, G. (1995). *Theory and practice of group counseling* (3rd ed.). Pacific Grove, CA: Brooks/Cole.

Cummings, A. L., Slemon, A. G., & Hallberg, E. T. (1993). Session evaluation and recall of important events as a function of counselor experience. *Journal of Counseling Psychology, 40,* 156–165.

Ellis, M. V., & Douce, L. A. (1994). Group supervision of novice clinical supervisors: Eight recurring issues. *Journal of Counseling and Development, 72,* 520–525.

Etringer, B. D., Hillerbrand, E., & Clairborn, C. D. (1995). The transition from novice to expert counselor. *Counselor Education and Supervision, 35*(1), 5–16.

Fenster, A. (1991). The making of a group psychotherapist: Needs and goals for graduate and post-graduate training. *Group, 15,* 155–162.

Gladding, S. (1991). *Group work: A counseling specialty.* New York: Merrill.

Graham, B. (1994). Mentoring and professional development in careers services in higher education. *British Journal of Guidance and Counseling, 22*(2), 251–271.

Haensly, P. A., & Parsons, J. L. (1993). Creative, intellectual, and psychosocial development through mentorship: Relationships and stages. *Youth and Society, 25,* 202–221.

Hazler, R. J., & Carney, J. (1993). Student-faculty interactions: An underemphasized dimension of counselor education. *Counselor Education and Supervision, 33,* 80–88.

Hillerbrand, E. (1989). Cognitive differences between experts and novices: Implications for group supervision. *Journal of Counseling and Development, 67*(5), 293–296.

Hillerbrand, E., & Clairborn, C. D. (1990). Examining reasoning skills differences between expert and novice counselors. *Journal of Counseling and Development, 68,* 684–691.

Jacobs, E. E., Harvill, R. L., & Masson, R. L. (1994). *Group counseling: Strategies and skills* (2nd ed.). Pacific Grove, CA: Brooks/Cole.

Johnson, J., Simpson, J. C., Williams, M. L., & Kotarba, J. A. (1993). New careers models revisited: The importance of mentoring. *Journal of Employment Counseling, 30,* 55–66.

Kivlighan, D. M., & Quigley, S. T. (1991). Dimensions used by experienced and novice group therapists to conceptualize group process. *Journal of Counseling Psychology, 38,* 415–423.

Lowe, D. W. (1994). Characteristics of effective graduate psychology courses: Student and faculty perspectives. *Teaching of Psychology, 21,* 82–85.

Miller, M. J. (1986). On the perfectionistic thoughts of beginning group leaders. *Journal for Specialists in Group Work, 11,* 53–56.

Newby, T. J., & Heide, A. (1992). The value of mentoring. *Performance Improvement Quarterly, 5*(4), 2–15.

Robinson, E. H (1994). Critical issues in counselor education: Mentors, models and money. Special Section: Critical issues in research in counselor education and supervision. *Counselor Education and Supervision, 33,* 339–343.

Rogers, J. C., & Holloway, R. L. (1993). Professional intimacy: Somewhere between collegiality and personal intimacy? *Family Systems Medicine, 11,* 253–270.

Ronnestad, M. H., & Skovholt, T. M. (1993). Supervision of beginning and advanced graduate students of counseling and psychotherapy. *Journal of Counseling and Development, 71,* 396–405.

Simon, J. D. (1992). The group therapist's absence and the substitute leader. *International Journal of Group Psychotherapy, 42*(2), 287–291.

Whitely, W. T., & Coetsier, P. (1993). The relationship of career mentoring to early career outcomes. *Organization Studies, 14,* 419–441.

Wiggins, J. D. & Carroll, M. R. (1993). Back to the basics: Perceived and actual needs of group leaders. *Journal of Specialists in Group Work, 18,* 25–28.

Wright, R. G., & Werther, W. B. (1991). Mentors at work. *Journal of Management Development, 10,* 25–32.

Author Index

A

Abramson, J. C., 172
Aburdene, J., 141
Adams, K., 84
Alschuler, A. S., 64
Alschuler, C. F., 64
Altshul, J. A., 60
American Counseling Association, 122
Amundson, J., 191
Anderson, C. M., 65
Anderson, H., 191, 192
Anderson, T., 200
Anderson, W., 18
Aplin, J. C., 141
Aponte, H. J., 26, 31
Arieti, S., 83
Armeniox, L., 84
Arredondo, P., 46, 48, 51
Association for Specialists in Group Work (ASGW), 117, 118, 120
Atkinson, D. R., 46, 212
Avila, D. L., 29

B

Baldwin, D. C., Jr., 29
Baldwin, M., 31
Barón, A., 48, 49, 51
Basescu, S., 26, 32
Bass, B., 172
Beck, A. P., 167
Benne, K. D., 140
Bennis, W., 154, 170, 172
Benshoff, J., 84
Berger, P., 186
Bernard, J. M., 22
Beutler, L. E., 31
Bion, W. R., 150
Blanchard, K. H., 19, 145, 146, 151, 152
Blase, J., 172
Blocher, D. H., 137, 143
Bly, R., 84
Borders, L. D., 22
Boscolo, L., 30
Bourdieu, 192
Bowman, R. P., 86
Bradford, L., 120
Bradley, L. J., 139
Braiotta, L., 170
Brasher, B., 196
Brinson, J., 44, 45, 211
Bruner, E., 186
Brusa, J. A., 167
Burke, W. W., 143
Burman, E., 183
Burns, J. M., 154

C

Cahill, A. J., 64
Campbell, T., 196
Carew, D. K., 151
Carkhuff, R. R., 139
Carlton-Ford, S. L., 172
Carney, J., 211
Carr, C., 120
Carroll, M. R., 224
Casas, A., 212
Casey, D., 140
Cecchin, G., 30
Cesa, I. L., 222
Chase, K., 93
Chau, K. L., 44
Church, A. H., 143
Clairborn, C. D., 216, 218
Clark, K. B., 46
Clark, M. P., 46
Clayton, G. M., 192
Coetsier, P., 212
Cohen, A., 121, 123, 124, 131
Cohen, S. L., 49
Coleman, N. C., 46, 48
Combs, A. W., 29
Conlon, I., 171
Conyne, R., 67, 117, 121, 139
Cora, D., 193, 196, 197, 199
Corey, G., 18, 19, 33, 47, 48, 49, 140, 151, 155, 211
Corey, M. S., 18, 19, 140, 151, 155
Covey, S. F., 171, 172, 173
Cox, B. G., 64
Craig, D., 123
Cross, W. E., 46
Crowley, R. J., 89
Cummings, A. L., 219
Cushman, P., 26, 27

D

D'Andrea, M., 83
David, A. B., 27
Decker, N., 64
DeLuga, R. J., 172
Delworth, U., 22
Deutch, M., 172
Dickerson, V. C., 186, 197
Donigian, J., 129
Douce, L. A., 220
Douvan, E., 49
Dreher, D., 106
Dufrene, P. M., 46, 48

Dunn, J. R., 88
Dustin, D., 19, 137
Dyer, W. W., 31

E

Edwards, D., 186
Ellis, A., 91
Ellis, M. V., 220
Eng, A. M., 167
English, J., 110, 115
Epstein, L., 26, 33
Epston, D., 183, 186, 187, 198
Erickson, C. A., 27
Erikson, E. H., 26
Etringer, B. D., 218, 219, 222

F

Fairclough, N., 186
Feng, G., 110, 115
Fenster, A., 211
Fiedler, F. E., 172
Fischer, E. H., 49
Fisher, P. P., 84, 87
Fleshman, B., 82, 84, 96
Fong, M. L., 64
Forsyth, D., 18
Foti, R. J., 172
Frank, J. D., 31
Fraser, S. C., 222
Friedman, W. H., 65
Fryrear, J. L., 82, 84, 96
Fukuyama, M. A., 46
Fuqua, D. R., 141

G

Gardner, J. W., 171, 172
Geertz, C., 187
Gergen, K., 29, 182, 183, 186
Gladding, S., 18, 19, 49, 60, 67, 82, 92, 141, 146, 155, 215, 220
Glassman, S. M., 142
Goodstein, L. D., 146, 153
Goodyear, R. K., 22
Goolishian, H., 191, 192
Gorelick, K., 82
Graham, B., 212
Grawe, D., 31
Guze, S. B., 64

H

Haber, R., 27, 35
Haensly, P. A., 212
Hallberg, E. T., 219
Hamilton, J. D., 64
Harper, F. D., 46
Harre, R., 183, 186

Harris, M., 172
Hartz, P., 115
Harvill, R. L., 60, 155, 211
Hater, J. J., 172
Hayes, B. A., 139
Hazler, R. J., 211
Heide, A., 212
Heider, J., 105, 108, 111, 115
Hellreigal, D., 138
Helms, J. E., 46
Herrera, A. E., 51
Hersey, P., 19, 151, 152
Hilkey, J. H., 68
Hillerbrand, E., 215, 216, 218
Hoff, B., 107
Hoffman, L., 29, 30
Hollander, E. P., 167
Holling, D. W., 19
Holloway, E. L., 143
Holloway, R. L., 213
Hollway, W., 186
Holt, G. R., 107
Hood, J., 120
Horne, A., 60, 68
Hoskins, M., 90
Hrebiniak, L., 121
Hulse-Killacky, D., 19, 129

I

Ishiyama, F. I., 50

J

Jackson, J. S., 49
Jacobs, E., 60, 82, 155, 211, 212
Jensen, M. A., 85, 147, 148, 151
Johnson, C., 46
Johnson, D. W., 18, 64, 140, 143, 151
Johnson, F. P., 18, 140, 143, 151
Johnson, J., 212
Johnson, S., 145, 146
Jones, J., 117
Jordan, J. M., 51, 52
Jurma, W. E., 171

K

Katzenbach, J., 120
Keltner, J., 141
Kenner, J., 120
Kenny, D. A., 172
Ketrow, S. M., 172
King, M. I., 172
Kirby, P. C., 172
Kivlighan, D. M., 212

229

SUBJECT INDEX

A

Acting out, 58–69, 61–66, 77
  successful steps with, 66–75
Adolescents in groups, 62–63, 67
Anger, 63–64, 193
Anxiety, 49, 67, 85
Apprentice model, 212
Assertiveness, 136, 137, 154
Audience for narrative, 200
Authenticity, 10, 22

B

Buddhist philosophy, 16

C

Caring, 69, 78, 123, 125, 136
Centering, 112–113
Certainty in counseling, 190–191
Change
  through group, 61, 68, 75,
    77, 84
  in organizations, 161, 170
  resistance to, 143
Children in counseling, 14, 38
Co-facilitator. See Co-leader;
  Leader(ship)
Cognitive dissonance, 9
Cohesion, group 65–66, 111
Co-leading (co-facilitating), 5,
  17, 127–128, 158, 210,
  211–213, 220, 225, 227
Collaboration, 15, 138, 167
Communication, 67, 146, 151,
  169–170, 186
  with client's family, 65
  through creative arts, 84
  intercultural, 50–51
  between leaders, 216, 220
  reciprocal, 150
  styles, 48, 172
  withholding, 61
  conceptual framework, 12,
    21, 22, 48, 129
Confidentiality, 94
Conflict, unresolved, 70
  management, 136, 137, 150,
    170, 172
  in mentor relationship, 223
  stage of group, 88–90
Confrontation, 65, 72
Consistency, leader, 78
Constructivist
  orientation, 26, 29–30, 186
  model, 182–183, 194
Control, 159
  in mentoring relationships,
    221, 223
  need for, 76–78

Cooperation, 177–178
Counselor characteristics, 22
Countertransference, 34, 78
Creative arts in groups
  limitations of, 95–97
  rationale for using, 82–85
Cultural
  biases, 43
  consciousness, 46, 53
  differences, 50, 184, 189
  diversity, 44–46
  identity, 27
  influences, 26
  differences in leadership, 171
  values, 47–49, 51–54
Curiosity, 191–192, 197
Cutting-edge behaviors, 20–21

D

Decision making in groups,
  123, 145
Deconstruction, 185, 192–194
Dependability, leader, 78
Developmental
  perspective, 49, 62, 183
  stages of groups, 147–150,
    151–153, 160
  stages in mentoring, 222–224
Discourse, 186, 188–190, 193
Diversity. See Cultural
Drawing activities in groups,
  86–87, 89, 93–94
Drumming in groups, 86

E

Eating disorders, groups for, 105
Eclecticism, 11, 48
Egalitarian approach, 16
Ego state, 26
Emotions, release of, 84–85,
  87, 96, 193
Empathy, 66, 90
Empowerment, 45, 46, 49, 51,
  52, 53, 85, 89, 150
  employee, 139
Energy
  motivational, 145–146
  Tao, 110, 111–112
Ethnicity, 51. See also Cultural
  and creative arts, 85
  and self, 27
Existential perspective, 47. See
  also Humanistic perspective
Externalization, 196–197,
  200–201

F

Family relationship, 65
Feedback, 10, 17, 19, 36, 65,
  96, 121

  in mentor relationships, 212,
    224
  by process observer/
    facilitator, 135, 136, 140,
    144–146, 161
Feelings, 84, 96, 126
Feminist theory, 16
FIRO theory, 150
Focus groups, 158

G

Gestalt methods, 7, 12, 16, 17, 92
Goal setting, 146
Group
  cohesion, 65–66
  development, 147–150, 151–
    153, 159–160
  dynamics, 68, 75, 79, 97,
    117, 135, 140, 147, 161,
    167–168
  expectations for, 76
  process, 126–128, 159–160,
    162, 167
  responsibilities, 128
  structure, 67
  task, 117
Group members
  difficult, 59–60, 62, 67, 69
  interactions, 83
Group mind, 111

H

Here and now, 10, 16, 70, 102
Humanistic perspective, 29,
  35, 61, 194
Humor in groups, 73, 88, 168
Hunches, 31–32

I

Immediacy, 36
Impasses, 35, 88
Inclusion, 90, 150, 159
Individual therapy, 11, 22
Inner nature, 108–109, 113, 115
Integrity, 172, 174, 179
Internalizing, 189–190
Interpersonal relationships, 21,
  66, 76, 90, 167
  cultural, 51
  in FIRO model, 150
  in mentoring, 221, 224–225,
    226
  in task groups, 123, 129, 144
Interpretation, 70, 154
Intuition, leader, 35, 106, 108,
  112, 113, 171
"I statements," 64